THE TEN TOUGHEST Leadership Problems

And How to Solve Them

THE TEN TOUGHEST Leadership Problems

And How to Solve Them

Dr Katie Best

First published 2025 by Basic Venture
an imprint of Hachette Book Group

First published in the UK 2025 by Macmillan Business
an imprint of Pan Macmillan
The Smithson, 6 Briset Street, London EC1M 5NR
EU representative: Macmillan Publishers Ireland Ltd, 1st Floor,
The Liffey Trust Centre, 117–126 Sheriff Street Upper,
Dublin 1 D01 YC43
Associated companies throughout the world

ISBN 978-1-0350-8219-3 HB
ISBN 978-1-0350-8220-9 TPB

Some of the names of people and organizations have been changed
to protect identities. The context on some of the cases and examples have
also been slightly altered for the same reason.

3 5 7 9 8 6 4 2

A CIP catalogue record for this book is available from the British Library.

Printed and bound by India by Thomson Press India Ltd.

To Patrick and Bobbie
L.Y.G-S.

Contents

Introduction

WHY YOU NEED THIS BOOK

Because I am a leadership coach and consultant who's been working with leaders for nearly two decades, it's typical for me to open my emails or LinkedIn and find a message from someone I've worked with before but haven't heard from for ages. Sometimes, they're just saying hi. Other times, they're wanting to chat about some new leadership problem they have run into that they need some help with.

This means it wasn't a surprise when one day, about five years ago, I received a "hello from the past" message from Simon. Simon was someone I'd worked with about a decade before, when he was responsible for business development for the business school I was then working for, and I was designing the programs he was (very successfully) trying to sell.

When he emailed me, as well as having moved companies a few times, he had moved up the ranks considerably and was now for the first time at C-suite level as the chief commercial officer in an organization selling consultancy and training. Throughout the intervening period, he'd done very well for himself. We went for coffee, and he reminded me why I'd enjoyed working with him before: he was friendly, very capable, and funny. I was happy he'd gotten back in touch. Initially, it was to ask me to coach him and some members of his team. I was very happy to.

However, this was during a good period for the company—things were going well. They were in a business where things could change quickly, and two months later, things were going less well and now the company couldn't afford coaching anymore. But Simon felt very frustrated—he could have coaching when everything was going well and he barely needed it, but as soon as things were difficult and he needed more help on how to motivate his team through the tough patch, and how to talk about strategy and change, and his team members needed more help on how to be resilient, there was no budget available for coaching! He was incredibly frustrated as, when he took on the C-suite role, they knew he was new to this level and he had been promised support. But now, if he wanted coaching, he would have to go through a lengthier justification process, pitching for the money that no longer sat in his budget. He feared that, by the time he got the coaching agreed, he would have made many suboptimal decisions as he tried to solve the problems flying at him as a result of the downturn in the market and of being new.

That's the irony of leadership coaching—many of the people who need it the most can't access it—their companies won't pay, or can't afford to pay. Or their companies are willing and able to support the coaching, but by the time the sign-off is given by a boss, and then HR, and then a purchase order is raised, and a contract is signed, the problem is worse, has headed off in a totally different direction, or has disappeared but without the leader learning how to handle it and fearing it coming back. It's hard for Simon, and people like Simon, to get leadership coaching because companies don't always understand the value that it adds—it's expensive, and it's hard to prove through numbers how much it adds to the bottom line. What was coaching, what was luck, and what would have happened anyway? And yet leaders who experience great coaching speak highly of it, many of them seeing it as critical to their success.

And it's not just about not being able to access help through a leadership coach. It can often feel like drawing attention to your weaknesses if you admit that you need help. In organizations with cultures that are reticent to admit problems, doing so can make you look like a poor performer (when you're probably just more honest!). Leaders write in to Dear Katie—my newsletter advice column–with a tough problem for which they feel they are receiving no organizational support. They receive an answer without having to admit to anyone else what problem they are facing.

There are lots of reasons then: a lack of budget, time pressure, a sense of failure if they admit that they need help, which means that leadership can feel very lonely. They can't admit to problems, they can't ask for support from their organizations, and they can't work out how to handle a situation they haven't faced before.

But don't worry! It's not all doom and gloom. What you are holding in your hands (or listening to on your headphones) is here to help you and others like you to handle your leadership problems. This book is going to support you as you figure out what's going on, what your possible solutions are, and how to choose one that fits your environment. Because the solution that is right for the CEO of a ten-person human rights charity may be quite different from the solution that's right for the store manager of a coffee shop or the HR director of a large accounting firm. It's going to help you figure out what further problems you could run into when you try to implement your solution and how to handle them. And, excitingly, it's going to show you how you can leverage the new skills you learn to improve your leadership ability well beyond the point of where you are now.

To help you improve your leadership, you'll be guided through ten leadership problems that are both tough and common, using my SOLVE framework. Then you'll learn how to use the SOLVE framework to figure out any other problem you face. Think of this book as a pocket leadership coach, because now that you own this book, it's here for you, ready to pull out when you need it and to help you get through the tough problems you are facing—or will be facing—as you continue your leadership journey.

THE SOLVE FRAMEWORK

Before jumping into the problem-solving, I need to lay out the model that you'll be using. This model is born from my coaching, advisory, and exec ed work in the past twenty years. The work that I do has, for a very long time, focused on the magic that can happen when leaders apply high-quality thinking to their problems. When I say *thinking*, I mean analysis, self-reflection, and conducting light-touch research to learn more. This model, as you'll now see, helps you to work through a tough problem with sharp thinking applied at each stage.

S = State the problem

WHAT YOU'LL DO

Former head of research at General Motors Charles Kettering is credited with saying, "A problem well-stated is a problem half-solved," and in this section, you'll work on stating your problem in one to two sentences. I'll give you some prompts to help you generate these sentences, because you'll want them to be a clear, focused summary of what the problem is.

WHY YOU'LL DO IT

This problem statement forces you to extract the main problem from a complex situation and to work out what you're going to try to solve. I often find that leaders come to me with a very complex web of problems, and we may even spend our whole first coaching session working on this stage—narrowing, clarifying, reducing, until they are able to state what's going on. By getting you to focus on just one to two sentences (which you can always go back and edit later as your understanding of the problem grows), you are laser-focused on what the problem is and therefore can make sure that your solution is designed to fit your specific problem.

O = Open the box

WHAT YOU'LL DO

You'll unpack your problem. What is going on, why, and how? Within this stage, you'll be encouraged to observe and research your situation, while also learning some of the key theories and ideas that have been researched by experts and that should help you gain a better understanding. There are two major elements that will intertwine:

Firsthand research: This is you, as a leader, asking questions and finding out more about the problem. How are people feeling? What seems to be happening? This stage requires you to become data-focused, using conversations with others, listening carefully, and seeing what other data you can gather to make sense of the problem.

Preexisting research: You'll use the research done by others on these types of problems to deepen your understanding of what might be going on and what a suitable solution might be. You may find that, having read the preexisting research in this area, you can ask more specific questions and gather particular types of data to help work out what's happening. For example, if you have read that hybrid working can particularly disadvantage younger staff members, even though they have the strongest preference for it, can you see these factors at play in your setting, or is there something else going on?

By the end of the section, you should have a much better understanding of the situation.

WHY YOU'LL DO IT

Too often, we rush to a solution without fully understanding the problem. I think this is because it seems easier—the idea of researching further what is going on feels time-consuming and potentially scary. *Do we really want to know more about this problem, rather than trying to solve it?* Yes! Yes, you do. Because by understanding the problem more deeply, you'll establish the underlying causes, the other relevant factors, and how it's unfolding in your context.

L = Lay out your solution

WHAT YOU'LL DO

You'll originate a solution based on the problem you've identified. You'll make sure that it's a solution that looks as though it will work for your context, of which you've gained a better understanding through the "Open the Box" section. Again, you'll make use of preexisting research as to what works well in this type of problem.

WHY YOU'LL DO IT

A problem needs a solution, and this is where you lay it out. However, you'll notice that—having spent time understanding what is going on—laying out the solution will be far less time-consuming than usual because particular options will suggest themselves more strongly based on the knowledge you have gained.

V = Venture forth

WHAT YOU'LL DO

In this section, you'll start to take action. At this point, it's a case of being brave and applying the plan you've made. However, you may run into problems. This section will highlight some potential problems or pitfalls you could run into and suggest some solutions or preventative measures you may want to take.

WHY YOU'LL DO IT

It is unrealistic to think that, in a complex organizational setting, a solution can be applied without consequence. This section will take a look at some of the common consequences and how to handle them, so that you are well prepared. This isn't to say that there won't be other problems, but it encourages you to think about these, too, and to be prepared for a range of eventualities.

E = Elevate your learning

WHAT YOU'LL DO

Through solving the specific problem you faced, you'll have learned new skills and gained fresh knowledge. In this section, you'll learn how to continue to use the skills and knowledge that you've gained.

WHY YOU'LL DO IT

Too often, we learn a new skill to handle a problem, and then when the problem is dealt with, the skill goes back in the drawer. However, this is a big missed opportunity for leaders, who can and should lean into their newfound proficiencies. You may have found a skill you excel in, or something you can teach your team, or a proficiency that could be useful in a much wider range of situations than just the one you used it in. This is about leveraging your knowledge to elevate your leadership, seeing yourself as a lifelong learner who can carry on developing and growing throughout their career.

HEARING ABOUT REAL-LIFE LEADERS

To maximize the usefulness of this book, I've packed it with real-life examples from organizations and leaders of all types. Alongside this book being based on my experiences of working with and for leaders on their problems, I have also spoken to around thirty real-life leaders so they could help me to bring the stories, theories, and advice to life. I've spoken to a well-balanced mix of leaders across genders, race, and heritage. Breadth of experience was my aim, so I spoke to a very wide variety of people, because leadership is incredibly varied. Leadership is not just about being in charge of a huge business; being a frontline leader in a branch of Starbucks or being the captain of a sports team or the person at the helm of a small charity is just as much leadership. My main criteria for choosing leaders was the quality of their leadership—I've either seen them in action, or they come highly recommended.

Wherever I could, I've referred to my interviewees and their organizations by their real names, but on occasion, I've had to anonymize them. Many of them also shared very useful hints and tips on how they've solved leadership problems, and I've passed on as many of these to you as I can.

FIT THE CONTEXT BOXES

Throughout the book, you'll also see boxes that I've labeled "Fit the Context." This is because, for particular problems or situations, there is critical specific advice. It's recognizing that being a leader in one setting is not the same as in another—your problems may sound the same on the surface but can emerge for very different reasons or need entirely different solutions.

Keep an eye out for these boxes, and if you feel that they fit your situation, apply them to your SOLVE.

TALK TO ME!

One of the things I love the most is the huge variety of leaders I meet and the privilege of speaking to them about their problems. If you are reading through this book and feel that you need some help, or would like to send a problem to Dear Katie, or would just like to make contact, then please do! You can contact me at www.katiebest.com/contact-me.

The time has come! Your problems are not just going to solve themselves! So let's jump in.

PROBLEM 1
Personal Effectiveness

"I'm drowning in too much to do, but with no energy to do it. And yet I've just got to keep swimming for the benefit of my team. Being a leader and having a massive workload of my own is so hard!"

"I don't seem to have the ability to focus on anything anymore! I constantly buzz from one thing to the other, checking my phone, checking emails, waiting for the next thing to land. I'm not sure if it's me or if it's my work, but either way, I can't get sustained quiet to focus on what I need to do."

"All these meetings, projects, and expectations are draining my time and energy, but everyone needs a piece of me! I just don't know how to say no!"

I WAS MEETING AMELIE—A SALES DIRECTOR FOR A WELL-KNOWN TECH firm—for our third coaching session, and she came onto our video call looking tired and sad. I asked her how she was, conversationally, and she shook her head.

"Don't ask. I've got so much going on. I know I always say that, but this week, it's the worst it's ever been. My team is hassling me about how slow I am at the moment giving them feedback on their proposals. It means they can't send them out to clients, and so they can't win work and contribute to their sales targets. My boss is pushing me to update the format of the monthly report I send her, because she says it's outdated and doesn't take into account how much the team has grown and how the data need to be more aggregated as well as being chopped in a variety of ways. I should have said no when she asked, and said it needed to wait a few months, but like the idiot I am, I said yes. And then there's my usual work, like staying in touch with clients, doing my own proposals, and all the rest. My to-do list is enormous, and it's making me panic! I keep checking my inbox to see what else I'm being asked to do and dreading how I'll fit it in. And that makes me feel so stressed, all the words start swimming on the page, and I can't focus. So I end up doing the easy stuff, and that's fine, but the big, ugly tasks on the list—like the report—don't get done." She stopped and looked at me. "Sorry. Did you just mean, how am I? I'm fine, thanks. How are you?" She grinned wonkily, but before I could answer, her phone beeped, and I saw it take her attention as she looked at the message. "Sorry. Where were we? Oh yes, shall we start the coaching now? I've got so much going on; I was hoping we could finish fifteen minutes earlier?"

I really felt for Amelie in that moment; the weight of expectation she felt to do everything and do it really well was sending her into a tailspin that was reducing her ability to focus and to cope. Rather than being a helpful motivator, the pressure was threatening her well-being and diminishing the quality of her work. But it's so tough for leaders to focus when endless distractions and high workloads threaten to undermine their personal effectiveness while the cult of overwork threatens to crush them with its perspective that perhaps they are never quite effective enough.[1]

And rather than being a bit of helpful pressure, this obsession with being personally effective can reduce our work performance—for example, through uncharacteristic errors or lapses in memory; it can increase our likelihood to clash or conflict with other staff; and it can cause us to withdraw from our work, our workplace, and our colleagues, creating a further decline in performance.[2] Untreated, work pressure and overload can lead to anxiety, depression, digestive problems, heart disease, and weight gain.[3] As things currently stand, 72 percent of leaders feel used up at the end of the day.[4]

So if you are facing personal effectiveness issues similar to Amelie's, what can you do? This chapter is here to help—ascertaining what, if anything, is holding you back and helping you to establish good working habits, which will mean that you have good levels of personal effectiveness that balance achieving a lot in the moment with maintaining good work habits and well-being, allowing you to continue achieving in the future, too.

STATE THE PROBLEM

If you're facing personal effectiveness problems, it's useful to state what you think is going on, at a high level, before you dig into the details. Try to summarize the situation in one or two sentences, using the prompts below to help.

- **Where are you noticing problems with your personal effectiveness?**
  - Are you struggling to focus?
  - Are you lacking the ability to find flow?
  - Are you struggling to do the amount of work others expect of you or that you expect of yourself?
  - Are you feeling too tired or burned out to do what is required of you?
- **When, if ever, do you say no to work?**
  - When it feels as though it's not the right fit for you.
  - When you have too much going on.
  - You rarely—if ever—say no.

You can come back to adjust your sentences as your understanding develops over the course of the chapter, but it's there to help you be clear on what problem you're trying to solve.

OPEN THE BOX

If you're suffering from a problem with your personal effectiveness, it'll show up as a problematic drop in quality, quantity, or both. It may be that others have picked up on it or that you've noticed it in yourself. But once you're aware of it, you'll want to discover the root cause so you can solve the problem.

Is there too much going on?

Work overload can make concentrating difficult. The pressure of being overloaded can make you feel skittish and anxious, both of which can undermine your ability to concentrate.

Consider whether you have:

- Too many small tasks—it's hard to juggle and/or work out what to prioritize.
- A few big tasks but with big expectations attached.

In Amelie's example in this chapter's introduction, she had problems with both. She had lots of big tasks to do, such as writing client proposals and overhauling the format of the monthly report, and she had too many tasks—her very long to-do list was an indication of this.

A consequence of a long to-do list is task-switching, where you flit from one task to another, perhaps half tidying your desk, then sending an email, before writing up some stats, doing a bit more tidying, trying to phone someone, carrying on with the stats, and so forth. Ticking off small, easy tasks or making small dents in bigger tasks might feel like progress, but it's not efficient. It also leads to higher levels of cortisol and adrenaline (our stress hormones), which can cause foggy thinking and headaches, further impacting your ability to concentrate, as well as diminishing your memory[5] and creativity.[6] It also means that your big tasks won't get the sort of sustained attention that they warrant.

Aha! you say. *But I'm not task-switching! I'm multitasking.* I hate to break it to you, but you are not. Brains cannot do similar tasks simultaneously. Our limited attentions can only focus on one complex task. If you think you're multitasking between writing an email and listening to a meeting, you're actually doing one after the other repeatedly. And as you switch, you are using up time and cognitive energy,[7] because task-switching is very draining. A study of Fortune 500 workers showed that, on average, they toggled between different apps around 1,200 times a day, and each toggle took two seconds. Over a year, this added up to five working weeks per worker, or 9 percent of their time at work.[8]

Are there too many distractions and interruptions?

Leaders face myriad interruptions and distractions, from staff members reaching out for help, to email alerts, or phone calls, or urgent messages from a family member or a peer. Historically, managers' primary role was to supervise and handle problems, meaning that these interruptions were their lifeblood. However, most companies now expect managers to complete their own work alongside supervising, meaning that your need to handle live problems may be clashing with your need to focus.[9] Consider whether you are regularly drawn away from the work you were planning on doing by someone or something interrupting you. Do you do anything to manage this, or do you allow yourself to be interrupted and distracted?

It is also worth considering whether the novelty bias we all have is making things worse for us than they need to be. The novelty bias prompts us to pay more attention to things that are new or unusual to us than things that are more familiar. We developed this bias to keep us safe in the wild, making us hyperalert to something out of the ordinary that could represent a safety threat. However, in your safe office environment, your novelty bias mainly hinders focus.[10] Do you find yourself gravitating to the fresh problem you've been presented with, or the email from someone you don't know, or the Slack message that sounds interesting? And when you do, can you feel that dopamine rush, rewarding you for responding to the novelty? If you are regularly distracted from the task you're supposed to be doing by the lure of the new, then you may be struggling to fight the novelty bias.

Are you cracking under pressure?

Some pressure at work is good—if it's short term and relates to a specific project or task that you are keen to complete. In this form, it's *positive stress*—giving you a little adrenaline boost and the push to achieve. When you do, you're proud of yourself, the task is complete, the stress goes away, and you have time to recover before something else comes along at some point later when you're ready for another bit of positive stress. All fine—nothing to be concerned about.

However, when the pressure lasts for too long, or when separate pressures pile one on the other, or when you have no recovery time between successful periods, positive stress can quickly turn into negative stress, which can also be called *strain*. Strain makes us feel as though we are being stretched too far, squeezed too hard, placed under too much pressure. It leaves us anxious, panicky, sad, tired, or drained, and the hormones that are released when we feel stress—cortisol and adrenaline—go into overload and flood our systems, increasing our panic and making us feel foggy and reducing our performance.

As well as reducing our productivity, the fatigue that sustained strain leads to can create more serious outcomes, such as *burnout*. Burnout is a state that occurs when we work too hard and are left drained, disengaged, and less effective as a result.[11] Fortunately, it's not a clinical diagnosis, nor is it considered to be extremely serious—with time, you can recover, but you need to take that time. Otherwise, it could spill over into more serious conditions, such as heart problems and stroke, which can both be triggered by excess stress. This is a point at which it's important to be very honest with yourself: Are you facing too much pressure for too long a period that it is turning into strain? If so, you need to act as soon as you can to protect your health.

One more area you'll need to understand, to work out what's going on, is whether the pressure is coming from others or whether it's self-created.

IS THE PRESSURE COMING FROM OTHERS?

To ascertain whether you are working for a manager who's expecting you to produce more work—or work of a higher quality—than you are, consider if any of the following are happening:

- You have a pile of work that's too big, but you feel you can't push back.
- You have a lot of work to do in an area you're not skilled at, but your boss won't listen to your concerns.
- You dread sudden emails asking you for work last-minute, often forcing you to work in your evenings or weekends to meet their demands.
- A peer or senior is questioning your performance or commitment, despite there being good evidence that you are working well.

IS THE PRESSURE COMING FROM YOU?

Sometimes, the pressure that you feel won't be coming from your boss, peers, juniors, or even your clients. It'll be coming from yourself. You'll think, for some reason, that you need to work harder, quicker, longer, or cleverer to please others, hide your shortcomings, or please yourself.

I have seen many senior leaders who are so worried about failing at work or being seen as being less good than their colleagues that they work extra hard to cover their backs. I've seen others who are obsessed with being the best and fixate on work-based targets that are punishing. Either way, they create a huge amount of personal pressure, which tips over into strain. When they hear others call them *superhuman*, *intimidating*, or (in hushed whispers) a *workaholic*, they sometimes brush it off or sometimes see it as a badge of honor. In other words, personally applied pressure comes in a wide variety of forms and happens for many different reasons, but if you are putting yourself under this pressure, it's important to be honest about it.

In its most serious form, this personally applied pressure becomes a form of work addiction, where a worker places unreasonable pressure on themselves through an addiction or compulsion to do so, and like any bad habit, it needs acknowledging and breaking before they do themselves serious harm.[12]

Does work feel boring and pointless?

Quite a different sort of problem to close this section out with—rather than the world of high stress and novelty, personal effectiveness can also take a dip when we are bored at work or can't see any meaning in it. If you find the work mundane or pointless, or you don't value what you'll be rewarded with for completing it, you may find it hard to put in the effort required. The quality slips, deadlines are missed, you start to question why you are doing this job at all. A senior leader in the not-for-profit sector who had been, up until this point, very engaged in her work, told me how she knew that it was time to look for another job because she couldn't work up the enthusiasm to contribute to a team project. She had the feeling that she had "been here before" and that they had done many similar projects, but nothing had ever changed. The work felt pointless and too similar to the past. If you, too, feel your work is pointless or boring, and you think this is reducing your personal effectiveness, it'll be an important area to work on.

FIT THE CONTEXT: THE ADDED PROBLEMS THAT KNOWLEDGE WORK BRINGS

In knowledge work, where outputs are intangible and hard to define (Is that a good report? Is the thinking behind that recommendation of a high quality?), it is common for managers to measure performance by looking at inputs instead.

If you can't see how many units are produced, you can at least see how many hours of effort seem to be expended.

The problem is that this approach leads to *performative busyness*, meaning that rather than focusing their attention on the important work that needs doing, team members stress about things like replying to their bosses and showing that they are at their desk for ten hours a day, to demonstrate just how busy they are at work.[13] The quick responses take time away from what they should be doing—getting the big, important stuff done. And the long hours often reduce work quality, as tired brains are less likely to come up with creative solutions or provide novel insights.

Many sectors are in denial about this latter point, but, for example, higher rates of suicidal thoughts in the legal sector linked to high stress levels and overwork[14] is leading to firms taking it more seriously.

A final burden faced by knowledge workers in a quest for better personal effectiveness is that companies fill their laptops with apps that are designed to make collaboration easier. Real-time messaging, the ability to call someone for a video chat at that moment, and being able to set up all sorts of work channels for different projects should mean that you are able to boss your to-do list. But often, what these systems give us in terms of better collaboration, they take away in terms of our ability to find focus and flow, as they are designed to interrupt us so we don't hold someone else's work up when they are waiting for an answer.

If you are a knowledge worker, you may want to consider the degree to which the culture is driving you toward a higher level of personal effectiveness than it is reasonable to expect. Are there moves in your industry or organization to take action on this? Is there anything you are particularly concerned about that you would like to factor into your solution?

BEFORE MOVING ON:

- What do you think the causes of your personal effectiveness problems are?
- Do you think that anyone is making your personal effectiveness problems worse? How?
- Have you identified any serious risks of strain or burnout that you need to prioritize dealing with?

LAY OUT YOUR SOLUTION

As you now work on solutions for your issues with personal effectiveness, you'll be focusing on how to improve your own behaviors but also how to handle others who are not helping you by asking too much of you or distracting you.

How to find focus and flow

CULL DIGITAL DISTRACTIONS

Get rid of those phone beeps, email pings, pop-ups, and impromptu calls that you feel you have to respond to lest you hold a project up or someone accuses you of not working hard enough. Sure, you still need to engage with these elements, but you should be actively choosing when, rather than them choosing for you. This will allow you more opportunity to focus and find flow. Turn off any notifications that you can. Social media notifications and email pop-ups are good initial targets. You should be able to turn them off in your settings. If your work phone is locked down and you can't, then turn off the volume, turn off vibrate, and leave it in your coat pocket while you work. As soon as you can see it, you're more likely to be tempted by it. If you can't switch them off on your computer, again turn the sound off, and stick a Post-it over the corner of your screen that notifies you when something has come in. There will be times when you do need notifications, so you can switch them on again, and you can also experiment with which ones are useful versus which are distracting.

You may feel odd to start with—it can even feel like a form of withdrawal. Your brain could well be addicted to the little dopamine rush it gets each time it distracts you with a new alert or piece of information. Just as with any addiction, breaking the habit will take some time and conscious effort. In this case, you are breaking your body's reliance on the nice feeling that the dopamine rush gives.[15] When you feel yourself wanting to be distracted (i.e., your body wanting the dopamine), you'll need to remind yourself why you're not going to let it happen (reduced personal effectiveness, higher stress, no chance to focus) and get back to what you were doing before your brain gave you that nudge.

CULL REAL-WORLD DISTRACTIONS

If you're working in an office, find ways to signal to colleagues that you don't want to be interrupted. Close the door to your private office if you have a door. If you're in an open-plan workspace and it's acceptable to listen to music, invest in a pair of noise-canceling headphones—people will soon realize that, when you have these on, you're trying to concentrate and you don't want to be interrupted. You don't have to play music—you can just have them on or put on some white noise or relaxing sea sounds or one of those spa-type playlists. Block out your calendar, too, and encourage people to check this before interrupting you. Tell them it's not them, it's you—you are struggling to concentrate, and you really need to.

If you want more focus than your office can provide, even with these ideas above, consider booking out a meeting room or a coworking space in your office, going to a coffee shop, desk hopping to a department where no one is in on that day, or even sitting out in nature. Computers these days are good enough that the shade of a tree is sufficient for you to be able to see your screen, and it's been shown that sitting in nature can increase your productivity and task performance, so you may find the benefit is bigger than you're expecting.[16] All these other places will put some distance between you and those people who threaten to disturb your focus.

If you're moving away from your desk anyway, consider leaning further into this and leaving your laptop behind if you can do some work that doesn't need a computer (brainstorming, writing a first draft or plan, reading). Being away from a screen for a bit can be really good for your creativity and for recharging your brain and eyes if they are tired of staring at pixels.

STOP TASK-SWITCHING

Remember that multitasking is rarely possible, and you are task-switching instead, which is using up extra time, rather than making you more efficient. And when you feel tempted to switch, remember that the idea that you are being more effective is an illusion.

To help your discipline in focusing on just one task at a time, highlight it on your to-do list, or write it out fresh and put it on your desk prominently (while hiding your to-do list). It also helps to clear your workspaces—digital and physical—to remove distractions that could prompt you to task-switch, allowing you instead to focus on the task at hand. This means you should close tabs, remove distracting to-do lists from your visual field, and put away documents or other items that remind you of other tasks to be done.

I have found moving my to-do list online has been great, as I don't then have my to-do list sitting on my desk, providing helpful suggestions on how I could switch tasks. Instead, I open the tab, choose an item off it, do the item, and then reopen the tab to delete it off the list.

GIVE YOURSELF PERMISSION TO FOCUS

If you recognize that your personal effectiveness isn't optimal but you are reading the above recommendations coming up with reasons why they may not work for you, I think you should check that you are not addicted to the busyness, or overemphasizing how important your immediate contribution is. Remember when you were ill, and everyone coped? Remember that two-hour meeting you were in last week when everything was just fine afterward? Attention management expert Cal Newport says that, at least once per semester at university, he takes himself to the cinema for an afternoon to remind himself that the working world can and does tick along quite nicely without him.[17]

Even if you've felt resistant until now, turn to your calendar and pick out a clear space at some point in the next fortnight of at least one hour long. Block it out for a task you know you need focus for. And then, when you get to it, block distractions and focus.

How to make your work more interesting

If you've been struggling to find work interesting and your personal effectiveness has suffered, try to reframe your work as important and meaningful. There is a whole section on this in Problem 5 where I look at the ways to improve engagement and job satisfaction. In headline form, you should be reminding yourself of how your work is critical to the organization's mission. If it's about work that is too easy, raise the stakes by working to a tighter deadline or setting a higher standard of quality. Easiness could also mean that a task is suitable for delegation to a more junior team member who may find it more challenging.

FIT THE CONTEXT: ARE YOU BEING ASKED TO DO THE HOUSEWORK?

In organizations, there are always tasks that don't allow any scope for being recognized or rewarded for their performance. Taking on a very small number is good—it shows you to be a good organizational citizen. However, don't take on more than your fair share. This can range from small, almost unnoticeable tasks like making the tea or printing the handouts for a meeting to much bigger tasks like writing Christmas cards to clients or booking everyone's tickets for a conference.

On the whole, women are far more likely to say yes to these tasks, setting an expectation that they will do them in the future. This has a negative impact on the time they have available to do tasks that *are* promotable. This may in part explain why they lose out on promotions to men more frequently than vice versa.[18]

If you find yourself about to say yes to the housework, consider whether this will mean you're doing more than your fair share, and if it will, say no.

How to prioritize

Four thousand weeks. That's the number of weeks in the average life. Gulp. When best-selling author Oliver Burkeman made that horrifying time frame the title of his book,[19] I had to sit in a room and think for a bit. That's a whole lifetime. Take out childhood, post-school training, retirement, holidays, and weekends, and the amount of time you have to make meaning from your work really shrinks. I don't think there's a better reminder that we need to be prepared to focus on what really matters to our work and cut everything that doesn't. But how?

- **Take all the pointless things off your to-do list.** If they're just there because you feel obligated, but they don't serve any real value, cull them. If someone needs to do them, but not you, pass them to the correct owner. Jo Farmer, joint managing partner at Lewis Silkin, could easily have an over-crowded to-do list, but she talked about the value of having peers and team members who are quick to say when a task shouldn't be a priority for her, or when it should be on someone else's to-do list. These peers save her from the things that otherwise might distract her from the firm's strategic intentions.
- **Be ruthless with meetings.** Most organizations have too many, they're too long, and they take people away from doing their proper work, so be brave and say no. Only go to meetings if they're important or compulsory. If you have to go, work hard to make them efficient. If you're in charge, insist on a proper agenda beforehand. And don't be afraid to cut them short if everything's covered.
- **Attack your digital clutter.** Delete apps you don't use, tidy up your desktop, have a decent filing system, and make it less likely you're going to be distracted while working by some unwanted notification or by having to look for a file you haven't actually filed.
- **Wage war on your real-life clutter.** The pile of papers on your desk you must look through to find that one thing you need, the work clothes you haven't worn for years, the collection of tea bags and biscuits you've picked up from meeting rooms for no discernible reason and that are arguing for space with your stapler in your top drawer. A tidy work landscape could save us hours a year not looking for papers or getting distracted by the clutter.

A simpler digital and physical life, with a shorter to-do list and a laser focus on what matters, will help you conserve energy, find your focus, and reach a flow state. I've kept this section intentionally uncluttered to hammer home my point. Enjoy.

How to handle pressure

As a leader, you'll regularly be in pressure situations, but remember that this is fine as long as you have sufficient time to recover between periods of pressure and as long as the pressure doesn't go on for too long. As such, handling pressure is twofold: building up energy supplies means that you can withstand pressure for longer, factoring in recovery time. You also need to be able to spot when the pressure has been going on for too long and know what you should do about it.

BUILDING UP YOUR RESERVES

To prepare for periods of prolonged stress, try to maintain a healthy lifestyle the vast majority of the time. That means eating well, having a good sleep pattern, exercising regularly, and looking after your mental health. These actions will foster good energy levels, a healthy body, and a good headspace. They'll mean that when you do find yourself under high pressure, you can endure it more successfully without it impacting your performance, like a well-trained athlete.[20] If we begin a period of stress with good blood pressure, great sleeping patterns, and low cortisol levels, we have some capacity to take on more stress without overloading too quickly.[21]

HOW TO REACT WHEN THE STRESS KICKS IN

When stress starts to kick in, double down on your good habits. Work hard to go to wind down in the evening and go to bed at a regular time, as good quality sleep will safeguard you from the negative stress for longer. Eat extra well, and avoid alcohol, caffeine, and other stimulants and depressants. Yes, they can provide temporary relief, but consuming them will reduce your performance and your ability to recover.

FACTOR IN DOWNTIME TO RECOVER FROM STRESS

These rest periods will look different for everyone. It's worth considering which activities, for you personally, are energy creators and which are energy sponges. If you're not aware of how your energy ebbs and flows—what tops it up and what depletes it—keep a note on your phone for a few weeks, recording the times of day when you are particularly high or low energy, as well as activities at work and outside work that boost or deplete your energy. After a few weeks, you should have a sense of what invigorates you versus what drains you, and when you typically have the most energy so you can use that time for the work that requires the most focus.

Megan Jones, a catering manager for BaxterStorey, has long, demanding days. When I asked her how she coped on a day when she woke up with low energy, she told me she would make sure she dressed in bright colors, had a longer chat with the baristas when she got her Pret coffee on the way in to work, talked to her team a lot at work, and then she would make sure she sat in an area of the office with lots of plants—an addition implemented by the facilities team after the COVID-19 lockdowns and very much appreciated by the staff. These are all small actions, but Megan knows that each one has a positive effect on her, topping up her energy and helping her to handle the stress of work.

MAKE SURE YOUR RECOVERY TIME IS SUFFICIENT

Remember: if you aren't getting enough recovery time and you are still under pressure, your stress will build. You'll need to watch this, to ensure you're not going to run out of reserves before the stressful period is over. If you are, plan to reduce the pressure now, or increase your recovery time to reduce the risk of burnout.

How to handle unrealistic expectations

WORK OUT WHAT *IS* REALISTIC

If you've identified unrealistic expectations, your first step is to work out what is realistic for you to achieve. How many hours can you commit, when, and what can you achieve in this time? Humans are good at estimating how long practical tasks will take, but much worse at estimating the duration of more abstract or cerebral tasks, so you should assume that all the major tasks on your list will take you 25–50 percent more time than you initially allow for.[22]

I would generally recommend honoring what is already on your to-do list, even if it means a few more weeks of hard work. It means you are not throwing others under the bus with tasks that haven't been completed, which can reflect very badly on you. Then, before taking on anything new, make sure you say no to tasks that don't fulfill your criteria for a task worth doing (return to the section on prioritizing if you need help with this). Also make sure that you're saying no to tasks that are unrealistic for you to achieve because you don't have capacity right now.

LEARN TO SAY NO TO OTHERS

Saying no to others is best done from a place of respect and appreciation. If the person feels as though their request was valid, and you have good reasons for saying no that are not suggesting that they or their work are not important, you will stay on good terms with them after the no. Here's how to structure a good no.

- **Show appreciation** that they have asked you, as opposed to someone else, by saying thank you.
- **Present a rational argument** about why taking on this task isn't in the company's best interests (e.g., will take your focus away from your main role, or a more important task,

or conflict with another project you're working on). Make sure you have a clear, rational reason before you say no.

- **Seek permission to say no**, whether you have the right to say no or not. If they're senior to you, asking before you say no respects the hierarchy. If they are equal or junior, it softens the message. The simplest phrasing of this is, "Is it going to be okay if I say no?"
- **If they're not okay with it**, suggest taking time out and returning to the conversation in the next day or so. It's remarkable how often someone will accede to a request if they are given time to think about it, as the time allows them to arrive at solutions other than you doing the work.

LEARN TO SAY NO TO YOURSELF

If you're unfairly putting yourself under pressure to achieve more, you need to stop. Now that you've clarified what's appropriate to expect yourself to achieve, you'll need to find a way to enforce it. I suggest a clear set of statements that you can test yourself against—not something vague like "I'll take less on," which you can't test yourself on or hold yourself accountable to. Instead, use specific boundaries, such as "I will volunteer to help with three recruitment days a year maximum," or "I will say no to work that isn't clearly related to the success of my team," or "I'll remove myself from the training committee." These sorts of statements are objectively measurable—you can clearly see whether you're sticking to the boundaries or not.

Amelie, the coaching client I introduced at the start of the chapter, always felt there was more she could do and struggled to clock off in evenings and at weekends. However, previous promises to "have an evening" were hard to put into practice. What did that even mean? But once she said, "I'm only allowed to work past 8:00 p.m. one evening per week," she could clearly check if she was actioning this plan or not.

KEEP A WATCHFUL EYE ON THOSE BOUNDARIES

When I coach leaders, I regularly see the pattern. They say that they are being overworked, or are putting themselves under too much pressure, and then set clear boundaries. They are great at enforcing them for a while, and then slowly, it slips again. Research shows that this is true for many of us and that work-life balance is commonly a cycle, not an end point. We go through phases where work takes over and phases where it's less dominant—either because we push back or the workload is less extreme.

What I find, though, is that the leaders who are better at maintaining their boundaries notice that they are heading for overwork because they have made their boundaries clear, and they take time to reflect on them. Perhaps they keep track of hours worked or notice the signs of stress in themselves, such as poor sleep or headaches, and take corrective action quickly.

If you find, over the coming months, that you cannot stick to the reasonable boundaries you have created, it may be time to consider if you do have a problem with workaholism. As we're heading into the territory of a recognized addiction, if you think you may have an addiction to work, because despite best intentions you are still overworking to a dangerous level, then reach out for help.

You could turn to a family member, a friend, or a trusted colleague. Make sure it's someone who's going to be sympathetic, rather than a boss who sees your overwork as a valuable organizational resource and doesn't want you to stop! You're looking for someone to talk through the issue with you and help you to get further support if you need it.

BEFORE MOVING ON:

- What will you do to solve your problems with personal effectiveness?

- What will you do to manage others' expectations about what is realistic for you to achieve? How will you manage your own expectations?
- How will you maintain good personal effectiveness and/or expectations management as you move forward?
- If you are concerned that you may have work addiction, or be a workaholic, where will you turn for help?

VENTURE FORTH!

The biggest obstacle you're likely to face when trying to improve personal effectiveness is yourself. You'll be breaking old habits and making new ones, both of which are hard to do. Here are three blockers you might experience and ideas for managing them:

If you accidentally drift back into bad habits . . . take a deep breath and start again

Some of the work you're expecting yourself to do *will* be hard. Old habits can be hard to break. And it can take up to three months to properly break a habit, depending on how long it's been a habit, your motivation to quit, and how integrated into your life it is.[23] And in that journey, you may find that you accidentally drift back into bad habits, scrolling on social media, working late, or saying yes to a task you really should be saying no to. What should you do?

- Acknowledge the misstep and think about why it happened.
- Choose to commit to the habit again immediately.
- Promise yourself interim rewards for maintaining the habit, such as a Friday afternoon matcha latte or a longer lunch break.

If you forget . . . set reminders

Forming new habits, even if they're going to have a positive impact, can be hard to do. You may need to remind yourself until they become habits. Set calendar reminders for focus time. Block out time in your calendar to clear your desk or declutter your hard drive. Set an alarm on your phone for twenty minutes after you usually wake up to spend a few moments focusing on your breath to increase your propensity to focus. Leave a cryptic Post-it on your monitor at work saying RTSN (Remember to Say No).

If you find you're trying to do too much at once, and you can't remember all the new habits in one go, focus on one at a time, starting the next one once you've made good progress on remembering to do the first.

If you find yourself sticking rigidly to a bad plan . . . pivot

Some of the best-laid plans turn out to be totally wrong. You might think that it's definitely going to work for you to have focus time every Thursday morning, and then the reality of the way your job works means this just ends up being plowed through and it's massively frustrating. Sometimes it will be about persistence, but sometimes it will also be about pivoting. Maybe your idea for what was going to help your flow was wrong and you need another strategy to achieve the same end goal.

It's okay to change your mind and decide to do something else. As long as you keep that important end goal in mind, it is less important which particular technique you use to get there or how you flex it to fit your own circumstances.

For example, in a C-suite workshop I ran recently, participants had vastly different attitudes toward time off. One said that he would rather check his emails for half an hour every morning of his holiday and pass the work on to colleagues so he knows what he's coming back to.

Another said she would rather pass it all over before she goes away and be uncontactable. Both had done a lot of self-reflection on their journeys to the C-suite to work out what was right for them.

I'd recommend writing down some notes as you make your way through your personal effectiveness plan as to what's working easily, what's proving harder, and what's impossible. And then you can continue to make changes as you head toward your goal. You can adjust your approach by revisiting the suggestions in this chapter.

ELEVATE YOUR LEARNING

Once you have executed your own plan to improve your relationship with personal effectiveness and begin seeing results, what next?

If you're enjoying your newfound focus . . . increase it further

If you want to be able to focus, you need to learn to focus. The good news is brains can be trained. Every moment you actively focus, you increase your brain's ability to focus. It is like working a muscle at the gym.

You can dedicate time to improving this ability through mindfulness and meditation. Neither requires any specialist equipment, and you can start immediately.

HOW TO INTEGRATE MEDITATION INTO YOUR DAY

Find a calm space, sit comfortably, and observe your breathing. To help you focus, count each breath. When you reach ten, or lose count, start the count again. You will, of course, lose focus, and the real work you're doing is acknowledging that your focus has wandered and gently returning your focus to your breath. Do this for ten minutes if you can, but even three or four minutes, on a busy day, will have an impact.

HOW TO INTEGRATE MINDFULNESS INTO YOUR DAY

Mindfulness is paying attention to what you're doing, when you're doing it, and noticing your actions without judgment. You could stop work for a moment and mindfully notice your surroundings—identify four things you can see, three things you can touch, two you can hear, and one you can smell. You can also pay extra attention to your lunch when you eat it, mindfully chewing. Or approach your email in a mindful way, observing the way that you type, how you move the mouse around, the words that you choose. It's all about living in that moment with more presence, and it can be incredibly useful for calming a stressed mind and for training you to have greater focus now and in the future.

If you can see the value for your team . . . share what you've learned

Share your newfound knowledge of personal effectiveness with your team to help them improve their relationship with it, too. Start by making sure that you are modeling good personal effectiveness behaviors. A key role of leaders is to be a role model, showing the way to their juniors. As such, leaders who recognize the need to find focus and flow, look after their well-being to maintain their energy, and are not afraid to say no stand a much better chance at fostering these performance-enhancing behaviors in their team.[24]

Reflect on ways that you can encourage or ratify choices that will increase personal effectiveness—for example, saying no to meetings, or turning off emails for an hour to get something done. If you hear that people are doing this and you notice good work comes out of it, provide positive feedback to them so they know they have your ongoing support.

You could even go a step further; increasingly, managers are advocating meeting-free days or lunchtimes or encouraging team members to block out time to complete focus work. Can you find a way to organize your team's working patterns so that they can take advantage of afternoons with no meetings, or hours when they are not expected to answer their emails?

We met Amelie, a sales director at a tech company, in the opening section, and she was struggling with the multiple demands she was being placed under, as well as the volume of work. It was all making her feel stressed and reducing her personal effectiveness.

Over the next few coaching sessions, the topic of how she could improve her personal effectiveness became a common theme. Amelie realized that she needed to prioritize looking at the proposals her team was sending her; otherwise, they would not be able to win or retain their clients. She also needed to prioritize reconfiguring the monthly report for her boss, as simplifying it as her boss had proposed would immediately start to save her a considerable amount of time each month.

She also recognized that, because her workload was so high, and her team was capable, she needed to let go of the clients she was still looking after directly, instead passing them on to trusted members of her team. Her boss had been encouraging her to do this since she'd stepped into the role, and it had only been the high expectations she'd had of herself and of being able to do it all that had prevented her from doing so.

Her final act—but a big one—was to turn off message notifications on her phone. She realized that rather than making her more effective, they made her less effective, interrupting her train of thought. She could never give them a decent response when she was away from her desk in any case, and it stopped her being attentive to what was going on at the time, such as a one-to-one with a team member, a meeting, or a coaching session. Stopping notifications had the added benefit of reducing her stress levels, stopping the little surge of panic she had each time a message came in.

REMEMBER:

- High levels of personal effectiveness are more likely when you reduce distractions, increase your interest in your work, identify what you need to prioritize, learn to focus your attention, and are able to say no when required.
- Handling pressure is key to ensuring high levels of personal effectiveness in the moment and avoiding burnout and reduced effectiveness in the future. Build up your energy reserves to help cope when times are tough, and factor in downtime to recover from periods of stressful overwork.
- Perceptions that your personal effectiveness could be better are not always fair; you may be putting yourself under too much pressure or allowing others to put you under too much pressure. Recognizing what is reasonable for you or others to expect will help you to establish and maintain appropriate boundaries.

PROBLEM 2

Decision-Making

"I have made a bad hiring decision, and I'm worried I'm never going to live it down."

"I'm not confident in the quality of my decisions, but I've just been put in charge of the marketing budget and want to make sure I'm making sound choices that I can justify."

"I feel like I'm in an echo chamber with my peers and my team, and I don't think anyone tells me what they really think."

MILO WAS FRONT-OF-HOUSE TEAM LEADER IN A RESTAURANT, AND XIA'S manager. Xia regularly arrived late, called in sick, and called friends from the staff room when she was supposed to greet customers.

It should have been an easy choice as to what to do: tell her to stop. However, she was the restaurant owner's niece. She also looked and acted like Milo's daughter, who had recently moved out, and he knew he would find it harder to reprimand her.

Rather than making a decision to handle the situation in some way, Milo just let the situation rumble on. However, he was in his office organizing the staff roster about six weeks into Xia's employment, and three furious staff members burst in: they had found Xia chatting in the staff room in a way they would never get away with. They felt it had had a big impact on the quality of service they were able to offer and on their diners' willingness to tip at the end of the meal.

Milo's decision to do nothing had been bad for the team, its performance, and its financial gain. His decision-making was faulty because he had let his relationship with his boss and his soft treatment of someone who looked like his daughter cloud his judgment.

If, like Milo, you are a leader whose decision-making isn't always great, read on. This chapter will look at decision-making problems from two angles: 1) what to do about a bad decision, and 2) how to improve your decision-making processes, with this helping you avoid bad-decision situations more frequently.

STATE THE PROBLEM

Can you state your decision-making problem in a few sentences? You can use these prompts to help.

- **What type of decision-making problem is this?** Is it that a decision has gone badly and you need to rectify the situation, or that you just need your decision-making to be better?
- **If it's a problem with a decision that's gone wrong, who has it affected?** How big a problem has it created for them? What have you already done to try to resolve the situation? Have any of your actions helped?
- **If it's a problem with your decision-making in general, what do you think is going wrong?**
    - You take too long to make decisions.
    - You make decisions too quickly, without sufficient consideration.
    - You don't always have the right data to make a good decision.
    - You don't have a good decision-making process.
    - You're worried you may let biases or illogical thinking reduce the quality of your decisions.

OPEN THE BOX

Are you in the aftermath of a bad decision?

If you've arrived here while dealing with a recent bad decision, as Milo was, you may be tempted to act immediately. However, this may make the situation worse: your emotions could cloud your judgment; you might overestimate the severity of the problem; and in trying to right wrongs, you may also overcorrect. Milo could have stormed up to Xia and fired her, which would not have helped his relationship with his boss, or he could've made a rash promise to the team that he would approach his boss about the problem, which he may have struggled to go through with.

Nick Rice, CEO of Consolite, a supplier to the defense industry, told me that if someone comes to him with a problem that makes him feel emotionally charged, he doesn't act immediately, but instead sleeps on it. He recognizes that as the CEO of a small-to-medium enterprise, he needs to make clear, consistent decisions.

Following a poor decision, take the space to work out what went wrong and what you can do to improve your decision-making in the future. Later, you'll learn how to structure a good apology and make amends for your error. First, we should look at where your decision-making is going wrong.

Are you making important decisions too quickly?

Busy leaders have plenty of good reasons for quick decision-making. Having too much to do can mean it's harder to find the space to deliberate over a decision, whereas if you just make a choice, you can move on. You might also have a natural action orientation, being inclined toward action over reflection. You may even have been promoted to leadership *because* you are a speedy decision-maker.

If you've been overloaded with decisions recently, you may struggle to process any more decision-making information, prompting a less careful, quicker approach, due to mental exhaustion or wanting to be done with thinking about decisions.

If you are making important decisions with big gaps in your knowledge or not weighing the evidence sufficiently before you do so, this could lead to weak choices that are reflecting badly on you as a leader. If this describes you, you're in good company. Research has shown that even professional project managers give too little time to the process of decision-making, then spend far too much time dealing with the overspend and late delivery of ill-thought-out decisions.[1]

Consider whether:

- You regularly feel you want to "get on with it," rather than checking if you have enough information to decide.
- You feel great when things are decided in a meeting, even if most other people seem to want to go slower, or spend longer considering alternatives.
- You often later gain extra information, which would have been relatively easy to access earlier, which makes you wish you could reconsider your decision.

Are you making decisions too slowly?

While good decision-making may require some of us to slow down, for others, it means they need to speed up, because good decisions require careful balance between speed and precision. It is not always good to go as slowly as possible; time used on one decision can't be used for something else, and the situation can change while you're still deliberating (quoted prices go up, candidates come off the job market), meaning you have to start your decision-making process again.

Causes of slow decision-making can include an overload of data and fear of making the wrong decision, each of which can lead to decision paralysis.

Consider whether:

- You labor over decisions, even small ones, considering your options extremely thoroughly.
- You mull over the data, or seek more and more data, more than is required for this sort of decision.
- Your team pushes you for a plan, feels held up by you, when you are still thinking through a number of similar options.

If this resonates, you may have a problem with slow decision-making.

Are you making decisions based on bad foundations?

A poor decision often comes about, despite all best intentions, because the assumptions or data it's based on are faulty. Below are a selection of common ways that leaders come unstuck, and you should reflect on which of these you have a problem with.

YOU'RE PERSUADED BY POOR-QUALITY DATA

If you're under time pressure or bombarded with information, it can be easy to take data or evidence at face value and assume it is correct.

However, if you are not looking at the nature of the data someone is using to convince you or that you are using to shape your decision, then this could lead to poor-quality decisions.

There are all kinds of ways that data can be poor quality—being too old, based on too small a sample size, or using a sample that doesn't reflect the group it claims to represent (e.g., talking about all women's experiences of work but only asking women ages forty to fifty in New York City) are three common problems.

The way that data is presented can be misleading—for example, starting the y-axis on a graph from a number to make differences between groups look big when they are actually very small.

Data may be intentionally biased to help the person presenting it to make a case to support a particular perspective or outcome, or it may be inadvertent.

Consider whether you are actively and bravely considering the quality of the data and evidence you use, or are presented with, to make your decisions. If not, this could be a major source of low decision quality.

YOU'RE IGNORING YOUR COGNITIVE BIASES

Cognitive biases cloud our judgment and, when allowed to dominate (rather than us noticing them and managing them), can lead to poor decisions.

Read the following list regarding decisions you have made recently. Which of these biases do you think you are succumbing to?

- **Availability bias** occurs when you assume that the data you have easily at hand is precisely what you need to make a good decision. You may decide who to interview based on the number of recommendations they have on LinkedIn, which may be skewed by how actively they've asked for recommendations from previous employers.
- **Confirmation bias** happens when you favor the data that confirms what you already believe. If you are a leader who's "noticed" that team performance has dropped this quarter, you notice a slight drop in Net Promoter Scores, while inadvertently ignoring the statistic that shows significant growth in repeat business. Therefore, you decide on expensive customer service training, rather than using the money to develop existing business relationships.
- **Status quo bias** kicks in when you take the course of action that allows you to keep things as close to how they currently are as possible. Rather than considering all options for a team restructure, you double down on your view that

everything is best how it currently is, without realizing you're doing this more through fear of change than because it is the best course of action.

- **Overoptimism bias** occurs when you view a course of action as more desirable than it is—for example, believing data that tells you a project will come in at a particular time to a particular budget. Regularly, these figures will be much higher, but we are inclined to believe the more optimistic version of events. It can prompt you to take on projects impossible to achieve within the stated budget and/or time frame, making you look like a poor decision-maker or a poor project manager.
- **The "I'm not biased" bias** is when you think you are in a nonexistent group of people who are not affected by cognitive biases. Thus, if you read through these examples and think, *Well, that doesn't apply to me*, you are experiencing this bias. It's part of a broader category of biases that lead humans to be overconfident in their abilities. It means that even if you do not think you are biased, you should from here on in assume that you are.
- **Experience bias** occurs when we become bewitched by our own view of the world and don't perceive that there are other ways to think about a situation. If you are a leader from a military background who's very keen to maintain their fitness levels, you're more likely to see spending on the workplace gym as a good use of money. To examine if you are someone who fails to explore how your context affects your decisions, reflect on whether you consider the impact your gender, sexuality, race, cultural heritage, status as a parent or carer (or not), hobbies, religion, country of upbringing, country of residence, job role, or personality has on your decision-making. If you let your own experiences dominate

your decisions, without trying to widen your perspective to take on board other people's perspectives, you will make decisions that suffer bias.

Do you feel that some of these biases influence your decision-making? Make a note of which ones and where you think they are having an impact. If you don't believe so, remember the "I'm not biased" bias and check again.

ARE YOUR DECISIONS GOVERNED BY POLITICS?

Organizational politics occurs when individuals push their own agenda, at the expense of what's best for the organization. Your own self-interests may also shape the decisions you take, perhaps favoring a bonus scheme where you can take a larger helping of the bonus pot than your team members.

If your decisions are overly influenced by your own agenda, or someone else's, this could slow down decision-making, or lead to bland or suboptimal outcomes as you try to factor in these self-interests.

To analyze whether your decision-making is excessively influenced by politics, consider:

- Are you consistently favoring certain people in your decisions to keep them happy?
- Are they lobbying you or putting you under pressure to concede to their demands?
- Are you letting your own self-interest override the decision that would be best for others—in particular, your team, peers, or organization?

If you've answered yes to at least one of these questions, organizational politics is likely to reduce the quality of your decisions.

Don't forget the role of bad luck!

So far, I've based this chapter on the assumption that bad decision outcomes are entirely avoidable. This is simply not true. Sometimes you will make a decision at the right speed, with high-quality data, and it won't go the way you thought it would. It might make the decision look bad in retrospect, but it's just bad luck that it didn't play out as you'd envisaged.

One interviewee, a senior leader in the public sector, told me how he had once been on the appointment panel for the CEO for a charity. She was great in the interview, her references were superb, but in eighteen months, she had bankrupted the organization. The panel went back to see if there was anything they had missed, any warning signs in her interview or in her past, so that they could learn from the experience. There was absolutely nothing. They chewed it over before concluding that, on the evidence that had been available, recruiting her had been the right decision and what transpired next was best characterized as bad luck.

If you are looking back at a bad decision, and you've been through this "Open the Box" section and you can't pinpoint anything you've done wrong, it may just have been bad luck. If so, there will be no benefit in creating a better decision-making process for that type of decision, as it was already good.[2]

You *should* stay alert, though, and if the same situation arises again, you'll need to revisit your decision-making process again with a more critical eye as to what went wrong.

BEFORE MOVING ON:

- Are you in the aftermath of a bad decision? If so, what was it? How is it impacted?

- How does your decision-making appear to go wrong and why? Too quick? Too slow? Bad data? Biases? Politics? What makes it more likely that you will make a poor decision?
- Are you struggling to see any faults that may have caused the problem and will now treat it as a case of bad luck, unless evidence arises to suggest otherwise?

LAY OUT YOUR SOLUTION

Decide how much care this decision needs

An optimal decision-making process would take every possible option and weigh it carefully using numerical weightings at various stages. However, as a busy leader, with most decisions you face, it won't be realistic to say, "Hold on! I'm just going to take a few days to consider all the options, think about all their outcomes, assign percentage weightings to the likelihood of each option under each scenario, and then be absolutely certain that we are placing our stationery order with the right company." Time pressure, and the decision often not being important enough to warrant that much time spent on it, means you need an approach that can flex to fit, and the confidence to analyze how much effort it's worth expending on this particular decision.

To understand how long you should spend, consider:

- How likely it is that something could go wrong if you don't consider the decision in detail?
- How bad would it be if something went wrong?

If it's likely to go wrong and it would be bad if it did, you'll want to follow a full, detailed decision-making process—for example, if you are tasked with choosing between two new structures for your team, which will affect everyone's employment contracts and may be sufficiently different, such that you can expect resignations from important team members whatever you choose. Here, the stakes are extremely high, and you'll want to weigh the decision carefully.

If it's extremely unlikely that something will go badly wrong, and/or if something does go wrong and it's unlikely to be all that bad, you can have a lighter touch to your decision-making process. Deciding on a new template for all client presentations is important, but extremely unlikely to go badly wrong. When picking a location for the office summer party, even if it's not perfect, no one will mind that much. You can make these decisions relatively quickly.

It's also easier to be light-touch in your decision-making when it's easy to reverse the decision or to pivot. This is another form of "it's unlikely to be all that bad," but in this case because you can change direction easily. Deciding whether to give clients a three-month free trial of your service may seem huge, but it's easy to remove the offer from future clients if it doesn't work out. Amazon regularly uses these sorts of experiments, calling them "two-way door decisions," because if it doesn't work out, they can just come back through the door, offering something different to future clients.[3]

Anchor to a good decision-making process

Some decision-making models include so many steps, they're not easy to commit to memory. As a leader, you need one that is simple enough to know by heart (or to be easy to read on a photo on your phone) and capture everything important on one sheet of paper in half an hour or so.

I've shaved the decision-making process that you, as a leader, should follow into five primary steps:

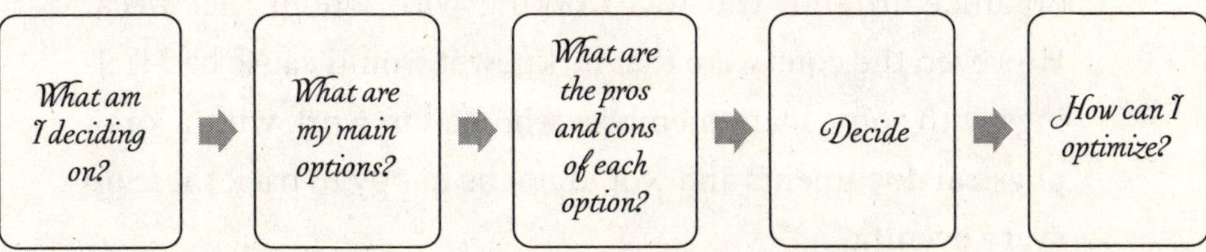

1. **What am I deciding on?** This is where you clarify the decision. You should be able to express your decision in a simple question, such as "How should we reorganize the office space to increase cross-team interaction?" This was a topic a client recently asked me to explore in a coaching session.
2. **What are my main options?** There may be many, many options or just a couple. If it's not a decision that requires extensive analysis, you can speed up by considering the main options. In the case above, Deniz, the director of online publishing for a textbook publishing house, was deciding how to reorganize the office space. It was not a high-stakes decision, because he could easily reorganize the space again, so he just weighed up hot-desking versus everyone having their own desks in cross-team pods. For a more important decision, you may want to slow down and consider some more unusual options. If he was looking to restructure their employment contracts or buy expensive new furniture on the basis of his decision, he may want to explore options such as full-time home working or fully flexible furniture that can be moved around based on needs.
3. **What are the pros and cons of each option?** With most decisions, considering the potential advantages and disadvantages of an option will be sufficient. You'll want to think about what will happen as a result and anything that stands a reasonable chance of happening. How do you feel about these possibilities? As far as Deniz could see, the main pros of the hot-desking option were frequent mixing and the ability to organize around who was working with whom that week. However, the cons were that he knew it would cause bad feelings with some team members who had to work with a lot of physical documents and would not be happy to pack these up every evening.

The pros of the cross-team pods were that people could settle into their desks; the cons were that it would take longer for sub-team interaction to build to the level he wanted, as people would not be moving around as frequently and work alongside other people as quickly. As sub-team interaction was the most important factor, Deniz saw a need to prioritize an approach that would achieve this. He wasn't confident that the cross-team pods would deliver what he felt was needed. The higher stakes the decision is, the more rigorous you will want to be in identifying the likelihood and desirability of each option. I lay out a possible method for you to consider in the "Fit the Context" box below.

4. **Decide.** You now have enough information to choose an option. Everything has been building to this moment, and now you can make the choice. Deniz was able to choose hot-desking. He reached this decision relatively quickly, as he knew it would be easy to swap approaches if hot-desking didn't work out.
5. **How can I optimize?** It can be tempting to make a decision, put it into place, and then wait for things to play out. You've done the hard work, haven't you? But making the decision is just choosing which door to walk through; there is still plenty of work to do on the other side. You need to focus attention on maximizing the success of that decision to increase the chances of it looking like a great decision. Deniz recognized that his choice would create challenges for team members who worked with big piles of paper, so he realized he needed to get them on his side first, as they could potentially bring the whole team down. By taking them to one side, acknowledging the challenges they were going to face with this, and asking them to come up with possible solutions, he was tackling one of the challenges

he'd spotted. To improve the chances of success, he also organized whole-department mixers so everyone could get to know one another better and so they would not be sitting next to a stranger when they hot-desked.

For some of us, this sort of process doesn't come naturally but can be critical to our success as leaders, so it's worth trying to build your comfort with it. Jo Farmer, managing partner at law firm Lewis Silkin, says she hates unnecessary process but knows that her role needs her to use processes when making big decisions, so they are well thought out and easy to justify to others.

FIT THE CONTEXT: INTRODUCING MEASUREMENT INTO A BIG DECISION

If you are faced with a big decision and need to spend more time and energy exploring the options and trying to understand how beneficial (or not) each one would be, and how likely they are to come to pass, bulk out two stages to create a more robust process:

What am I deciding on? (Stage 1)

At this stage, you should identify the problem but also establish outcome criteria. Outcome criteria state what you want to achieve from the decision you make. They will be the basis on which you judge the quality of the decision.

If you are considering how to manage Xia's poor performance, identify the outcome you are hoping for. Is it that you want Xia's performance to improve, or that you want team performance to improve, or that you ultimately don't think she can improve and want her to leave? Let's say, for this example, the outcome you are hoping for is that Xia's performance improves.

What are the pros and cons of each option? (Stage 2)

At this stage, having established outcome criteria, you can determine how well you think each option might lead to the outcome criteria being met.

Suppose you have identified three major options to manage Xia's performance:

1. **Doing nothing:** This will likely lead to no performance improvement and bad feelings from the team as they keep filling in for her. The chance of her improving herself feels very low. This has next to no chance of helping with team performance.
2. **Having a casual chat with Xia over coffee to talk about the problems with her performance:** This may help a little to improve her performance and temporarily improve the team's performance due to her increased effort, and their sense that something is being done to address her behavior, meaning they are not demotivated. However, you feel that any change is likely to be temporary at best and return to a place of poor team performance.
3. **Start Xia on a formal performance management process:** There are two possible outcomes here. One is that Xia's performance improves as she realizes how serious it is and uses the guidance offered on how to improve her performance. Team performance therefore increases because she is pulling her weight and the team is happier to continue with her as a member. If her performance does not improve, you have begun the process of managing her out and to be able to replace her with a better-performing team member.

In this example, Option 3 emerges as the most likely to achieve the outcome criteria. Decision scientists advocate following a process where you assign percentage likelihoods of each outcome happening and how desirable it is, but this is beyond the patience or scope of most leadership roles. If you are interested in learning more about this process, I strongly recommend *How to Decide* by professional gambler Annie Duke as a well-researched, easy-to-read, and entertaining book on more detailed decision-making processes.[4]

Tackle your biases and blind spots

If you've identified that biases, bad data, or organizational politics affect your decisions, important methods for tackling these issues include:

WELCOME THE POSSIBILITY OF BEING WRONG

If a leader can be open to the possibility that they are wrong, they create an environment primed for great decision-making because it forces them to keep an open mind.[5]

Scientists are great at being wrong; they approach experiments with the sense that they could be surprised, actively seeking out data that may challenge their views because it helps them to refine and improve their understanding of the world.

Act like a scientist by welcoming the possibility that you could have your mind changed and that what you're about to find out could challenge the status quo. Try to dispense with your ego and instead show flexibility when you are presented with something new.[6]

SEEK OUT OTHER PERSPECTIVES

Work out where you can find views other than your own, and seek them out, listening carefully to what they would recommend.

- **Your colleagues:** You are likely not the only expert on a particular subject in your organization—your team, your peers, and your boss may also have expertise. Share what you'd like their honest take on. Reinforce your desire for honesty so they don't deliver a less honest, more palatable message. Listen openly, ask clarifying questions, and thank them for their input.

- **AI:** Ask a generative AI tool like ChatGPT to suggest limitations or options for your ideas. If you find a prompt or question that extracts useful information, make sure you keep a note of it so you can use it again.
- **Third-party research:** Check journals, reports, and books in the area you're trying to make a decision on. Check the quality of the data and publication, and that it provides appropriate insights that fit your context. If deciding whether to expand, using research that is old or looks at growth in a slightly different industry won't be as helpful as a big study from last year that focuses on your specific industry.

CONFRONT, REMEMBER, AND MANAGE YOUR BIASES

Guard against biases that threaten decision quality, such as biases caused by your cultural heritage, a fear of your boss, a tendency to be optimistic about the cost of a project, or anything in between. It can be hard to keep biases front and center, so you may need a decision card that you use when making important decisions. List the biases you think you're subject to and keep it updated as your understanding of how your biases and viewpoints shape your decision-making develops.

Undertaking de-bias training, reading books about biases, listening to podcasts, and talking to colleagues about how bias affects decision-making will also help remind you that your biases are there and need acknowledging before making important decisions.

BUILD BIAS CHECKS INTO TEAM PROCESSES

Consider what biases your decisions are most commonly blighted by and build your team's processes in ways that prevent you, and others, from falling prey to these biases.

In the UK government, many team processes have built-in safeguards against common biases, such as the overoptimism bias. Mark Etherington, project manager in the UK Civil Service, told me that rather than allowing people to progress assuming a project will be delivered quickly and on a low budget, the available data is subjected to a series of questions—for example, to consider whether their timings are realistic and to question whether their analysis of the data is correct.

Another way they spot and manage bias is through multi-stakeholder meetings (up to around thirty people), all of whom read the proposals, prepare, and then question and challenge. Because the organization is proudly diverse, and everyone is expected to voice their opinion if they have one, blind spots are reduced. It can make decision-making slow, but in a setting where decisions are as high-stakes as government finances and national livelihoods, this is appropriate.

FIT THE CONTEXT: WHY SENIOR LEADERS SHOULD ASK MORE VULNERABLE QUESTIONS

Seeking alternative perspectives is difficult for senior leaders—they are isolated from the truth by people who don't want to deliver bad news. At a recent workshop, the CEO discussed feeling isolated and struggling to receive honest feedback from senior managers. He sensed his decisions were often suboptimal, but no one told him when or why.

However, the next day in the office, a topic came up he didn't know much about—expanding to Greece—but rather than asking the room to share their expertise, he said this was a bad idea and moved the conversation on quickly. There was actually someone who had run a satellite office in Greece for his previous company, but he didn't have the chance to speak, and so the opportunity to expand into a new terrain was lost for fear of looking vulnerable.

While senior leaders may not want to erode trust in their competence by admitting gaps in knowledge, the downsides of making decisions that are ill-informed from a fear of appearing weak are potentially much greater, as we can see from the example above. In addition, research suggests that showing some vulnerability can even increase a leader's standing and likability,[7] assuming they have already established a foundation of trust.[8]

USE, AND EXPECT, HIGH-QUALITY DATA

To make good decisions, you need good data. Here are four questions that I encourage leaders to use to improve their critical analysis of evidence they plan to use:

- **What is the motive of the person presenting the data?** We often receive data that has been gathered, compiled, and presented by others. It may be that, in this process, their own agenda has crept in. Your team may have presented a report with selected stats to showcase their performance this month, leaving out stats that make them look less good. Check the motive of the author and presenter to see how their motives may twist what they present to fit their agenda.
- **How sound do the methods used to gather and analyze the data appear to be?** Have the data gatherers used methods to gather and analyze the data that seem sound

and appropriate for what they are trying to work out? For example, does asking customers how easy they find it to use your company's new chatbot seem like a good method to determine how good the chatbot is, or would it be better to observe customers using it or measure how long they spend on the platform? Considering this question should help you to highlight anything that seems off.

- **How reasonable are the claims being made, based on the data?** Based on the data that the researchers have ended up with, is it okay for them to make the claims they are making? For example, if they have surveyed ten new employees on their experiences of the company, could they claim 67 percent of employees like working at your firm? Or would it be better to gather data from the whole firm, if possible, or at least a bigger sample? Wouldn't a better claim for the data they *have* gathered be that 67 percent of *new* employees like working at your firm?
- **Is the data from a trustworthy source?** This can be a useful shortcut. If the data is from a trustworthy source, such as a high-quality newspaper, a well-known academic journal, or a report from a major consultancy or finance house, you can be more confident in the quality of the data, the methods used to gather it, and the claims that are being made for it.

As well as holding yourself accountable for high-quality data, if someone you work with uses data for decision-making and you're not convinced of the quality, gently get them to check the quality of the research.

Now you can make up for a bad decision

By now, you've learned what causes decision-making issues, and how to improve. If you have a bad decision to handle, you can now start to take action.

1. APOLOGIZE—REALLY WELL

Couple a clear "sorry" with specific details of what you feel you did wrong. This helps those receiving an apology to see it as well thought out and sincere.[9]

Susan, a recent coaching client and partner in an American-owned law firm, needed to apologize to her team for keeping them out of the loop on a big restructuring decision, which changed the nature of over thirty people's jobs. The team focused on providing legal services within the firm, such as contract review and insurance negotiation. In the past, the team had been organized around similar work types, such as contract review. However, this was inefficient, as some team members had little to do, while others had a lot of work. Instead, the team needed to be one big pool of people who could pivot between different work types as the business' needs changed. Susan's perception was that she needed to keep this quiet until she had gotten agreement from the managing partner. However, the team members felt she had acted behind their backs. Susan took some time at a facilitated session I ran for her and her team to apologize deeply. She didn't just offer a generic "I'm sorry." Instead, she included meaningful specifics: "I'm sorry for feeling I couldn't let you know. I can see the upset that the secrecy caused, and it's understandable, as it must have felt sneaky. I'm sorry I couldn't find a way to bring you into the conversation." Making sure your apology shows empathy is critical—in the example above, Susan didn't just apologize but also reflected on the feelings that the situation had created in her team. She recognized the emotional impacts and found a way to reference them in her apology.

2. PROMISE CHANGE (AND THEN ACT ON IT)

Share what you plan to do differently, demonstrating how you are making amends. Use the ideas we discussed around improving your decision-making in the future to offer promises of how you will change.[10]

For instance, at the end of her apology, Susan added the following remark: "I'm sure there will be future situations that the managing partner would like to keep quiet, but I will push hard going forward to be able to share information with you more quickly. You are all senior enough that you should be part of the conversation, and your input would actually have been useful." Note that she can't promise something huge—as she can't guarantee she can influence her seniors—but she will try.

3. GET IT DONE AND START TO MOVE ON

Show evidence of your promised changes as soon as you can, showing you to be trustworthy in a crisis and able to take corrective action when you make a mistake.

And then it's okay to move on. As long as you continue to apply what you've promised, you've done what you can.

It's very easy to feel regret in these situations, because it can appear so obvious in the rearview mirror that it was a bad decision.

Remember, though, that you did not have access to all the information at the time you made the decision and you were not as good a decision-maker. People make mistakes, and a good colleague should accept your apology graciously and allow you to move on, too.

BEFORE MOVING ON:

- Have you identified how much care this decision needs and made use of a decision-making approach that allows you to take the appropriate amount of care?
- Have you confronted and worked on managing your biases and blind spots in the decision-making process?
- Have you used high-quality data in your decision-making?
- And if you're trying to make up for a previous bad decision, have you apologized well, acted on a promise to change, and started to move on?

VENTURE FORTH!

Executing your plan for improved decision-making will help you justify your reasons for making a decision and feel more confident in the decisions you propose. It will also provide a basis for saying sorry and promising change. However, there are a few common problems when people start to use a more robust decision-making process:

If a "good" decision is unpopular... handle the fallout

If you feel you've made a good decision but others are challenging you, you'll want to take action quickly, as this sort of dissent can bubble up and out of control. If you find this happening, you should:

1. **Check it's actually a good decision:** Ask, open-mindedly, why they think it's bad and weigh up the merits of what they say. Remember to check that their justifications or data is of good quality. Return to your data in light of the new evidence they've brought to you to see if the decision needs adjusting.
2. **If the data still justifies your decision:** Share your rationale with them for why you made the decision you did and present their information in the broader context of the decision you made. For example, imagine you've decided not to tender for a new client, as you believe the odds are too long and it's too time-consuming. A team member tells you they think you're wrong. They think that you should be tendering because a friend of theirs is on the panel that will decide which contractor to use. You would want to explain that it doesn't change your mind, because you are still very inexperienced as a firm at working with insurance companies. You know at least two other companies who will likely tender who *only* work with insurance companies. You would need to be prepared for their disappointment, anger, or frustration and be ready to empathize.

3. **If the data suggests you need to change the decision:** Thank the person who presented you with the information that's changed your view. Share your decision with the stakeholders. Explain why you have changed your mind. Evidence suggests that rather than this making you appear weak, as long as you do not change your mind too frequently, this preparedness to be wrong can help build your reputation as a high-quality leader.[11]

If you're tempted to take longer to decide... weigh up if that's the right call

You are right to take your time, if you can, to make important decisions, but at some point, action will be required. If you want a little longer to decide but want to work out whether it's a valid call, consider the following questions:

IS THE DECISION IMPORTANT ENOUGH TO TAKE MORE OF YOUR TIME?

Important decisions require more time than less important decisions, and you need to be honest with yourself about how important this decision actually is. Does it warrant taking more time and occupying more headspace, or has it already had the time it deserves? If you're still struggling to decide, think about what other stakeholders would say about you taking longer to make a decision. Would they be impressed that you were taking it seriously, or would they be rolling their eyes at your lassitude?

IS THERE A BENEFIT FROM DECIDING NOW?

If deciding now can help you to optimize the quality of the decision, then it's a good incentive to act. If you decide whom to send to a sales conference, a decision soon will help them prepare. Also, if the decision landscape will change soon, meaning you have to review all the information you've gathered, without it making a significant difference to the outcome, it's also better to decide now. For example, if you need to decide whom to recruit, and you know that if you don't decide soon, some candidates will get jobs and you'll need to find new people to interview, there's an incentive to act.

ARE YOU LOOKING FOR AN UNREALISTIC LEVEL OF CERTAINTY?

You may be holding out in the hope of that perfect statistic or insightful comment from your boss that will make the whole situation fall into place. However, often, you will have to make decisions without that ideal input, because it doesn't exist. One interviewee, an executive director at a large global investment bank, told me how in her industry, people often like to see a lot of data to feel reassured in a decision, but because the data is based on the past and the decision is in the future, there will often be a level of uncertainty anyway because where you are making decisions about a novel project or new situation, you will usually have to decide based on data that feels inconclusive. If a decision still needs to be made, despite uncertainty, you will need to find the bravery to make it, and a few more days is unlikely to help.

ELEVATE YOUR LEARNING

If you're interested in decision-making best practice... learn to recognize tilt

Tilt is defined as "when a bad outcome causes you to be in an emotionally hot state that compromises the quality of your decision-making."[12]

The advice from poker, which I'll carry over to leadership, is that when you feel your emotions are interfering with your ability to make a good decision, step away. Grabbing a coffee and taking a walk around the block may be enough to reset you, or you might need to step away from the decision until another day.

If it's a decision that needs to be made right now, and perhaps the pressure is adding to the emotions, this is an excellent moment to seek an outside view to help you think through your options and prevent you from making a terrible mistake. If you can't discuss it with a work colleague, a friend who you know will challenge you and hold you to account can also be a good thought partner.

Good decision-makers learn to spot tilt, or heightened emotions in their body, and learn to pause, walk away, or get an outside view at these times, to reduce their chances of making a mistake due to their emotional state.

If you found value in using AI to seek the outside view… find further uses

There are other ways that generative AI, such as ChatGPT, can help decision-making. You can treat it as a "sparring partner,"[13] helping surface ideas you haven't considered, challenging your thinking and refining your decisions.

- **When you're coming up with options:** Ask AI to come up with additional suggestions, refine your suggestions, or combine current suggestions to create more complex scenarios. Ask it what sort of biases people typically fall into when making a decision like this.
- **When you're narrowing options:** Ask it to list the merits and demerits of each option to see if you already have them covered. Don't be tempted to let it do the work for you, as it may miss important angles that you struggle to see once you've read its seemingly comprehensive response.
- **When you have made your decision:** Ask for refinements. For example, if you have decided to reorganize the office to increase sub-team interaction, you can ask it what else you

could do to enhance this plan and increase its chances of success.

The key to success is to be playful and experiment with the prompts you give it. If you come up with a good prompt, write it down so you can adapt it for use again, as this is often the key to unlocking the value of generative AI.[14] It will not always have the right answers, as it will not have a deep read on your context, but it can open up new avenues and help you to refine others, or close them down.[15]

In the introductory case, Milo, front-of-house team leader in a restaurant, was concerned about the poor performance of Xia, the restaurant owner's niece. The team was fed up with filling in for her when she was on the phone in the bathroom. He mapped out his choices to "Continue to do nothing," "Have a formal chat, recorded by HR," or "Ask her to leave." Once he'd weighed up the options and realized that it was primarily fear of his boss's reprisals and his own biases in thinking she was like his daughter, he decided a formal chat was the best action because she had not been properly told the severity of the situation and it would not anger his boss as much as asking her to leave.

He also renamed the recruitment folder on his computer to "Is this person right for the job?" This prompted him, each time he had to print an interview form, to remember to look at the candidate through a critical lens, not letting his biases sway him into recruiting someone unsuitable.

He also apologized to his team and told them he was taking action. They grumbled that it was too little, too late, and he showed regret at being swayed by his boss's hold over him. While this level of authenticity might not be comfortable for some managers, Milo felt very comfortable being vulnerable in this way with his team, and he felt it helped win them back around.

REMEMBER:

- If you're in the aftermath of a bad decision, step away until you've considered how you're going to improve your decision-making process going forward. Then you can apologize and explain how you'll change your behavior in the future.
- Biases, blind spots, and bad data lead to subpar decisions. Raising your awareness of which of these you're subject to will improve your decision-making process.
- A simple decision-making process of 1) What am I deciding on? 2) What are my main options? 3) What are the pros and cons of each option? 4) Deciding, and 5) How can I optimize? will be adequate for most situations.
- Weighing up the need for speed versus accuracy will help you scale up or scale down your decision-making process to fit the circumstances.
- There are times when, rather than you having made a bad decision, you've just been subject to bad luck. If you can't find evidence that your decision-making process is bad, you may choose to do nothing to correct at the moment, but be careful if this problem emerges again, at which point you should revisit the possibility of taking action.

PROBLEM 3
Influence

"No one on my team is getting their work done—they just seem to ignore me and do what they feel like—even though I'm their boss!"

"All this organizational power and politics stuff just isn't for me. The idea of having control over anyone is creepy. I just want to do a good job and have people listen to me because of that."

"The senior managers humor me but don't do anything I ask them to. I've got to get better at managing up, both for my own sake and that of my team."

NASRIN WORKED FOR AN INSURANCE FIRM AS A SPECIALIST DIRECTOR. She had worked in the sector for over a decade but had recently been promoted to director level. She had a large team below her, comprised of seven unit managers and their own teams. Above her, there were three levels: the director of claims; the UK CEO; and the global CEO. It was a big, busy hierarchy, and she was struggling at this new level for her voice to be heard.

She felt that rather than her power having increased with the promotion, it had decreased, as her new boss was easily distracted and perhaps even a little distrusting of her as a newbie. Even when she brought well-evidenced ideas to him, he tended to go with ideas from more established team members whose arguments looked weaker on paper.

And even though she was more senior than her team, because she had worked alongside them at the same level for so many years, they were cynical of what she wanted them to do. She had tried being nice and she had tried just telling them, but both strategies had failed with various team members. She felt helpless.

This situation caused her personal sadness and professional distress. She had gone from feeling as though she had power and influence to being more senior but feeling as though her power and influence had been eroded, both above and below. She told me that she felt like a cog in everyone else's machine—they would only do what she wanted them to if they felt like it. Her voice didn't seem to matter at all.

Nasrin's problem isn't uncommon! Establishing and using power and influence at work is always hard. And our increasingly flat hierarchies, which mean people aren't keen on being told what to do, have made it harder.[1]

But without power and influence, as Nasrin found, you won't be a great leader. It will be hard to get your point across or to get anyone to do anything! So how to resolve power and influence problems so you can be a more effective leader? This chapter will help you to work out where your problems are and help you to course correct. By the end, you'll have a clear improvement plan with immediate, meaningful steps to get your power and influence back on track.

STATE THE PROBLEM

Try to state the problems with culture and values that you are facing in one or two sentences. Use the prompts below to help.

- **Who are you trying to influence?** Are they a junior, a peer, a senior, or a client?
- **What have you done, if anything, to try to get them to do what you want them to?** Why do you think your approach hasn't worked?

- How do you think they see you? **Do they see you as someone they are prepared to be influenced by?**

You can come back to adjust your statement as your knowledge develops in the following sections, but it's there to help you to be clear on what problem you're trying to solve.

OPEN THE BOX

You're using the wrong influence approach

As a leader, when you try to influence others to take an action or to change their minds on something, you can use a wide variety of techniques. These range from using data, to appealing to their values, to letting them know that others whom they trust are planning to take this action, to insisting that they must do it because you are the boss. However, you may find that, if you are struggling with influence, it is because you are not using the full range of techniques available to you, and you are choosing techniques that are ill fitted to the situation. Read on to work out if this may be true of you.

YOU'RE USING YOUR PREFERRED TECHNIQUES (NOT THEIRS)

Influence attempts are often unsuccessful when, rather than analyzing what the person you're trying to influence may want or care about, you default to an influence technique, or combination of techniques, which you feel comfortable with.

Look at the list of common influence techniques below, all of which can be successful in particular circumstances, and consider when you last used each of them and which of them you tend to use the most. I recommend doing this before moving on to the next step.[2]

- **Rational influence:** You use facts, evidence, and logical arguments to show the feasibility and value of a request.

- **Inspirational appeals:** You appeal to the person's values or ideals when you influence them, trying to harness their emotions.
- **Consultation:** You ask for their input into the idea, perhaps suggesting improvements or helping you to plan the change you're suggesting.
- **Personal appeals:** You ask for a personal favor before saying what it is, or ask the person to carry out a request or favor based on your friendship with them.
- **Ingratiation:** You use flattery or compliments, or express enthusiasm that they are the right person for a difficult task.
- **Exchange:** You offer to trade favors, to reciprocate at a future time, or incentivize your request.
- **Legitimating:** You refer to rules, policies, formal documents, or your place in the hierarchy to justify why you are able to make this request.
- **Coalition:** You get others to support your suggestion and then use their support as a reason why the person should agree to your request.
- **Pressure:** You use demands, threats, frequent reminders, or regular checking to influence the person.

Paulo, a leader I worked with recently, was struggling to influence upward. He was one level below the C-suite in a law firm known for being extremely shrewd and loaded with highly intelligent lawyers and support staff. Paulo's instinct was to default to ingratiation to get what he wanted, as well as building up really good relationships with the people he works with and using personal appeals. When influencing his team (downward influence) and his peers (lateral influence), this was absolutely fine. However, he found it much harder to influence the C-suite in this way. When we conducted an influence audit, running through the styles above to see what he tended to use, he found he was missing out on rational influence and legitimating, both of which would have helped him to influence those he knows less well. Ingratiation can seem very shallow with someone you don't know well, as you are basing your praise and compliments on insubstantial evidence and you do not have a friendship to fall back on.

Just because you prefer a technique or are used to it, it doesn't mean it is the right one, as the next section will highlight.

YOU'RE MISINFORMED ABOUT WHAT WORKS

You may default to a particular method because it's been very effective in the past, and you are not confident in some of the other methods that feel less suited to your way of managing, or that you have not had much of a change to practice. Below are some common patterns that leaders fall into when trying to influence. Are you making any of these mistakes?

Are you using pressure, which is creating resistance?

When you need someone to do something for you, and you are worried you're not going to get anywhere, it can be tempting to apply some pressure. However, pressure is the least successful type of influence technique and more likely to lead to situations where people resist what you are asking them to do, perhaps through annoyance, or trying to retain their sense of control, or because you haven't tried to win them over. You are telling rather than selling, pushing rather than pulling, and as soon as people feel that they are being coerced, they are likely to resist.

Are you ignoring emotion?

Leaders have a tendency to overuse rational influence attempts, assuming that data trumps everything. It may be a surprise to learn that this is not always the most effective way to influence, because our brains respond better to emotional arguments than rational ones.[3]

If you appeal just to the head and not to the heart, you may get compliance, but you are less likely to inspire enthusiasm or commitment.[4] People are more likely to just go through the motions, rather than putting their whole selves into the task.[5] So if you suggest an exchange, or you legitimate your request, or you create a coalition to try to force the situation, you may achieve compliance, but you are less likely to achieve enthusiasm.

In the case I opened with, Nasrin was struggling to influence her team and her seniors. She felt that presenting them with evidence should be sufficient to get them to act on her behalf. And she had upped her approach to be more authoritative so that she was no longer seen as "one of the team" following her promotion. However, this seemed to be backfiring, as she was eroding the high-quality relationships she had with the team, meaning that personal appeals weren't working. She had also wanted to show that she knew what she was doing, so she did not consult her team in making decisions. As such, she was underusing soft techniques, overusing rational influence, and when rational influence wasn't working, she was upping her hard influence techniques, which was making the problem worse.

Do you worry about appearing manipulative?

Some leaders shy away from using warmer influence techniques, such as ingratiation, personal appeals, and inspirational appeals (appealing to someone's values), seeing them as overly manipulative and worried that their motivations, if discovered, will undermine the influence attempt. They may also avoid them because they are more time-consuming, with building a relationship taking far longer than telling someone to do something.[6] Are you scared of using a warmer, more personal influence technique for reasons such as those above? If so, you may also be missing out on the opportunity to inspire deep commitment.

YOU'RE BEING UNREALISTIC ABOUT YOUR ABILITIES TO INFLUENCE

Do you feel as though, despite your best efforts, you just don't seem to be able to get someone to do something you want them to? It may be that, based on the current situation, you are being unrealistic about how much influence you have with the person in question.

This doesn't mean you can't change your abilities to influence in the future, and indeed, that is what the "Lay Out Your Solution" section is largely about. But right here, right now, you do not have the necessary tools to influence the other person. Here are some reasons why you may not be getting what you need.

YOU ARE TRYING TO PERSUADE THE WRONG PERSON

When you decide whom to influence, a key element is making sure that they are actually the stakeholder you need. Is it really their mind you need to change, do they control the resources, or are they the person who can sign off your request? If not, then it may make what looks like a successful influence attempt from the outside fall short of what's required. It may be, also, that there is more than one person you need to influence.

Recently, I ran a workshop for the senior leadership team of a fast-growing tech company. In this company, the senior leadership team is one layer below the C-suite. My brief was to get this senior leadership team to put together a charter of how they would work together, to be signed off by the chief people officer. They framed their charter, and requests for C-suite input to it, around the assumption that the CPO had the ability to sign off on it. As such, they organized it around topics they knew she cared about, such as alignment with organizational values and leadership principles. However, after the workshop, when they presented it to the C-suite, it emerged that the CFO was not prepared to let the CPO have final sign-off and questioned where the data was to justify their approach, as he was much more data-driven. He felt he had the right to have a say because 70 percent of the senior leadership team (SLT) fell under his reporting line. Clearly, in this case, the CPO was misinformed, and the CFO also needed to be influenced.

Have you incorrectly identified the person or people you need to influence? Is this leading to problems in your influence attempts?

YOU HAVEN'T WORKED OUT HOW TO PERSUADE THEM

Having the right person is just the first step. As you can see from the example above, the team did know that the CPO would like a charter that was values-aligned, and they would have known that the CFO would want a data-driven charter. However, this is not always the case, and frequently, we spend too little time thinking about the person we are looking to influence and what might shape whether we are successful in influencing them or not.

Have you given due thought to what they care about? What does their specific context, functional role, temperament, or position in the hierarchy tell you about what matters to them? What else do you know of them that you can use to understand how they might be influenced? What are their values?

If you are not spending time building up a picture of who you are planning to influence, you are less likely to be selecting an influence technique suited to the situation. As the SLT tried to convince the CFO that this is a good charter with no data to back it up, their work was rejected.

You may find that if you are looking to trade favors or exchange resources, you are wrong in your belief that they want or care about what you are able to swap. For example, are you trying to exchange good work for an extra day off, when the person in question has more holidays stored up than they think they are going to be able to use? Or are you suggesting that they could do a favor for you and you can return the favor further down the line, but they don't see you as being able to do them any favors that they would find valuable?

YOU AREN'T SEEN TO BE WORTH FOLLOWING

Just as beauty is in the eye of the beholder, leadership is in the eye of the follower. In other words, if your team, peers, or seniors don't see you as being worth following, then they won't. I realize it may sound strange to talk about your seniors or your peers following you, when actually they are above or parallel to you in terms of power, but when you are trying to influence them to take action or change their minds, you are looking for their temporary followership. If you are not perceived by them to be worth following, your success will be limited. You will be worth following if you hold formal hierarchical power and as such can offer rewards or punishments. They will also be more willing to follow you if they trust, like, and admire you, if they value your expertise, or if you hold information they are interested in.[7]

Ask yourself how often they do the following as you consider your interactions with them:

- Default to your judgment.
- Ask your opinion.
- Engage you in warm, friendly conversation.
- Confide in you.
- Appear interested in information that you have which they do not.

If the answer is "Not very often," then you may have found why you are struggling to influence them.

BEFORE MOVING ON:

- With each situation where you are struggling to influence, what, based on the evidence described here, appears to be going wrong?
- Are there any influence techniques you rely on too much or do not use at all? What impacts do you think this could be having on your success levels?
- Are you being unrealistic about your abilities to influence? How?

FIT THE CONTEXT: WHEN *POWER* IS A DIRTY WORD

Some of you will be finding this chapter uncomfortable reading, not wanting to think about your power at work, as it seems wrong to be thinking about having such control over another person. To you, the idea of soft influence may even seem ugly, as though you are manipulating others to do what you want by pretending to be nice.

A recent participant in a workshop I was running on finding your power and influence said to me, "It's horrible to think that being nice to someone is a form of influence!"

"But is it?" I asked. "If you want a friend to do a favor for you, how do you ask? In a grumpy voice that makes them feel begrudging and maybe even say they can't help? Or in a happy one, having already asked them how their day has been, because you're trying to reinforce that you're a great friend whom they want to help?"

We all manipulate, or influence, or encourage, or try to get people to do things all the time. It's the nature of being a human in the world. And when you are a leader, you are actively agreeing to get people to do things. Even the design of an office building is subtly manipulating us to sit at our desk, stare at our computers, and talk to the people we're sitting closest to. But these are just the actions that keep the world moving, removing friction, making it a more pleasant place to be. Yes, someone is using their power to get us to do something, but it's not with a terrible action as a result.

Of course, it is good to be aware of the problems that having power can bring—it can reduce your ability to see other perspectives[8] and make you dismiss expert advice,[9] and not being totally comfortable with it can be a good thing. But to reject it altogether means you won't be as good a leader as you could be.

But if you feel uncomfortable about the very idea of power and find it to be a dirty word, then you should reflect on how this could be holding you back and whether leadership is even right for you. You can choose what to use your power and influence for, but to deny them altogether is to deny your leadership.

LAY OUT YOUR SOLUTION

Build up your influence muscles

Being a better influencer is in large part about preparation. Some of this preparation needs to happen just a few hours or days before the influence attempt; other elements can happen months or even years beforehand. Because if you have identified that you are using a narrow range of influence techniques, you need to widen the range. And if you have discovered that people don't tend to see you as being particularly worth following, you need to improve their perceptions of you as a valid influencer.

INCREASE THE BREADTH OF YOUR INFLUENCE TECHNIQUES

As you will remember from the "Open the Box" section above, there are a wide range of influence techniques that can be used, and if you found you weren't making use of all of them, now is the time to broaden your approach.

To increase your use of . . .	You could try to . . .
Rational influence	Use facts, evidence, and logical arguments more frequently when you are constructing an influence attempt. Prepare in advance with high-quality evidence, but rather than overloading with lots of different data points, focus on a few that help to drive your point home. If you're presenting them in a report or on a slide, give them lots of space to shine out from what you're saying.

To increase your use of...	You could try to...
Inspirational appeals	Identify what the person's values are, or what fires them up, and look at how you can make use of this in your influence attempts. If you know they are someone who values community, emphasize the benefits of a project for improving their network and embeddedness in the company. If you know that they came to work for the company because it is more creative than their last firm, talk about the project you're asking them to be involved with in terms of how it's going to allow the company to be even more creative in the future.
Consultation	Ask for their input into the idea or to suggest improvements. It's important, if you do this, that it's genuine, as saying that you are consulting and then doing what you want anyway can seriously affect morale and reduce their trust in you. Often, it's good to be clear on the what in advance (e.g., what the end point is) but to give lots of consultation space on the how (e.g., the steps to get there).
Personal appeals	If you have a good relationship with a team member, ask them for a personal favor before saying what the personal favor is. You might text them to say, "Can I ask you a favor?" which might prompt them to say yes before you then reveal what it is. Don't overuse this, as people can get tired of being called upon for favors, particularly where it's a one-way relationship and you are not easily able to reciprocate by helping them with favors.

To increase your use of...	You could try to...
Ingratiation	Use flattery or compliments to get someone to do something. You could tell them why they are the right person for this job and how you only trust them because they have proven themselves to be so brilliant in the past. Be careful that the compliments feel genuine; otherwise, it can seem manipulative and can create resistance rather than commitment.
Exchange	Offer to swap favors or to reciprocate at a future time, or offer a reward for them acceding to your request. You may offer them your parking space for the next two weeks or promise them that you'll step in to help the next time they are overworked.
Legitimation	Consider which rules, policies, or formal documents might help you to land your request. Is it essential for someone at their level to do up to three days of last-minute overtime a year? Is your appraisal overdue so your boss needs to organize it as soon as possible? Be careful with legitimation—it can make you seem quite aggressive and rules-driven, which, in some company cultures, is frowned upon.
Coalition	Find others who can support your suggestion and use that support to get the person to agree to your requests. If you're trying to influence a peer, can you get others at the same level to come on board with what you're suggesting, so it's just them who is not on your side? However, use with caution. As with pressure (below), coalition can feel coercive and can lead to resistance more than 50 percent of the time.

To increase your use of...	You could try to...
Pressure	Can you use demands, threats, or regular reminders to get someone to concede to what you want? Note that this technique should be used very sparingly and only when time is of the essence, as it leads to resistance far more than any of the other techniques listed here. This is perhaps one not to actively practice but to be aware of in case all else has failed and you need to get a project over the line by the end of the day or you face large negative repercussions. It's also safer to use it when you know that everyone will eventually be okay with what you've asked. For example, you need them to stay late to finalize the budget for the year, but you know that, when the budget goes through, it will be more generous than last year and lead to positive benefits for all.

You should also look at ways to combine these methods. A great combination is to combine rational persuasion with inspirational appeal. You win over the scientists and the poets with this approach, tapping into the head and the heart.

One interviewee, a management accountant with a focus on performance improvement, explained how she influenced people to make the necessary changes by "storytelling with the data." She'll tell a negative, cautionary tale with data of the past and an upbeat call to action with the projections of the future. No longer are these dry financial figures—these are numbers that dance off the slide, winning hearts and minds with their potential for change. In a subtle way, she is making the workers heroes of a narrative, inspiring them to take actions that they care about.

BECOME SOMEONE WORTH FOLLOWING

Remember that, whether you are influencing down, across, or up, people need to be prepared to listen to you and follow you for that moment, in relation to that particular issue.

As such, strengthening in advance people's perceptions of you as someone who is worth following is a valuable use of effort.

You should focus your attention on these dimensions, taken from the work of social psychologists John French and Bertram Raven.[10]

Work on increasing your likability and trustworthiness

French and Raven call this *referent power*, and it appears in plenty of work on how to influence and lead. More recently, research has shown that, to be really influential, you should show yourself to be trustworthy and likable *before* you show yourself as competent. If you are competent first, you can come across as cold and untrustworthy. But if you are likable and trustworthy, and then competent, you are much more likely to be seen as a convincing leader.

As such, you should try to do the following:

- Be warm, kind, and happy, as people want to be around others who are this way, as it creates a sort of "emotional contagion."[11]
- Find common ground to increase the quality of your relationship. We are more likely to like people who are similar (or who we perceive are similar) to us.[12]
- Work on showing that you are a leader who is trustworthy but also competent. This combination is what we desire most in leaders and makes us more likely to follow them.[13]
- Show a small amount of vulnerability, as a leader who's "too perfect" can feel intimidating and hard to like. If you are seen to be largely very competent, but have vulnerabilities, you will trigger the pratfall effect, which will make someone like you more.[14]

This is not about spending months being likable before turning to increasing your competence but rather just about making sure that you put in the effort to start with to make a warm first impression on people and then maintaining this throughout your relationship with them.

Megan Jones, a general and catering manager at BaxterStorey, said how important it was in her work for her team to like her. Working with frontline catering staff, she said that a huge part of her role was dealing with people's feelings—her staff's and customers'—and much of her day was taken up with talking to people, asking how they are, smiling, complimenting them, and acting warmly. She also talked about the importance of her being able to admit mistakes and say sorry, showing her own imperfections and making it more likely that her team will own up to their mistakes before they become a real problem. Her referent power is central to her work, and through plenty of small, daily actions, she builds this sort of influence significantly. But rather than it being manipulative, it's nice. Megan likes the people she works with and wants to build a rapport. It's a positive benefit that also means she is more able to influence them as a result.

Work on increasing others' perceptions of your competence

You can demonstrate competence by doing a good job, doing what you say you will, and highlighting your success. In addition, establishing yourself as an expert in your field, function, organization, or other related area can increase your power. French and Raven refer to this as *expert power*, and to build it, you need to find ways to increase others' perceptions of you as an expert:

- Identify the area or areas in which you already have expertise that may be of value.
- Demonstrate this expertise where you can, showing how you can make a useful contribution to the success of the organization through the application of your knowledge.

This could be through relevant contributions in meetings, mentoring less experienced staff members, creating on-the-job learning resources, or being ready and available to help colleagues who are facing problems or need advice in your area of expertise.

- Find ways to publicize your knowledge—for example, through the company's internal blog or external media outlets.
- Identify areas where you could usefully grow your knowledge and skills that are needed by those you are looking to influence, to continue to increase your opportunities to gain expert power.

If we return to Nasrin, you'll remember that she was newly promoted but struggling to influence. She recognized that she had let her referent power slip—people were finding her harder to get along with as she was trying to be strong and rational, rather than maintaining the high-quality interpersonal relationships she had always had with the team when she was at the same level as they were. She started to work on rebuilding relationships with her team members, in particular putting time aside for one-to-ones, which she started by asking them how they were and really listening to the answer, as well as remembering to thank them and praise them for high-quality work. She made sure that she followed through on any promises that she made them, as well as demonstrating her extensive knowledge, which had been the primary reason for her promotion, and thus building her expert power, too. She noticed that her team was listening to her more and already more likely to do what she asked them to do, even with just these small changes.

Prepare for a specific influence attempt

For an influence attempt to be successful, you should be spending time planning. In particular, you should be considering whom you are planning to influence and then picking a suitable influence attempt.

HOW TO ANALYZE YOUR TARGET

In the language of influence, the person who you are planning to influence is your *target*. I usually avoid this language, as it sounds quite hostile (!), but for this particular stage, I think it's helpful, as it reminds you to be laser-focused on the person (or people) in question.

You should consider:[15]

At what level are they?

You're particularly interested in whether they are above, next to, or below you in the hierarchy, as it will dictate if this is an upward, lateral, or downward influence attempt. If it's a downward influence attempt, all the influence strategies are available to you, but you are likely to inspire more commitment if you avoid applying pressure and you don't call in personal favors too often.

If you are influencing laterally or upward, then building good relationships and using data and evidence to back up your requests will be more likely to inspire action. If it's a lateral influence attempt, exchanges can also be very effective, as you are likely to be able to offer exchanges of a similar perceived value.

Consultation can also be effective with downward and lateral influence, giving people a meaningful role in shaping the request. And if you do take their ideas on board, give your team members credit because often ideas that emerge as a result of consultation or feedback are overlooked for praise.[16] This can undo the hard work you've done in getting them involved and may make them cynical of your use of consultation in the future.

What seems to matter to them?

If you are looking to influence someone who's junior to you, it's easy for you to build up an understanding of who they are and what they care about simply by asking them. It is likely that they will be happy to give you their time and will be largely honest about what they care about. The more you can understand what matters to them, the better you can offer rewards they value and create inspirational appeals that relate to their values and concerns, evoking their emotions.

If it's lateral influence you're after, it's again useful to get to know your colleagues to work out what matters to them, so you can shape your requests around inspirational appeal. However, you may also be able to explore what resources you control that they would like to have access to and see if you can factor this into your influence attempt. For example, if you want a manager on the same level as you to assist you on a project, you could offer them some of your most experienced team member's time. You may know they've been keen to enlist this team member to help with their data analysis, as they don't have an expert on their team, and so this is a good arrangement. Particularly because you know your team member is more likely to want to get involved if this other manager is also involved, as they are keen to learn what that part of the business does.

If it's senior influence, understanding, for example, how they like data to be presented and whether they like to receive papers before a meeting may seem like small details but could help you to catch them in a good mood and make them more likely to accede to your request.

How likely are they to resist?

Understanding how likely they are to resist your attempts to influence them may help you to prepare counterstrategies—for example, organizing data to back up your requests, or considering something you could offer in exchange for their compliance. You will want to consider if they are likely to have a good reason to want to block or resist your proposal, if they have the ability to do so, whether they share your perspective or have a different view on the matter at hand, and whether there are political issues at play that may make it hard—or against their best interests—to agree.

Some of these may be beyond your ability to control, to counteract, or to prepare for in detail, but being aware of what may come up and seeing if there are strategies to counteract could be the difference between a hard no and them conceding to think about it.

Remember that, with someone who's your junior, they may have to comply, but they may be able to resist more subtly—for example, only doing the bare minimum. If you spot that they are agreeing but not particularly enthusiastically, you may also want to use another influence strategy to try to move them from compliance to enthusiasm. For example, can you throw in an inspirational appeal, or add some ingratiation into the mix, telling them how great you know they're going to be at this?

Now you're ready for an influence attempt! We'll cover the practicalities of what to do and how to handle it if things go wrong in the next section.

FIT THE CONTEXT: EVEN IN EVIDENCE-BASED PRACTICE, EMOTIONAL ENGAGEMENT STILL MATTERS

In some roles, the need for expertise will be very high, and influence attempts must include data. For example, in legal, medical, scientific, or government settings, data is critical to decision-making, which must be evidence-based.

Former Labour MP Barry Sheerman, who has during his career led multiple social enterprises, Westminster commissions, and charities, recommended that if you want to win people over, get the best experts you can, but don't forget the heart, too.

When he was leading the campaign for compulsory seat belts, he worked with leading researchers, vehicle manufacturers, and victim groups, including the parents of children who had had accidents when not wearing seat belts. The scientists were experts on what worked; the parents were, sadly, the experts on the grief of a lost child. The ability to use their expertise paid off, and compulsory seat belt wearing was passed in the UK and has likely saved hundreds of thousands of lives.

So find ways, even when it feels like an environment where only cold, hard data is going to cut it, to marshal emotion to your benefit and combine rational and soft influence techniques.

BEFORE MOVING ON:

Developing your influence bases:

- How are you going to improve your bases of influence?
- Which influence techniques are you going to work on making better use of? With whom? How?

Preparing for a specific influence attempt:

- Whom do you want to influence, and what matters to them?
- How will you organize your influence attempt? What do you need to prepare to maximize your chances?
- What backup influence attempts will you have ready in case the first one doesn't work?

VENTURE FORTH!

The previous section should have set off two concurrent processes for you: developing your influence bases, and helping you to prepare for specific influence attempts.

If you're still worried about this influence attempt... what else can you do?

If you are ready for your influence attempt, but want to do more, you can think about what you will say and how you will act in the moment, too. In particular, you can consider working on the content of what you say to improve your chances of success:

- **Use humor:** A 2023 study of nearly 2,500 TED Talks showed if you use humor in a public presentation, you are more likely to be seen as a leader. This is especially true for female speakers. It works by increasing perceptions of warmth and, hence, raising likability.[17] Find ways to weave funny anecdotes, callbacks to previous conversations, and levity into your talk.
- **Use sets of three:** Humans respond positively to groups of three, recognizing them as satisfying patterns and complete sets. When you are trying to convince, give three short reasons why you should get what you're asking for: "It'll increase the team's chances of success, it'll increase the company's chances of success, and so, it'll increase *your* chances of success, too." The rule of three has a long pedigree having been used in ancient Greece but more recently proved by neuroscience to be effective.[18]
- **Consider mirroring:** We tend to like and trust people who are the same as we are, and a way to create this sense in the moment can be to mirror the behaviors of the person we are looking to influence. This can include taking a cue from how they usually dress (if they are smart, go smart; if they are casual, tone it down on the day you meet them), how they use their body when they talk, and the type of language they tend to use. If they have a particular way of referring to the new project you're discussing, or talk a lot about feelings, or data, or the concerns of the C-suite, mimic their language

and show that you are really listening and are aligned with them. If they are sitting back relaxed, try to do the same. If they are leaning forward, looking urgent, give a similar sense of purpose to your actions. It sounds bizarre, but the data backs up repeatedly how successful it can be during influence attempts.

- **Make eye contact while speaking:** We all know that we should make eye contact when we are listening to show that we are attentive and engaged. However, research shows we should also make eye contact while speaking—we tend to make less eye contact when we speak if we are more junior in the relationship. We can therefore "play" with this rule and increase the eye contact we make to signal that we feel we have, or deserve to have, a high status in the relationship.[19]

Your action will be divided into your longer-term attempts to develop your power bases and actions you can take during influence attempts to increase your chances of success. But what obstacles might you run into, and what can you do about them?

If your influence attempts still aren't working... are you being realistic?

Influence techniques are not perfect—they raise your chances of success but don't guarantee it. Resources are finite, and there's a limit to what people will agree to. You should know this from personal leadership experience: at some point in the past, a team member has no doubt approached you with utterly unrealistic demands for a salary increase, or a promotion, or a project proposal that's unfeasible. So you know, particularly with upward influence, that there is a limit to what can be asked for, before it's just a hard no.

You should also return to what you are asking for and check that it is realistic. This is not about being self-limiting—it is fine to have audacious plans. It is instead about working out how far you really can push it before you are likely to meet a no, and pushing it all the way up to that line! As you grow your power bases, this will help, but growing them will take time. You can't start to work on your power bases on Monday and expect to be the most popular and influential member of the senior leadership team by Friday. Give it time and keep trying. Positive changes will come, I assure you.

If they're not working, but it's critical... have you pulled out all the stops?

If it's super important to you to encourage a particular behavior or drive a change through, you should pull out all the stops. This isn't about appearing desperate but rather about putting all your efforts into increasing your influence to, for example, get a project past the post.

Think additionally about other ways to get what you need. Sarah, who's a middle manager in a city bank that is very hierarchical, says that she sometimes feels like she's getting nowhere with her direct boss on a staffing issue. She needs something to change, but her boss won't help. She can't win on that problem—the battle is lost. But the next time, she realizes it will be better to go to the head of HR instead, with whom she has a great relationship. Are there ways to sidestep someone who's blocking you and find another route to yes? Use your newfound skills of influence on them instead.

ELEVATE YOUR LEARNING

If you're better at influencing now... help your team to upskill

If you have found it helpful developing your power and influence techniques internally, there is no reason to limit their use to internal contexts only. The same techniques are just as valid in a wider context with clients and other stakeholders, and even with family and friends. With client relationships, you likely want to deepen the relationship, widening the number of products and services they buy from you, and turning clients into advocates of you and your organization's work. Focusing on those power bases that allow you to establish yourself as indispensable (expert and informational power) and a decent human being (referent power) will give you much better leverage in getting what you need.

If you want to increase your expert power further... become a "trusted advisor"

Expert power has real traction in most workplaces, as people see you as having the necessary skills and knowledge, and you can influence decisions as a result. You can improve your expert power further by looking to become a "trusted advisor" to your clients. If you are working in an internally facing role, then your clients are those within the business who are availing of your services.

According to an excellent piece of thought leadership by consultancy practice KWC Global, to become a trusted advisor, you should focus on:[20]

- Emphasizing excellent service over making a sale (or pushing your service on a colleague).
- Demonstrating passion and enthusiasm for your work and that of your clients.
- Working hard to understand and solve your client's problems.
- Generously sharing knowledge, expertise, and experience to help build your client's business or work output.
- Understanding the importance of being liked and working hard to achieve this.
- Connecting emotionally and understanding your client's challenges and successes.

If you can weave these elements into the way that you engage with your clients, using your knowledge to help them move to a better place, you will find that they increasingly come looking for your expertise and that your power base with them, and your impressed colleagues, grows!

REMEMBER:

- Your influence may be lower than you would like because you haven't worked on establishing your power in advance or because you are relying too heavily on hard or rational influence techniques.
- Working on power bases can take some time, and you will need to flex your approach depending on how senior or junior you are in the relationship. If you are junior, you won't be able to make use of legitimate power, and reward power will be harder to establish, too. Everyone can try to build expert, informational, and referent power. No one should be looking to use coercive power.
- In any specific influence attempt, you should give priority to soft influence techniques, such as inspirational and personal appeals, and consultation. These are the most effective and can also work well alongside rational, data-based influence. You should not make use of hard influence techniques unless you are very short of time and it's business critical to push a decision through.

PROBLEM 4

Individual Performance

"I have a team member who's failing me and themselves with work that's just not up to the standard. My boss has noticed, and they're putting me under pressure to turn the situation around, but I'm not sure where to start."

"I hate performance management. I think it's partly because measuring performance is so hard and partly because I hate having those difficult conversations."

"I have a team member who has low confidence. I think they're great, but they constantly undermine themselves by acting underconfident and telling others they don't think they're good enough to be operating at this level. This makes everyone else think they're a weak performer, but they're just misunderstood!"

LAST YEAR, I PROVIDED COACHING FOR A MEDIUM-SIZE CHANGE consultancy firm, FlipSize. Tom was a director of consultancy with two problematic staff members. The first was Charlotte, a newish consultant. Before FlipSize, she'd had just one consultancy role in a bigger firm. Her incentive for moving to the firm had been to have a bigger stake in the projects. She had been very convincing at the interview and had great people skills. However, when it came to the technical analysis and research elements of her role, she was very weak, barely appearing to be trained in any of the major research methods typical in this area of consulting. But Tom hated giving developmental feedback—it seemed so harsh. Each time he tried, her face fell, and he could see her fighting back tears. But he needed her to upskill quickly, as she was not fulfilling the role he needed her to.

Jayden had different performance issues. He had come straight from completing a PhD at a top business school, specialized in the psychology of change management, and was confident talking about this on a one-to-one basis with Tom. However, as soon as Jayden was put in front of clients or more senior staff at FlipSize, he would start to shake, mumbling responses and sitting hunched up. Tom knew he needed to find a way to help Jayden, too, but save for strong medication or intense therapy, he wasn't sure what he could do.

I'm sure you'll know that these sorts of performance problems are common, and you're likely reading this chapter thinking of ones within your team right now. The secondary problem for you as a leader is that if your team isn't performing well, it can make you look bad and reduce your boss's perceptions of your team's performance more generally.

This chapter will look at why poor performance happens and how to handle it when it does. As a leader, you can do much to turn things around. It's a case of first working out what's going on and then making a plan to improve matters that is realistic and fits the context.

STATE THE PROBLEM

If you think you have a problem with a team member's individual performance, working out the basics before you start to untangle it further should help you to stay focused on what matters. Answering the following questions before you start to "Open the Box" will help:

- **Who is the team member whose performance you are concerned about?** What are your concerns?

- **What evidence do you have that the team member is performing poorly?** Robust evidence and data? Observations? Hearsay? Are you comfortable with what counts as good data for performance measurement?
- **How skilled are you at giving positive and/or developmental (negative) feedback?** Do you find it awkward, or are you okay with it?

OPEN THE BOX

Identify where their performance is weak

If you suspect an individual performance issue, you need to get your evidence straight. What is it that you feel is a problem, and does the evidence back it up? You should focus your research on the following areas:

Are they falling short on the job's requirements?

Someone who has been in their role for a while should be doing everything the job requires. Someone newer, or whose job has changed recently, may be in the process of receiving training, learning, or development to help with some elements, but there shouldn't be anything required of them that either they can't do already or that they aren't learning to do.

You should have an up-to-date job description and be able to use that to compare their capabilities to what's required. If the job description is less up to date or if there have been recent changes to their role, you'll need to update what you have.

Are they failing to complete the necessary volume of work?

They may be doing their job, but not enough of it. Check that your assumptions about what is possible are reasonable and can be completed in a "normal" working week. What constitutes a normal working week will differ between settings, so make sure your analysis of what is reasonable fits your context. You could do this by comparing to others who are undertaking similar roles, either within your team or in other teams across the firm. Considering how much work they are able to complete in a set time frame and comparing it to the colleague you're concerned about should provide you with reasonable data to decide if this team member is pulling their weight.

Is their performance below their targets?

Many of your workplaces will be wedded to KPIs (key performance indicators). KPIs are clear, quantifiable metrics. Your workplace may have other ways of setting targets or objectives and call them something else. In all eventualities, you should compare employee performance against their targets.

TYPES OF DATA THAT MIGHT HELP

When you're trying to work out how good their performance is, try to focus on data that is as robust as it can be. You could see performance data types on a continuum, between those that are harder to trust and those that are really robust and reliable:

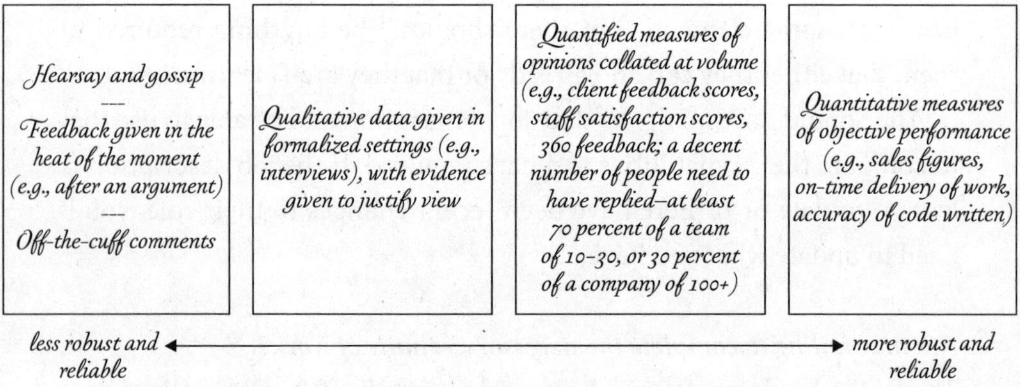

Hearsay and gossip — *Feedback given in the heat of the moment (e.g., after an argument)* — *Off-the-cuff comments*	*Qualitative data given in formalized settings (e.g., interviews), with evidence given to justify view*	*Quantified measures of opinions collated at volume (e.g., client feedback scores, staff satisfaction scores, 360 feedback; a decent number of people need to have replied—at least 70 percent of a team of 10–30, or 30 percent of a company of 100+)*	*Quantitative measures of objective performance (e.g., sales figures, on-time delivery of work, accuracy of code written)*

less robust and reliable ←——→ *more robust and reliable*

In some settings, quantitative measures of objective performance won't be available—there won't be a measure of work quality or quantity that fits the bill. However, in all settings, it should be possible to gather quantified measures of opinions collated at volume. What do people think of the person's work? How well are they doing relative to their colleagues? How successful are they at managing client relationships, at delivering work on time, at delivering work of the necessary quality? If there is not already a survey that goes out, or a way to gather this type of data, it may be time to talk to HR about creating one or a range of resources that you can draw on, as a manager, to get ratings of your staff members' work performance, particularly if you are concerned.

You may not want to flag someone's performance or make them feel bad by singling them out, so you may need to conduct a more general team performance review.

Ascertain the causes of underperformance

If your research has found evidence of underperformance, you will want to consider where it's coming from.

THEY LACK THE NECESSARY SKILLS

This is the most obvious source of underperformance. A gap in skills or knowledge will hinder an employee's ability to meet expectations. As a leader, you'll need to determine the cause of the gap.

Has it always been there but overlooked?

If someone is strong on other aspects of their role, a skills deficiency can be ignored for some time before becoming a meaningful problem that can't be ignored anymore.

A common manifestation of this is where someone has the technical skills required for their job but lacks the softer skills. We saw this with Jayden in the opening example. He was great at the technical analysis his job as a consultant required but was not good at talking to the client or senior members of staff. This might come about as a result of a lack of confidence, or just a lack of training as to what is expected, which means that your team member can't deliver, as they just don't know.

You may have overlooked it, as the other elements may have been easier to develop, but now that they are skilled in the other areas, the deficiencies are showing more clearly.

Has something changed in the individual or the job that has created a gap?

Many companies found, as tech grew, that the traditional secretaries who had worked as assistants to the leaders no longer had the skill set that was needed! The leaders needed savvy internet shoppers, people who could solve their phone woes, and people who could use pivot tables on Excel. Some were able to plug the gap with training, but others had no interest or propensity to learn the tech skills required and faced retirement. It can be stressful if the world moves on and your team doesn't! Are there areas where the role has changed but your people have not?

Has the person been overpromoted?

Sometimes people will be promoted into a new role and seem unable to do the job because it's too difficult or too different compared to what they've been doing before. For example, a person promoted to a marketing leadership role may be great at the marketing but less good at the coaching that is now required of leaders at this level to bring the best out of their team. They are falling prey to the "Peter principle," a well-evidenced phenomenon where people get promoted to their level of incompetence and then get stuck there.[1] This means, in companies that promote based on someone being good in their current role rather than matched to the more senior job, they get stuck with lots of managers who aren't great at what's expected of them.

Look at the staff member in question. Have they been overpromoted before you were certain they have the skills that are needed?

THEY ARE UNAWARE OF WHAT'S EXPECTED

If a team member is not aware of what they are supposed to be doing, it is not a surprise that they may be underperforming. Unclear job descriptions, ill-defined KPIs, and poor objectives make it difficult for employees to know where to focus their efforts. Failing to give someone useful feedback can also hinder performance, as whether you expect them to do better or want them to do more of the same, they may not know and just carry on, as you haven't told them otherwise.

An absence of expectation setting can leave employees confused as to what matters and how to perform well. It can also create demotivation, because if no one seems to care about what they are doing, sharing either praise or developmental feedback, perhaps it's not important anyway?

The CEO of a tech firm had significant complaints about his senior leadership team. He called me in to address their "very weak behavior" and lack of commitment.

I offered one-to-one coaching for each of them to help performance improvement. However, in my first meeting with each of them, every single one said they were totally unclear on expectations, which were woolly and regularly changed. There was a frantic yearly dash to create business-level KPIs and cascade these into individual objectives, but then these weren't followed up on by the CEO, who would change what he cared about a few months later, but not update the objectives to match. It meant weak performance from his team, who were confused and, in some cases, angry that they were trying to do their best and being criticized for it.

As a leader, you should ensure employees are clear on expectations. If you feel they do not have a clear sense of expectations, updated when business needs change, ensure that this is one of the first areas you tackle!

FIT THE CONTEXT: FEEDBACK PROBLEMS IN MATRIX ORGANIZATIONS

If you work in a matrix organization (one where employees are "lent out" to project teams and then "returned" to their home team for people management and appraisals), it can be hard for those individuals to receive meaningful feedback from managers. Poor team performance may be due to lack of quality feedback from managers who have borrowed them for projects,[2] sometimes caused by not knowing what is expected in the first place due to poor initial briefing on joining a project.

One interviewee, a senior HR professional at a global finance company, talked about how they work hard to try to achieve this, but how it's very hard and there will always be some staff members who fall through the cracks. They emphasize the importance of taking feedback seriously to project managers, but it's difficult when they are busy and projects run one into the next.

If you are in a matrix organization and are either someone's line manager or the manager who borrows people for projects, you will want to consider if the mechanisms through which you give and receive feedback are robust enough and whether you are taking them seriously enough. Even if there is an organizational culture that makes it seem as though feedback doesn't really matter, you should ignore this; if you want to get the best out of your team, you should take the feedback process seriously.

WORK IS TOO PRESSURED (OR NOT PRESSURED ENOUGH)

Work with no pressure can be boring (see Problem 5: Engagement). Work with too much pressure can be hard to cope with (see Problem 1: Personal Effectiveness). Both scenarios can lead to underperformance.

Check if you're asking too much

Are you placing team members under so much pressure that they are experiencing stress, anxiety, burnout, or overload? It is okay for staff members to feel stretched—challenged by projects that are slightly more demanding than usual. However, when they feel that it's too demanding, it can take a toll on performance.[3] These questions should help you to ascertain if your high expectations may be leading to performance issues:

- Is the work they're doing at the moment a long way outside their comfort zone or the skill set I know they have?
- Have they expressed concerns about their ability to do the work, which may be justified?
- Have they been under pressure to deliver at this level or volume for a long time?
- Are they showing signs of work stress or burnout, such as higher levels of absenteeism, ill health, or mood changes?

If the answer to any of the questions above is "Yes," "Maybe," or "I think so," then it may require some further investigation with the person in question, asking them these questions directly and seeing how they respond.

Check if you're not asking enough

Conversely, are you giving them such an easy time that their sense of achievement and motivation has reduced? Being bored at work, or feeling that it's too easy, can reduce performance. This is also covered in more detail in Problem 5: Engagement, but these questions should assist you in working out if a team member has a problem with being bored or not stretched enough:

- Do they appear disengaged in meetings, discussions, or collaborative document creation, not showing much enthusiasm or not pulling their weight?
- Do they seem to be easily distracted from the task at hand—for example, regularly checking their phone, looking on the internet, or undertaking non-work-related tasks?

- Do they appear to be more negative or lethargic toward work than before, perhaps taking less initiative or acting more critically?
- Have you noticed physical signs of boredom, such as yawning, slouching, or appearing lethargic?

If the answer is yes to any of the above questions, you may want to ask them directly how they are feeling about work and ask them if they are finding it interesting enough and challenging enough.

PERSONAL PROBLEMS ARE AFFECTING PERFORMANCE

Relationship issues, illness, housing issues, and financial challenges can be too big to leave at the office door on the way in. You may be aware of issues team members face that could have an impact on performance, but if you suspect personal problems but haven't been told, what should you do?

It is not a team member's obligation to inform you of factors outside work that may be impacting their performance, but if you notice sudden drops in performance, particularly if accompanied by uncharacteristic periods away from work, or arriving at work late, or looking stressed, or if you are noticing any other unusual signs or behaviors from the individual, it may be worth gently inquiring if things are okay. You don't need to let on that this is a performance issue; rather, you can just say, "I've noticed you don't seem your usual self. Is everything okay?"

Remote working has made it harder for leaders to keep abreast of individuals' personal lives[4] and makes it easier to hide issues. For example, if you are helping to care for your father, but you can fit in your responsibilities on the two days you work from home, no one at work need ever know. But as a leader, you can wonder why Jeremy is never free to talk at 4:00 p.m. on a Tuesday or Thursday.

Some cultures also dislike discussing home problems at work, preferring to keep the two separate. One UK-based coaching client, who worked with a lot of Russian staff, felt frustrated that she never even knew where they were going on vacation, let alone what their family situation was or if they were having problems. As she was the chief people officer, she found this hard, as she could not support them, but also needed to respect that they preferred not to bring their home lives into work.

This can all mean that it is important to be very sensitive as a leader when inquiring, and if you sense that you may cause any offence, back away and chat to HR to see what can be done to find out.

Are you wrong in your view of poor performance?

There are occasions when a team member's way of presenting themselves leads us to undervalue their performance.

For each role, there will be a sense of how someone should perform in that role: how they should talk, how they should dress, how they should act. If we feel that people are not acting the right way in the role, we can see their performance as worse than it actually is.

Perhaps you take someone's quietness as a sign that they don't know what they are doing rather than it being that they are concentrating. Maybe you see their sensitivity and tendency to get involved in the emotional life of the office as a sign of weakness rather than as a marker that they have great people skills. Maybe you've seen weak performance from them in the past and you haven't updated your view to take account of how they've changed. Or it may be that someone's gender or culture sets off a bias in your way of thinking—someone from that country is too chatty and never gets any work done; someone of that gender is too bossy and doesn't ever listen.

These sorts of prejudices and biases can be hardwired into our brains and, without conscious effort, stick there, wrongly shaping our view. What we don't want, as leaders, is for our view of someone to be shaped by these unconscious brain biases, which means we are seeing something different from what is really there and therefore unfairly judging someone's performance as bad when it isn't.

If you have measured someone's performance objectively and found that it is good, but have asked people's opinions and they have been more critical, it may be that they have a harsh view of the person based on some aspect of their past experiences with them, or their biases. You will also be subject to these biases, so if you find you are rating someone more harshly than others are or that your perspective of their performance is worse than the data suggests, you should explore whether any biases or prejudices are clouding your view.

BEFORE MOVING ON:

- What data were you able to gather?
- What sorts of performance problems did you identify?
- What do you feel is causing the performance problems?
- Do any solutions already suggest themselves as potentially being appropriate?

LAY OUT YOUR SOLUTION

Leading efforts to improve individual performance will focus on performance improvement itself, but should also, if necessary, look at how to set clear requirements, give helpful feedback, and manage your biases that affect your perspective of performance. All of these will be covered in this section.

Get clear on requirements

If underperformance is emerging because the individual isn't clear on what they should be doing, you can easily change this. Make sure that what is expected of them is clearly specified and that this is reiterated, discussed, and updated on a regular basis. From experience, I've seen that the areas that underperforming employees need clarity on are:

- **What** the task, project, or role is.
- Any necessary **background information** to complete the task or project, or to perform their role.
- The **level of authority** that you're granting them.
- The **standards of performance and measures of success** that they should be working toward.
- The **timeline** (they have agreed that it is feasible and can work to meet the deadlines).
- The **process of feedback and follow-up**.
- If and **when you would like to be involved** or informed.

You will also want to make sure that the data you are using measures the sort of performance you want to support. When Elon Musk took over Twitter, he used lines of code as a measure of effectiveness and laid off employees who had not written as many lines of code.[5] He did not consider the impact of the code,[6] which would have been a far better measure of performance.[7]

Emphasizing quantitative measures too heavily can mean that employees start putting all their efforts to meeting them, to the detriment of other, nonmeasurable elements of their work.[8] For example, if you could measure how many projects someone delivered each month and used that as a metric, they might maximize the number they deliver at the expense of quality.

Get better at regular, helpful feedback

If you want to improve performance, giving regular, helpful feedback is the single best way to achieve this.[9] To create a climate of well-received feedback, take the following steps.

PRIORITIZE POSITIVE FEEDBACK

You want to clock up lots of goodwill by giving praise. The more you give positive feedback, the easier people will find it to accept corrective feedback when it comes.

Where feedback could be seen as negative, or corrective, see if you can find ways to change it into a more positive message. If employees receive positive feedback, they are four times more likely to remain engaged than after receiving negative feedback.[10]

To enact a more positive approach, instead of saying, "You talk on the phone too much," say, "You are really strong at understanding clients. I would love you to spend more time getting these great insights onto paper. I think you could find the time by shaving down how long you spend speaking to clients—you're going above and beyond what we need. Thank you, but are you okay to try a slightly different way?"

This is not about just giving everything a positive spin but about working to our strengths, and it's easier to play to a strength than trying to turn around our weaknesses.[11]

GIVE POSITIVE FEEDBACK IMMEDIATELY, AND OFTEN

Positive feedback should happen as soon after the moment as possible. Better to deliver great, positive feedback on the phone straight after a client pitch or the day after someone has sent you a report than to wait.

This is because the action that you are giving feedback on will feel fresher in the memory, and the person receiving the feedback will be more able to take the learning from it as a result. For example, if you say to someone, "I really like the way you phrased your presentation—the way you described the new product really resonated with me," they are going to be more able to recall how they did describe it and look to repeat their success.

Giving positive feedback very often can build a climate of goodwill, where they like you more as a leader and are prepared to do more for you, but also where they are more comfortable in receiving developmental feedback from you, as they are confident that you value the work that they do.

CHOOSE YOUR MOMENT FOR DEVELOPMENTAL FEEDBACK

Developmental feedback can be harder to receive, and so, in many situations, you will want to deliver it in one-to-one settings away from the moment to stop team members feeling embarrassed or defensive, which can make it harder to take action on the feedback received.

However, there is a real benefit to being able to deliver developmental feedback in the moment, if the context is right, to enable on-the-job learning. You should consider if it's acceptable by thinking through the following questions:

- Is it a minor point and one that will not embarrass or cause defensiveness?
- Do you have a good relationship with the team member?
- Is this a team member who responds well to feedback without becoming too defensive or embarrassed?
- Is there a benefit to giving it now (e.g., they can repeat the action or task better immediately and learn on the job)?
- Have you delivered lots of positive feedback to this team member recently, so there is goodwill for receiving developmental feedback?

If you're unsure, act cautiously and deliver the feedback later, one-to-one, out of the earshot of others. If you haven't given a lot of positive feedback recently, frame it in terms of authentic positive feedback, such as, "You are a really valued member of the team, whose work is excellent. I'd like to talk about one area of development to help you and the rest of the team. Is that okay?"

EVIDENCE THE FEEDBACK

Developmental feedback needs a solid evidence base. What facts or data can you speak to that back up what you are saying, if you need to? You don't need to lead in with this—no need to say, "On May 20 at 9:37 a.m., I saw you roll your eyes at Connie," but you need to know what your evidence base is if it's called on. If you were to say, "I have seen you act in an unfriendly manner to your colleagues," you need to be able to back it up if asked. Remember that hearsay and gossip are not good evidence bases! Don't just pass along a complaint from someone else before checking that it's a valid complaint.

Positive feedback should feel as though it also has an evidence base, but you can further raise its power if you make it clear that it's coming from you, is authentic, and should be taken as a well-grounded compliment: "I was impressed when you presented your pitch deck" or "I could see the client loved your enthusiasm for the project." If it's owned and evidenced, it will feel truthful, make the recipient happier, and likely raise their view of you at the same time.

Offer learning, training, and development to improve performance

Use learning, training, and development to help team members improve their skills and reduce knowledge gaps, including off-the-job and on-the-job training, self-driven learning, mentoring and coaching, and job shadowing.

To create a suitable intervention, specify the knowledge or skills gaps, then identify appropriate solutions to bridge the gaps.

IF IT'S STRAIGHTFORWARD INFORMATION ACQUISITION

Self-directed learning or off-the-job training can be a cost-effective solution. Learning how to use a new piece of software, read a financial statement, give high-quality feedback, code, or give a good presentation are all examples of areas where information acquisition can be very helpful.

IF YOU NEED SOMEONE TO IMPROVE AT SOME APPLIED ELEMENT OF THEIR JOB

On-the-job training or job shadowing can show precisely what to do in the moment (e.g., how to talk to customers or deal with exceptions to the usual manufacturing process). Job shadowing arrangements can save time trying to learn how to do things from a book—instead, your team member can emulate someone who's already mastered that skill. Remember that job shadowing is harder when people are working hybrid, so you'll need to sync the staff members' calendars to ensure the person shadowing has enough access to the expert.

IF IT IS AN AREA OF PERSONAL DEVELOPMENT

Coaching can be helpful, particularly where the person has shown a motivation to change. Areas ripe for coaching might include building greater resilience, reducing your reliance on colleagues, developing leadership skills, or improving time management.

In all scenarios, you'll need to align your desired outcomes with your staff development budget. There's no point setting your sights on a year-long coaching intervention if your budget is only for group training or the pot for individual development is very small.

FIT THE CONTEXT: TACKLING IMPOSTER SYNDROME

Barely mentioned in coaching sessions a decade ago, today it feels as though imposter syndrome is everywhere. In the informal way the term has come to be used (rather than in its original psychotherapeutic definition), it is when an employee has a sense that they do not have the requisite skills or knowledge to be there.

The concept originated in 1978, based on female-focused research.[12] However, while it may be more likely to be experienced by women, it's certainly not limited to them.[13] A recently promoted male team lead of risk analysis I have worked with regularly spoke about his horrid feeling of being an imposter and how he thought it was impacting his performance, as it stopped him wanting to contribute to debates with fellow team leads regarding a joined-up approach on how to measure and control for risk in their insurance products. These debates were central to his role, and his performance was suffering as a result.

Feeling like an imposter can seriously affect performance, either by reducing confidence and willingness to step forward or speak up, or by others picking up on the lack of confidence and perceiving their performance as worse because they do not seem to trust their own abilities.[14]

As a manager, you can do more to help them feel accepted by creating an environment where a wider range of behaviors is accepted.

If someone lacks confidence in a situation, don't take it as a sign that they aren't competent—check to see if they do actually have the skills that are needed, as often they will surprise you. Pay particular attention to those from groups that are in the minority in the organization, as it may be harder for them to find the confidence to take a seat at the table. You may need to help them to envisage that seat as being theirs and help them to occupy it.[15]

If it's a skills gap, that's solvable. Interviewee and former head teacher Dame Mary Marsh suggests recasting imposter syndrome (which sounds uncurable) into imposter awareness, which reflects that it's a temporary state. Yes, we may *feel like* we are not supposed to be there, but we use that awareness and learn and grow until we don't feel like an imposter anymore. So if a team member is talking about imposter syndrome, encourage them to have a rethink: What could they do to start to turn things around? How can they see self-doubt as a feeling that reminds them that there is always room to grow?

Help team members to be perceived as more competent

To appear more competent, team members should try to appear more confident as a signal that they know what they are doing and have a right to be there. You should encourage your team members to:

- **Appear confident in their views:** Encourage them to resist the urge to waver or show genuine uncertainty in meetings. They should trust their experience and share their opinions confidently. Try to avoid too much hesitation or overly justifying their opinion before a justification is asked for.
- **Assume confident body language:** An open posture (shoulders back, head high, making eye contact) signals confidence. Encourage them to take up room and convey a right to be there. Research shows that if we can stop from shrinking into ourselves, instead being more open, it can make us feel more powerful and convey this to others.[16]
- **Speak slowly and clearly:** Use a wide vocabulary and avoid mumbling. If you are working to fit in, using expressions or terminology specific to the company or industry (as long as it's widely understood by your audience) can helpfully signal that you are a "member of the club" and confident using the vocabulary.

There are, however, important caveats to all of this: one interviewee talked to me about a coaching client of theirs who had consistently been told that she did not fit with people's visions of a senior leader. She wore pink, had a high-pitched voice, and was seen to be "too bubbly." She had even been given the advice to try to lower her voice, be more like a man, and dress differently. In the end, this act felt distressing, and she decided to return to who she really was, no acting. She should not have been forced to choose like this, and I don't like that we live in a world where we have to choose. But sometimes this is the uncomfortable reality, and we can decide how important the various aspects of our identity that appear to be holding us back are.

In my case, I may get less work because I typically wear sneakers to work. Yes, they're usually crisp white sneakers, but they're still sneakers. But I feel as though I'm cheating on myself if I wear pumps, or court shoes, so I've made my choice. I make my life harder, but it means I work with clients who like me for me. You should only do those things that do not cause you emotional stress, and if something feels like a personal deal-breaker, then absolutely do not do it. Fight it and be you. But realize that you'll need to do other things to convey your high-quality performance. For me, it's playing up my qualifications and knowledge to show that I have a right to a place at the table, even if I am wearing sneakers.

Fight your biases

If you have a biased perspective of someone that is tainting your view of their work, you need to manage this. First, it's hurting their career. Second, it may come back to bite you if they bring a case against you for discrimination. Having realized that you are holding a tarnished view of the person should be enough for you to course correct, but you'll need to find ways to continue to remind yourself that you have a potential bias here that could creep in and find ways to handle it.

One interviewee talked about how she struggled to judge people equally if they held opposing political views to hers. She could not help but think that they were less smart, and it made her feel more critical toward them. As she was in an organization dominated by people who were aligned to her political views, it was easy for those in the minority to feel isolated and poorly treated, and she could see that it could lead to a higher turnover and more negative work experience for these people.

She had, since realizing this, made a conscious effort to treat these individuals like individuals, rather than representatives of their political views, and had found that she had got on much better with them as a result. She had made an effort to get to know them, been out for coffee, and looked for common ground. She had discovered a lot of shared interests with one of them and that she had a top performer who she'd overlooked that she had now promoted.

We need to fight biases by being honest with ourselves, keeping them front and center of our minds when we are making decisions or judgments that invoke them, and taking on the challenge to manage and minimize them. Find a way to remember them each time you're about to evaluate performance or conduct an appraisal. Is it a note in your diary, or a helpful prompt from your partner or personal assistant?

BEFORE MOVING ON:

- What performance improvements do you expect from team members? Are your expectations fair?
- If relevant, how will you improve your feedback?
- Are there any skills gaps that need to be addressed through learning and development?
- If necessary, how will you help team members to convey more competence?
- Going forward, how will you spot and manage any biases that lead you to judge team members too harshly?

VENTURE FORTH!

Addressing performance issues can be uncomfortable for you as the leader and for the team member in question. While the techniques and ideas described here should help guide you into relatively calm waters, you may come across some ripples that, if you are not careful, could turn into storms. What might you run into, and how can you handle it?

If people react badly to feedback...

Developmental feedback can be hard to hear. Even if you try to frame it around leaning into strengths, they may still go on the defense. What to do?

TAKE YOUR TIME

Give the person plenty of space to ask follow-up questions, particularly those that are looking to clarify what you've told them—for example, sharing your evidence and observations again. Remember, keep your feedback OPOI! (observed, positively framed, owned, immediate, and emphatic!).

VALIDATE THEIR FEELINGS AND RESPONSES

Agree that it can be hard to hear feedback and that you can understand why they are reacting in this way. Acknowledge their feelings of anger, sadness, or frustration, trying to share with them that you would find it hard in their shoes, too.

DON'T TAKE IT PERSONALLY

If they say something mean or difficult in the heat of the moment, try to discount it as their defensive response. If you find that you cannot let it drop, you can return to it in a few days or weeks after the situation is resolved and ask them to explain it more carefully. Focusing on it at that time would likely just escalate the situation.

REMIND THEM (AND YOURSELF) WHERE YOU'RE BOTH HEADED

The end goal of developmental feedback is improvement, which should ultimately benefit them and you. You have delivered this feedback to help them improve, not to be unkind. In fact, you can think to yourself that good feedback is a kindness, as it allows us to grow into a better version of ourselves, and this person will hopefully see this in time.

If their performance doesn't improve... and doesn't improve... and doesn't improve...

We aren't all going to be good at everything. Sometimes, even the best efforts don't work. Coaching, training, job shadowing, clearer objectives, better feedback, and working on executive presence may not cut it, despite lots of help and support.

At the stage where you are starting to doubt their ability in the role and think it might be time to explore offboarding them, or demoting them, you will need to get HR involved. The requirements in terms of how to do this will vary from country to country (it is generally easier to fire someone in the US than the UK, for example, where even the expression "firing someone" seems harsh—managing someone out on the basis of poor performance can take six months or more). Whatever your country culture, you will want to start a relevant performance management or offboarding process with the support of HR, who will make sure that you do not fall foul of any legal requirements.

This may seem harsh, but if you have done all you can, it is better for everyone. You cannot expect your team to pick up the slack or for that person to be paid a salary commensurate with being competent if they are not. It's joyless doing work that you constantly struggle with. And a poor team member whose performance cannot be turned around will ultimately reflect badly on you as their manager.

ELEVATE YOUR LEARNING

As you've learned to deal with individual performance, you'll have improved your feedback; become better at diagnosing training, learning, and development needs; and learned to perceive people more accurately. How else can you put these skills to use?

If you enjoy performance management... consider building out this element of your role

So many leaders today despise the performance management element of their role, feeling awkward about having to have these conversations. But there is a small proportion of leaders who really enjoy this work, seeing it as an opportunity to help people grow and thrive in their work.

Patrick Connolly, academy director at Mishcon de Reya, looks after learning and development for the law firm and really enjoys the performance management work he's required to do, having intentionally stepped into a role where he could help people be better versions of themselves at work. And it's powerful work—with a blend of coaching, leadership development, and staff enrichment programs, including talks from iconic speakers such as MPs, members of the Spice Girls, and one of the few remaining Holocaust survivors. This work helps him to lead staff by filling in their skills and knowledge gaps, as well as making them better-rounded lawyers and support staff. When he is asked to coach someone who is struggling in their role, he enjoys this, seeing an opportunity to turn their career around.

So if you are someone who leans into this sort of work, see if there are ways that you can make use of your skills in your company, as they may make the working lives of many of your colleagues a lot better as a result, rather than it being left to managers who dread having feedback chats and don't want to do very much to help to develop their staff because they are too focused on their own careers.

If you want to encourage even higher performance... design for it

As a leader, you will be looking for performance gains in your team members wherever you can find them. An area of particular personal interest is the impact of the workspace on performance. This was what first got me hooked on the topic of leadership—how leaders can shape workspaces to improve outputs.

Lewis Silkin, a law firm with whom I have worked a great deal over the years, recently moved into a new building that is designed for high performance, and the joint managing partner is already noticing the positive impact. Coworking spaces, quiet areas, spaces where staff can come across one another and engage in ad hoc conversations about what they are working on (which are central to business-critical cross-selling), smart meeting spaces that save time on room setup and tech issues, and views that increase the perceived status of the building and therefore the firm all play a significant role. Jo told me how, in the new coworking space, where she sat on the same bank of desks as many junior lawyers who could hear her calls, she was undertaking a client negotiation. When she had finished, three heads popped up enthusiastically. That was the first time they had heard someone negotiate in front of them—whereas this used to happen all the time pre-COVID. They were impressed, and they'd learned something from a highly skilled lawyer, due to the design of the new building, which will raise their own performance as a result. These open-plan areas sit alongside beautiful quiet spaces, clad in blond wood and with great noise-proofing, for deep work and for confidential client work, and each type of space brings its own performance benefits.

Think about how you could redesign your own space to encourage high performance. As per the example above, the most obvious one is providing spaces that allow for different types of work, from open spaces that give opportunities for less skilled staff to learn from you and other, more knowledgeable peers; to quiet spaces that allow focus work;

to spaces that allow ad hoc conversations across functions to reduce silos and improve cross-working and performance.

In the opening story, Tom was struggling to turn around the performance of two team members, one who was suffering from a lack of confidence and the other who lacked necessary skills. Tom was able, by following the steps described here, to improve the way he gave feedback to both of them. Charlotte was shocked to hear that Tom had seen problems with her performance, and together, they decided she should enroll in an online research methods course. The change was quick and dramatic—just a couple of months later, she was teaching other, new members of the team how to use research tools and was delivering great analysis off the back of her own research.

Jayden's issue, which came down to confidence, took longer to solve—it is still a work in progress. But incorporating positive feedback into his regular interactions with Jayden meant that Tom could build up his confidence. Tom also assigned a senior consultant as a mentor for Jayden. The senior consultant helped Jayden to see that his knowledge was valuable and showed him how to act with clients and how to talk to his strengths in meetings. Eight months after Tom realized Jayden's problem and started to help with it, Jayden took his first major role in a client presentation, and he did very well. He was extremely nervous, but the progress has been big, with Tom's proactive approach to performance management.

REMEMBER:

- Make sure that your performance expectations are reasonable and that any performance problems are well evidenced before taking action. Check that your biases are not getting in the way of your reasonable judgment.

- Positive feedback is far more helpful than developmental feedback—create a climate for performance improvement by giving lots of positive, immediate, and evidenced-based feedback.
- Where developmental feedback is needed, consider how to deliver it in the way that will be of most value—ideally in the moment, but not if there is a chance that you will make team members feel embarrassed or defensive.
- Reduce the chances of a team member being perceived as incompetent by helping them work on coming across as confident.

PROBLEM 5
Engagement

"They say they care, but they're not putting in any effort—it feels like quiet quitting."

"I can't find a way to get them inspired and engaged—everything I've tried doesn't seem to work!"

"Leading is different from ten years ago—the things that used to motivate seem to have stopped working."

JOHANN WAS A CARDIOLOGIST IN A LEADING PRIVATE HOSPITAL, SPECIALizing in cardiac imaging. He managed a team of imaging professionals and was concerned about Bruna, who seemed to fluctuate between boredom and exhaustion. He felt the long shifts and high levels of energy required were the probable reason: she was just exhausted. To help her attitude, he had tried to recognize her hard work regularly. He felt that in a similar situation, this was what he would want.

However, this hadn't had an impact, with her brushing off the comments with, "It's my job." One day, after a particularly blunt brush-off, Johann asked what the matter was. He was surprised to learn she thought her work was pointless. She scanned sick patients, passed the images and initial analyses on to the clinical team, and never saw the patient again or heard the outcome. "I always have to take someone's word for the fact that I'm helping others, and when I'm shoved in this windowless room on ten-hour shifts, I struggle to believe them. Sometimes I wonder if my scans and assessments just end up in the trash. I dreamed of working in medicine and helping people, and now it's come to this."

Johann wanted to take Bruna's complaint seriously but was not sure what to do. Johann felt sure that disengaged team members made more mistakes in their analyses. He was aware that this was high risk in a cardiac environment, where precision is critical.

Johann is one of many managers I've spoken to who've had serious concerns about disengagement in their team and the potential negative effects it can have. He, and they, are right to be concerned. Untreated, disengagement issues significantly reduce performance. Disengaged employees are estimated to cost the global economy $8.8 trillion in lost productivity each year.[1] That's more than the GDP of Germany and the UK put together.[2] If you think you have a team member suffering from disengagement, well done on reading this chapter, as it means, like Johann, you're recognizing that you have a role to play in solving this problem. Too often, managers bemoan team members' workplace apathy or disengagement rather than seeing it as an area where they can and should be looking to have an influence.[3] Read on to diagnose what the causes might be and what you can do about it.

STATE THE PROBLEM

Work out the headline problem, as you understand it, so that you have something to look back on as you read through the chapter and stay focused on what you're trying to solve. You can use these questions to help craft this problem statement. Try to keep it to one or two sentences.

- **Who appears to be disengaged?** What evidence do you currently have to go on?
- **How is their disengagement showing up?**
    - They seem bored or switched off from their work.
    - They're delivering their work late or at a substandard level, despite being capable of doing it well and on time.

  - They're getting in late, leaving early, or taking more sick days than you'd expect.
  - They're quieter or more distracted than usual, not contributing much to conversations.
  - They're coming across as negative or dismissive about the organization, the team, or their work.
- **What do you think might be causing their disengagement?** Have you asked them?

OPEN THE BOX

If an employee is disengaged, you need to determine the cause. This is about understanding what combination of the job, the organizational environment, and what they want from work is causing their disengagement.

The job has the hallmarks of a bad job

Ideally, we would skip to our desks each morning, ready to show how passionate we are about this job, this team, this organization!

However, the reality for many of us is different. Think back to Bruna in the introduction: she was deeply unhappy with her role, despite it being a lifelong dream to work in health care and help people.

Our unhappiness can come about because there are qualities of a job that can make it difficult to like:

- **The job lacks a sense of importance:** If it is hard to see how the job delivers anything important to the organization or its stakeholders, it can make workers feel disengaged from the role. If you ask an administrator to polish a presentation for a client pitch but they never find out if you won the work, their work can feel unimportant. They don't realize that they were part of a team that won the biggest contract that year.

- **The role is highly prescribed:** If a job requires a high level of prescription in terms of precisely what to do, potentially coupled with a high degree of oversight from a manager checking that it's being done precisely to specification, this can make a job feel tedious and routine. Being a burger flipper in a fast-food chain, a mail sorter, a scripted call center worker, or a chatbot operator are highly prescribed roles that lack opportunities to use creativity or initiative to get the work done. It's also easy for a manager to notice and reprimand a step out of the routine.
- **The job is low in development opportunities:** If a role doesn't provide opportunities for an employee to grow, repetition can disengage. It could be lacking in developmental feedback, formal opportunities for learning, or mentoring. It could also lack the space for challenge and growth through progressively more difficult work, if you aren't providing that space for supported stretch. Ed Hayward, an operations director in contract research, told me how he's seen teams that aren't challenged stultifying. As a leader, if you're not providing substantive professional challenge and occasionally "holding their feet to the fire," individuals and teams can find their jobs or contributions extremely tedious.
- **The workload is too great:** Having an excessive to-do list and having to work excessive hours to handle it can prompt disengagement to cope. Rather than giving everything, they have to dial their effort back to save themselves from stress and exhaustion. They may do this as a self-preservation mechanism before they burn out, or may have already burned out and lack the energy to invest in the role. In her experience as executive director at a large global investment

bank, one interviewee told me how a lack of engagement is rarely caused by not liking the work. It's often about a lack of capacity to handle more, which prompts someone to pull away.

- **The job is too challenging:** While challenging work generally gets the best out of people, if work is too challenging, it tips over from being motivating to being stressful. They may also feel this way if the job is more difficult or skilled than they can cope with, either because they lack training or experience. Have they been promoted too quickly? Has the skill set required in their role shifted over time into an area they are less familiar with? Has training promised at the time of recruitment not been forthcoming, and so they have a knowledge gap?
- **The job is low in recognition:** If there are few opportunities for praise and reward based on good-quality performance, workers can feel their efforts are leading to nothing and disengage. This can happen if your organization doesn't have a healthy discretionary reward budget, such as a bonus pot or pay raise fund, or if you don't have good visibility over an employee's work and so it is hard to give meaningful praise. It also happens when managers are necessarily hands-off due to high workloads, or project-based workloads, which mean they lend team members to other projects and don't have clear oversight of the quality of the work being done.

Consider which of these factors apply to your disengaged staff member's current role as far as you can tell. However, remember that what feels too prescriptive to one worker will feel fine to another. Where one team member wants a lot of career progression, another might be happier working their way up the career ladder more slowly. Some people won't care either way. We'll look at this later in this section, after we consider how the organizational environment can lead to disengagement.

They don't like the organizational environment

Alongside the job itself, there is the broader working context that is a catchall for any other aspect that may impact engagement. If aspects don't gel with what they are looking for from work, this can be particularly disengaging. Some factors to pay particular attention to, in my experience, are as follows:

- **The organization's mission doesn't align with what they see as important:** If the company's main purpose is to provide a service or product that the employee doesn't see as creating meaning or purpose in life, they may disengage.[4] If they point out the problems with the mission to colleagues, this can be contagious and cause further disengagement problems.
- **It's lacking community:** The workplace community can be a big decider how engaged we feel. If your employee isn't part of a strong, cohesive community that works well together, this can lead to a sense of disengagement. Notice whether they seem to have workplace friends, talk to their colleagues, volunteer for team projects, or attend work socials; these can be good indicators of how embedded they feel (or not) in the workplace community.
- **They feel badly treated compared to others:** Employees often look at what rewards they are given relative to the effort they are putting in and then do the same for their colleagues. If they feel the rewards they receive for their efforts

are less than those others receive, they will disengage to redress the balance.[5] A good question to probe this without creating problems where there aren't any is "How's the workload on the team?"

- **The workspace is unpleasant:** An unpleasant physical environment in which to work can, for some people, be difficult to handle. Day in, day out, it can lead to disengagement. It may be that the workspace is bland and feels unhuman, leading employees to feel disconnected with the mission—greige filing cabinets and static-causing carpet tiles. A dirty, cluttered workplace can reduce concentration with their constant distractions. Individual offices with doors closed can create a sense of isolation from colleagues. These are just some possible ways that a workplace can prompt worker disengagement.

Again, to make sense of whether these factors are at play for the employee in question, the best approach would be to ask them. This doesn't need to be a heavy conversation, and you should definitely work hard so it doesn't sound accusatory. For example, if someone doesn't feel invested in the work culture, inquiring in a kind, curious way rather than in a way that feels judgmental will help them to open up. In turn, it will help you to understand what's going on for them and put you in a better position to find a solution if you can.

FIT THE CONTEXT: DEALING WITH DISENGAGEMENT WHEN IT'S CAUSED BY NONWORK PROBLEMS

Conversations with team members about low engagement often reveal something big going on in their personal lives, such as a serious medical diagnosis for them or a family member, money problems, milestone occasions such as a house move or a child's wedding, a court case, or pretty much anything else! How should you handle it?

1. Start by empathizing (or celebrating!). Recognize their challenges before you turn it to workplace engagement, possibly even returning to the engagement chat on another day.
2. Work with them to find what support they need during work hours, and more generally, to handle the problem.
3. Seek permission to make a plan with them for how to cover the shortfall of their work, if there is likely to be one.
4. Ask them to keep you informed. They don't have an obligation to do so, but if you've shown compassion, you will increase the chances that they will want to.

Providing support to employees often pays dividends, with a team member finding that the support offered allows them to reengage with at least some aspects of work. Additionally, if your team members believe you wanted to help them because you are a nice person, they are likely to repay the kindness, perhaps going to extra efforts to complete future work for you.[6]

If you are aware that the problem may rumble on for some time, it is worth seeking advice from your human resources department on how to handle it, if the time has come to suggest a period of extended leave, dropping down to fewer days a week, or similar. They may have a contingency budget in place, which you can tap into for temporary staff or support to cover the shortfall or be aware of where in the organization such money could be found.

Occasionally, you may feel that an employee is exaggerating the problem or leaning into it for a little too long. If so, this is also worth seeking advice from HR, as they can take on an investigation behind the scenes or explore what might be the best recourse in such a situation.

The job and environment don't align with what they want

The benefits that paid work brings aren't just the tangible elements of salary and bonuses. They're also the intangible benefits, such as praise, greater autonomy, a better job title, a sense of being expert, great work-life balance, and plenty more. Each of these can motivate, or not, based on our personal circumstances. Employees' personalities, their stage of life, and their broader context will have a big impact on what they want from work right now. One interviewee, a senior leader in a consultancy firm, reflected that early in his career, he liked rewards that focused on interesting work and knowledge growth. At mid-career, promotion was a bigger driver, as he wanted to become a partner before he was thirty-seven. In his current career stage, he was more motivated by bonus opportunities to top up his retirement fund.

It's difficult to guess a team member's priorities, and we can't assume they share our perspective. Yes, there *are* factors that make a job a turn-off to many, but they aren't universal: one person may love the simplicity of a very routine job (or not care as long as it pays the bills); someone else may be prepared to accept a lower salary as long as they can have a highly creative role.

When I interviewed Mark, the tech director of an online holiday company, he said he wished his whole team was motivated by growing revenues and would focus on designing tech to achieve this. However, he's noticed that some team members care much more about the tech working well or how much recognition they get from senior managers. To motivate his staff, he has to find out what they care about, and when he tries to do otherwise, he fails.

To figure out if there is a problem here, you should talk to them. Share that you've noticed they are less keen than usual, and because you value them as a staff member, you want to try to work out what's going on for them. Ask if they have any idea of what's happened that has shifted their engagement. If they can't give you an answer, I have found the following exercise extremely helpful.

1. Ask the team member to look through this list of motivating factors and rank them from most to least important.
    a. Being part of a team
    b. Being in charge
    c. Being seen as an expert
    d. Higher levels of autonomy
    e. A higher salary or a bonus
    f. More interesting work
    g. More learning opportunities
    h. Praise and recognition
    i. Career advancement
    j. Great organizational culture
    k. Good work-life balance
    l. Happiness
    m. Having an impact
2. Ask them to reflect on whether work is currently delivering on their top five for them. If not, why not, and what could help?
3. Make sure they are clear you're not making immediate promises, but thank them for their honesty and tell them that you're keen to try to help them find work more engaging again, if you can. Let them know you're going to think through what they've said and will be coming back to them soon with ideas on what to do next.
4. Reflect afterward on what they've said is important to them, how they feel work currently stacks up, and what they've proposed as solutions. Read through the next section, "Lay Out Your Solution," to see if you can see the value of what they've

suggested or if you can see better ways to achieve what they say they are looking for.

BEFORE MOVING ON:

- What appear to be the likely causes of disengagement for your team member?
- Have you checked with them whether your analysis is correct?
- What aspects of work would your team member find most engaging? Are these present or missing from their current work?

LAY OUT YOUR SOLUTION

Align their work with what they want

Now that you've understood where your team members' disengagement is coming from, you can look to address the problems. If you are a junior leader with less ability to change the job role or work environment, focus initially on what you can change while tabling a conversation with your boss on any wider issues the team member has raised that you think they should be aware of.

Improve the role

MAKING THE ROLE FEEL MORE IMPORTANT

If the team member says it doesn't feel as though their work matters, and you know it does, then show them how. At Consolite, a firm that manufactures lighting for defense vehicles (e.g., naval ships and military aircraft), each person who works on a given project (which in a small business is everyone) is awarded a medal at the end of the project with a picture of the vehicle commending their contribution. Even if they are just performing a small or tangential role, it's recognition that everyone's role has mattered. And it is important work, CEO Nick Rice told me. It's not just making lights. In a submarine, their lights will be the only light source for six or nine months. It's not "just a light" anymore, and the worker is not "just an administrator" working in a manufacturing company—that person is helping keep other people mentally and physically healthy.

INCREASING ROLE VARIETY

If someone has described the work that they are doing as repetitive or boring, or saying that they don't find it a challenge anymore, look at how you can increase the number of different skills that are included within the role. Asking paralegals to take on a wider range of work is a common practice in law firms to ensure that their work doesn't become routine and they remain engaged. Encourage task rotation in a team, and have job swap days to tap a wider range of skills.

INCREASING ROLE AUTONOMY (MAKE THE ROLE LESS PRESCRIPTIVE)

This is about giving workers more freedom in when and how they complete work. Fozia Raja, chief people and culture officer at Stenn, told me that she has found autonomy to be an effective motivator. Granting autonomy demonstrates trust and empowers her team to use their discretion in delivering the best results. It allows them creative freedom and doesn't curb innovation, because her lens doesn't need to be the dominant one.

If you're a leader who struggles to give autonomy, force yourself to take measured risks by delegating tasks well, leaving precisely how the team member completes the task to their discretion, with guardrails in place that you have set. See it as a learning opportunity for both of you—you might discover better ways to handle this work through your team member, and they will develop new skills. Pret a Manger, the main street coffee and sandwich shop, provide their staff with high levels of autonomy compared to rivals, giving them the right to hand out a certain number of free coffees, snacks, and sandwiches over the course of the week. This doesn't just make customers happy; it provides a way to make the work more meaningful and autonomous to the workforce.

CREATING MORE DEVELOPMENT OPPORTUNITIES WITHIN THE ROLE

Create a culture where team members welcome clear and regular feedback as a path to growth by making sure that a high proportion of the feedback you give is positive. Positive feedback is a great way to learn the right things to do. Mark Etherington, project manager in the UK Civil Service, told me that he tries to make a conscious effort to "shine the spotlight on someone who's done good work." He recognizes it's not just about saying, "Well done," but also about highlighting the tangible difference the person has made on the project and focusing specifically on that.

Balance it with developmental feedback, which, when delivered well, can be valuable and welcomed by staff. When I interviewed an executive director from a large global investment bank, she explained that high-quality feedback, which highlights what you still need to improve to be considered for promotion, is particularly helpful in her environment, where there are clearly delineated career paths. I covered more on how to give high-quality feedback in the "Lay Out Your Solution" section of Problem 4: Individual Performance.

PROVIDING NECESSARY LEARNING

If the individual is disengaged because they don't currently have the skills, knowledge, or experience the role requires, address this through learning. Off-the-job training, on-the-job learning, skills coaching, or being mentored (by you or an experienced team member) are interventions that can help individual development.

On-the-job learning, supported by on-the-job mentoring, can be particularly powerful. Give them tasks that get gradually harder as their ability grows, while offering the developmental support that on-the-job mentoring can bring.

For example, if they are receiving skills coaching on how to speak to a client, you might initially provide them with team members to practice on, followed by some friendly, well-established clients, then some lower-stakes clients, before letting them loose on your most important but high-maintenance clients. Their on-the-job mentor may sit in on some of these meetings to give feedback, provide the staff with opportunities to watch and learn from them, and provide stretch tasks when they are ready for the next step up.

SHRINKING THEIR WORKLOAD

If their job's to-do list is too great, you should help them to:

- **Cull work:** There are plenty of tasks on most people's to-do lists that do not need to be there. Focus on removing tasks that are not important enough to warrant the team member being stressed.
- **Prioritize work:** Focus on the work that is important and/or high impact. If work needs to be done but not right now, push it to a future time when everyone is less busy. Make good notes on what's been done and what's still to do before shelving it, so the future recipient of the task doesn't waste time getting back up to speed or repeating work.
- **Distribute work:** Explore whether they can share some work with other team members with capacity. If no one has capacity and the work is important, consider whether it's time to recruit another team member. If their salary is high

and you can't justify that much expense, take easier tasks from them and recruit a junior, and possibly others, too, so you can rejig workloads.

These actions should give them space to reengage by making it less overwhelming. If you have team members who are prone to overwork, check regularly with them on how they are coping. It's easy for the workload to creep up and disengagement to drop again.[7]

PROVIDING MORE RECOGNITION WITHIN THE ROLE

There's a strong incentive for leaders to give verbal recognition: in an analysis of thousands of 360-feedback assessments, leaders who were rated in the bottom 10 percent for giving recognition such as praise and appreciation were considerably more likely to have disengaged employees than those leaders who were seen to be better at giving recognition.[8]

Verbal recognition doesn't have to be a public display of appreciation—it can be delivered in a one-on-one or spontaneously in the coffee queue. For recognition to be valued, it should be specific. "Great job!" is not enough—make it about a specific action, such as, "Well done on the work you've done with the new staff member—they told me how much they are enjoying being a part of your team."

And it shouldn't always be about an outcome. Impressive hard work doesn't always deliver the desired result; perhaps it was a tough project or bad luck interfered. Effort is more controllable than outcomes, so focusing on the effort someone has gone to, the creativity they've shown, their tenacity, or their smart thinking can be more powerful than congratulating them on a great result.[9]

Tangible recognition should be tied to what an employee is personally motivated by. If they are motivated by money, then a bonus can be great. If they've identified learning as a reward they value, ask them to propose some professional development they would like to do. Make it clear that this is recognition for a great job. It should also be linked to what you as a leader can practically offer. If you don't have a budget to afford training or bonuses, can you offer a discretionary day off?

FIT THE CONTEXT: COULD JOB CRAFTING HELP?

Job crafting is when an employee is given creative control over improving their job. It works only in situations where there is enough discretion within the role regarding what is done, how it is done, and when it is done for an employee to take advantage of this flexibility.

It appears to increase engagement in two ways: it allows the worker to create a job that they find more engaging, and the act of being put in control itself increases engagement by increasing the employee's sense of autonomy.[10]

An important success factor is helping employees understand what makes a job engaging so that they are crafting in the right ways. For example, staff who are less familiar with this idea may make a job too easy or low pressure, when some challenge and development can be beneficial for engagement, as I discuss above. As such, you could share this chapter with them or turn it into a lunch and learn.

If and when you decide to go ahead with job crafting, make it clear what they can alter and what they can't. For example, if working hours are set company-wide or there is a particular process prescribed by law in terms of how much professional development they are required to do each year, these would be areas where they could not make changes.

Notably, with job crafting, the responsibility for change is put in the employee's hands, so only call it *job crafting* if it really is. If it's just you saying they should come up with some suggestions and then you'll choose which ones they're allowed to do and push them through, then this is just getting them involved in the change process, which is still good but not the same as job crafting. Use job crafting when you are comfortable giving them lots of control over how they alter their job and what they ultimately decide to do. You will also need to be ready to give them support to put the changes they decide upon in place, not being a blocker just because what they have chosen is not precisely what you hoped they would choose or what you would have opted for.

It is also more likely to work if you have employees who are naturally proactive and therefore want to make changes and see them through, finding these processes motivating in and of themselves.[11]

Improving the organizational environment

As before, this category encompasses everything other than the job itself. Here are some actions to take to improve areas of the organizational environment you may have identified as responsible for your staff member's disengagement.

HELP THEM GET BEHIND THE MISSION

You can't change the organization's mission, but you can explore ways to help the team member see it in a more positive light.

Pharmaceutical company Pfizer has peppered the walls of their buildings around the world with photos of patients whom their drugs have helped,[12] trying to narrow the distance between the worker and the end user. Could you apply a similar strategy to narrow the distance between their work and the service or product being provided to a grateful end user?

By showing them how the company provides meaningful value to its stakeholders, the team member may be reminded why this work is important and help them support the mission.

Telling positive customer stories can help. Returning to Consolite, which manufactures lighting for defense vehicles, CEO Nick Rice uses storytelling to say that these are not just lights but life-supporting necessities that keep people safe and healthy when they are at sea (or undersea) for months.

The worker may not feel particularly aligned to the values of the defense industry and therefore may see the work Consolite does as less than positive. However, the story of a submarine crew who can eat nutritious food due to hydroponically lit vegetable gardens is powerful. They can return home to their families healthy.

EMBED THEM IN THE WORKPLACE COMMUNITIES (AND IMPROVE THEM IF NECESSARY)

If your staff member doesn't feel embedded in the workplace community, look to strengthen their ties. Encourage them to work on collaborative projects with other team members to increase their embeddedness in a work-appropriate way. Identify projects likely to have high levels of interaction between team members, and emphasize this as a key feature when setting up the team. Create buddying and mentoring programs to forge deeper work-focused bonds between team members, as these can have a meaningful impact on engagement.[13] Encouraging their attendance at wraparound activities and events can also be beneficial—for example, after-work socials, informal lunches, and coffee breaks can all be a great way to feel more embedded in the community.

If your company has special interest groups, these can be a good tool. I worked with KPMG to develop the leadership of their special interest groups and was impressed by the variety of groups and the sense of community they brought to members, from sports clubs to book groups, to social groups for those who were ex-military or Francophone, to support groups for those who had personal struggles in key areas, such as a carers group and a disability group. Gently encouraging the team member to find and join these groups, if available, can be beneficial. Or if there isn't one they are interested in, could they set one up with your support? Not only will this improve their embeddedness, it will also help others.

IMPROVE THE PHYSICAL ENVIRONMENT

If the physical environment is a perceived cause of disengagement or if you've been told they feel distanced, improving the workplace can help. It can also help with other elements of disengagement:

- **Improve the space's suitability for engaging work:** Focus on creating spaces that are clean, bright, and comfortable for work, providing optimal work conditions, reducing distractions, and thus improving in-the-moment engagement.
- **Increase feelings of comfort and well-being:** Elements that soften the harsh office space, such as plants, pictures on the walls, and comfortable furniture in common spaces, can increase feelings of well-being, which in turn can improve engagement.[14]
- **Improve the sense of community:** Common spaces that are user-friendly and suggest collaboration can increase the development of workplace communities and someone's sense of being embedded in them. Creating great hybrid meeting rooms where those who are not in the office can feel as much a part of the meeting as those who are can be helpful. I talk more about this in Problem 7: Hybrid and Remote Working.
- **Add features that reflect the brand or mission of the organization:** Photos of happy customers, well-used products in display cases, or the deeds to the first shop you opened framed in the cafeteria are touches that I've seen used to build a sense of purpose and brand.

The ways you can enhance a workspace to create a more engaging environment are almost boundless, and I would recommend thinking hard about what you want to achieve and making sure that your choices will allow you to deliver on these aspects. Getting in a specialist office design company can be expensive, but a trip to your local IKEA, hypermarket, or superstore with a well-thought-out shopping list can deliver a good result for a fraction of the price and can even be a nice reward for junior staff members who you know are engaged by roles that are varied or creative.

IMPROVE THE SENSE OF FAIRNESS

To increase their sense of fairness, you should ensure that they believe they are being paid fairly relative to their inputs, compared to their colleagues and other people they might measure themselves against. If you've discovered they feel under-rewarded relative to their effort, you could:

- **Alter workloads:** If you think they have good reason to feel they are doing more than others but not being rewarded for it, you can redistribute work. You'll need to check this isn't going to have the secondary effect of causing feelings of unfairness in others. If it does, this is not a good option, and you should look to your other choices.
- **Alter their rewards:** Another option is to up their compensation package, which includes salary, bonus, and any other rewards. Only do this if your research shows it's justified. If you can, ask them to come to you with a proposal of what they think is fair, based on evidence they have gathered. This places the onus on them and gives a starting point from which you can bargain. Don't agree in the moment—take some time to double-check the veracity of their data. If you don't have much budget to increase salary, are there other rewards you can give, such as more vacation days or better health insurance?
- **Change their perceptions:** If your research shows their rewards relative to their workload to be fair, you'll need to adjust their perceptions. You'll need to share with them as much as possible the information you're using to arrive at your perception of fairness and see if it adjusts their perception. I worked with a leader who was being badgered by a

team member who felt under-rewarded. The leader decided through coaching that the only way out of this was to meet with the team member and let them know that they were far less qualified and capable at their work than the people they were comparing themselves to. When the leader delivered their view, the team member went quiet for a while and looked close to tears. They asked for the meeting to finish, and the leader expected a call from HR saying the staff member had complained. However, the next day, the leader received an email from the team member to thank them for the honest feedback. The team member started working hard to correct the imbalance and within eighteen months had received the salary increase they were looking for. While I can't guarantee that all perception-adjustment conversations will have such an easy fix, it shows the power that sharing your view can have for adjusting someone else's view.

It's important to note that feeling fairly rewarded will stop an employee from feeling disengaged and will create circumstances that allow them to feel engaged, but wouldn't create engagement itself. It's a necessary factor for engagement, but not a tool to actually foster engagement. In other words, you'd better get it right, but don't expect additional loyalty, commitment, or engagement for doing so.

Reflect carefully on how much to change

As you take actions to improve engagement, remember one important caveat: *changing heavily to suit one person may not be in the best interests of you, your team, or the organization.* You could end up taking on a lot of extra work to try to keep one team member happy. Other team members could feel that someone else is receiving unfair special treatment and disengage. Make sure you are not overstepping in any of these ways. To assess the situation, ask yourself two questions:

- Is this an action that is feasible to scale up to other team members?

If yes, this sounds like a good solution. You can then reflect on whether you want to do that preemptively or wait until someone prompts or requests the scale-up.

If this is not an action that's feasible to scale up, consider this question:

- Is it fair to offer this to just this one team member?

If no, you may want to rethink your approach if you cause mass consternation. If yes, then this sounds like a good solution.

BEFORE MOVING ON:

- How will you improve engagement for the team member in question?
    - How are you planning to improve the role?
    - How are you planning to improve the work environment?
- Have you reflected on whether your planned changes are fair and realistic?
- How will you determine if they have a positive impact?

VENTURE FORTH!

If you can't improve one element... focus on others

In every setting, there will be some elements you can't change, but this may not stop team members telling you that this element is what's stopping them from engaging. Working on an oil rig will always be isolated and noisy; being an ER nurse will always be stressful and require long hours; working for a charity will rarely bring a high salary; being a junior lawyer will involve your work being highly prescribed. If you were a manager in those settings and a team member told you they were feeling demotivated because of those factors I've stated, you would not be able to make the changes they feel they need.

If someone insists they are unhappy with an element you can't change, it's likely not a good role for them. However, before deciding this, talk to them about what you could do to improve other elements and whether these might make a difference.

If you can't alter the job much, can you improve the working environment and/or the rewards? If it's a necessarily unpleasant working environment, how can you improve the quality of the job and/or the rewards? And if it's hard to offer high rewards, how can you ensure that the job and working environment are great?

I worked with a charity recently that offered lower salaries for functional roles than people might achieve in other sectors. For example, their IT professionals were paid less than they would have been in most for-profit settings. The work was also stressful, focused on eradicating abusive behavior online, and meant IT staff were exposed to lots of difficult content. To maintain engagement, the CEO worked exceptionally hard to create a positive, friendly office environment. Staff found it easier to cope with the stress and tolerate the lower salaries while remaining engaged because the culture was amazing. It gave them a buzz to work with amazing colleagues and feel they were making a big difference in people's lives.

If they're expecting more than you can give... help them with an attitude adjustment

If whatever you do to improve things for this worker doesn't seem enough, you may need to explore whether they need a reality check regarding what is feasible to expect from this organization, and from work more generally.

Work is a major source of identity for many people, meaning they pin their hopes on it being perfectly aligned to who they are. Perhaps the work you do can provide this perfect alignment, but more likely it can't because perfect alignment is likely an unrealistic expectation.

Simone Stolzoff, author of the book *The Good Enough Job: Reclaiming Life from Work*, describes how work should be just one part of our identity,[15] because it can rarely give us everything, and we need other sources of identity outside work, whether it's being a great friend, a community gardener, an enthusiastic martial artist, or a jigsaw puzzle fanatic. We become more rounded as a result and place less emphasis on work having to be perfect.

One interviewee, a senior HR leader at a global bank, explained how she sometimes had to reassure and encourage staff who were largely aligned with the company's mission not to worry too much about small areas of misalignment. As long as they can get solidly behind the mission, it may even be unrealistic to think that their values could be totally aligned.

Help a team member adjust to this way of thinking by gently questioning why total alignment between them and the role is critical to them, or whether they are in line enough and contributing sufficiently to the mission that they believe in for the differences not to matter.

If they feel that they need the work to be closer to what they want than it can provide, it may be time for a conversation about whether this is the right role or organization for them. The interviewee above talked about how, in that situation, she would want them to vote with their feet and leave because total misalignment can be too hard for them, and for the company, to absorb. As their manager, you could do this informally, exploring what they want from the future and whether the role can provide it—or, if you think it's needed, get HR involved for a more formal exploration of how their disengagement affects their performance with the intention of letting them go if their performance doesn't improve.

ELEVATE YOUR LEARNING

If you've seen the value of a particular intervention... consider scaling it

Your efforts to improve engagement with one team member may reveal approaches that you think could be of benefit to the team, function, or organization more generally. For example, if you have seen the engagement improvement caused by increasing the sense of community that a disengaged employee feels, can you find ways to strengthen the bonds between other team members through more collaborative projects, or provide opportunities for more socializing between employees, or start some more special interest groups?

Letitia is a leader in the pharmaceutical space who had experienced problems with the engagement of Sian, a team member. Letitia asked Sian what was the matter, and Sian said she felt underappreciated. She had been working hard every day but hadn't received any recognition for all the effort she'd put in. "But I always tell you you're doing a good job!" Letitia had replied. Sian had shrugged, and the conversation had ended. Letitia brought this problem to a workshop I was running and asked me what I thought was going on. I asked if she made sure her praise was specific—telling Sian exactly what she was doing well and thanking her for her specific efforts. Letitia said she didn't currently do this and would give it a try. I am sure you can guess what happened: the next day, Letitia tried this, and it worked almost immediately—it was one of the most powerful turnaround stories I had seen. Within hours, Sian was back into a good headspace, and it gave Letitia a moment to reflect: Could this be a strategy for unlocking higher engagement and productivity in other team members? She tried it, giving specific, meaningful recognition for high-quality work and high-quality effort. In her 360-degree appraisal, for the first time ever, she was ranked as "highly supportive" by her team.

What have you done to try to turn around the engagement of one team member, which could be valuable for other team members? If it's feasible to scale it, then go for it!

If everyone needs better working conditions... develop an impressive employee value proposition

An employee value proposition (much more regularly referred to as an EVP) is a statement of the unique benefits that an employee will receive and experience when they choose to work for your organization. It covers both tangible and intangible benefits.

Creating an EVP can prompt a powerful, organization-wide conversation. Start by identifying what you can offer employees uniquely. You should look for perks or opportunities that you can create for your employees that other companies who might try to recruit the same employees cannot offer. What makes your organization a unique, desirable employer? Ask current employees and interviewees for their take on this to develop your understanding and further embrace your unique employee offering.

The answers will likely focus on culture, values, mission, career progression, development opportunities, working environment, colleagues, salaries, and other benefits. Decide which are unique to your organization and which you want to support and turn these into a truthful statement focused on what you offer.[16] It can then be beneficial to use this statement to have further conversations around where you want to improve and how. If you are a more junior leader, you may not have the necessary sway to advocate a company-wide EVP. However, you can use this concept to think through your own team-wide or function-wide EVP.

Use the resulting EVP—whether it's company-wide or specific to your function—at recruitment to help job candidates understand your offering and increase the chances of recruiting people keen on your offering.

Remember Johann from the opening case? He was a cardiologist whose team member Bruna had lost sight of how her work was important and had become disengaged as a result.

Once Johann had ascertained the cause of Bruna's problem, he was keen to help Bruna reengage with the importance of her work. He asked the more agreeable cardiologists to provide feedback to Bruna and the team when the imaging helped someone. Johann also asked if Bruna could sit in on some patient consultations where her images and analyses were used. From sitting in, Bruna spotted a number of ways that she could improve how she presented her analyses, which would make the consultants' lives easier, meaning it had an additional benefit to the cardiology department and its patients.

However, this was not the end of the story: other team members became envious of the "special treatment" Bruna received, so Johann needed to change his approach. The process of asking the consultants to send written feedback to the team proved too onerous to maintain when the whole team now wanted it. However, he was able to ensure that each team member could sit in on at least two patient meetings a month, and the consultants continued to appreciate how it helped the imaging specialists do better work.

REMEMBER:

- Disengagement can emerge from poor-quality jobs, such as those that are too prescriptive, lack autonomy or importance, have insufficient opportunities for development and recognition, or require too much work or work that is too hard.

- Disengagement can also be caused by a lack of alignment between what the organization cares about and what the individual cares about, not feeling embedded in the organizational community, a sense that the rewards they receive for the efforts they put in are insufficient compared to others, and a poor-quality workspace.
- What you see as a reason to disengage is unimportant: it's what they see as a reason to disengage. Ask them what would engage them so you can narrow your focus to the elements that are important to them.
- To improve job quality and/or their perceptions of job quality, you can increase the importance of their role, their autonomy within the role, the role variety, the recognition they receive, and the development and learning opportunities. Shrinking the workload to a manageable level can also improve job quality.
- To improve the work environment and/or their perceptions of it, you can help them to get behind the organization's mission, improve their connection to workplace communities and the physical environment, and improve their sense of fairness.
- Focus on what is within your control and take particular care of providing anything to the individual team member that there may be an expectation you will provide to everyone.

PROBLEM 6
Teamwork

"My team's split into two warring groups, and I just don't know what to do about it."

"We're so disorganized! No one on the team ever seems to know what anyone else is doing. Stuff is always being forgotten, repeated, people step on each other's toes, and all this chaos and rush means we deliver substandard work a lot. It's embarrassing!"

"The team I'm leading is performing poorly, and I think it's because everyone's too nice! No one challenges anyone else; there's no sense of urgency or importance. We all just rub along comfortably."

IN THE PAST FIVE YEARS, I'VE WORKED REGULARLY WITH LOGAN, THE leader of the learning design team in a London-based university, to help him improve his team's performance.

When Logan first approached me, his team—split between India and the UK—was in a mess. Rather than seeing themselves as one team that happened to be based in two places, they saw themselves and acted as two totally separate teams.

It didn't manifest as conflict, though. Quite the opposite! As Logan pointed out to me early on, it was a bit *too* nice: only the UK team members felt that they knew each other well enough to challenge one another—but the Indian team members didn't challenge the UK team members or one another. And yet, away from the team meetings, Logan heard both the Indian and the UK team members grumble about the others. The UK-based team members thought that the India-based team members were too rules-driven and not creative enough. The India-based team thought the UK-based team was too slow and over-developing ideas and missing deadlines, which their India-based coworkers then had to pick up.

This meant that the UK team felt the India team often overstepped, taking on work that wasn't technically theirs, and meaning that Logan would end up with two versions of the same learning resource and have to pick between them, creating further tension and wasting everyone's time. Despite having really competent team members, he could see how the team problems were eating into performance.

Team working can be really difficult, and it can be hard to voice concerns or complaints for fear of making things worse. Whether you are part of the team you have concerns about, or whether you just manage them, you may have an important role to play in defusing problems and fostering great team performance. Because team problems left unmanaged can be disastrous: small troubles can grow into huge challenges, and so what starts as a miscommunication over who's doing what, made worse by a time-zone difference, can foster full-blown resentment and mistrust. But being front-footed about teamwork and investing effort in creating great team practices and a culture of high performance can result in a level of excellence that puts your team ahead of the pack. But how?

STATE THE PROBLEM

Before you get stuck in the details of your problems with teamwork, laying out, at a top-line level, what you think the problems are can be helpful. It will mean, as you start to read through the next few sections, you remember what you are trying to solve.

- **Who appears to be the problem?** Is it just one or two people in your team who seem to be causing problems, or a broader issue across multiple team members, or even the whole team?
- **What type of problem does it seem to be?** Use the sentences below for inspiration, or write your own short summary.
    - Everyone's too nice to one another: there's no challenge.
    - The team isn't acting as one, instead pulling in different directions.
    - There's a lot of unhealthy disagreement and conflict between team members.
    - Performance isn't even across the team.
    - There's confusion as to who's supposed to be doing what.
    - Hardworking team members are resentful of team members they think are slacking.
    - There is a lack of trust between team members.
    - Our meetings are ineffective and inefficient.
- **How severe is the problem?** Is it that team performance is slightly subpar, or that full-blown conflict threatens to shred the team apart, or somewhere in between? Often, with team problems, it can also be a number of problems at once, and if you have a number of parallel problems, include them all.

OPEN THE BOX

Is the team lacking psychological safety?

Psychological safety—when team members feel as though they are able to express their opinions freely without the risk of punishment or humiliation—has been shown to be a key factor in whether a team will perform well or not.[1] In a study by Google, to ascertain what makes a great team, psychological safety was shown to be the foundation of team function: without psychological safety, a team will struggle to get everything else right. They won't trust one another, they won't take risks, and they will subsequently pull away from challenging one another and fail to drive for better performance.

Identify how your team is doing on psychological safety by reflecting on these questions. If you do not instantly know the answer, observe them over the coming few days:

- **Handling problems:** Do team members speak up when they spot problems or mistakes?
- **Seeking improvement:** Does the team look to improve, asking members for feedback, ideas, and knowledge to grow? Do they accept these ideas graciously?
- **Asking for help:** Do team members ask one another, and those outside the team, for help when they get stuck?
- **Avoiding blame:** Does the team focus on finding solutions? Do they avoid attributing blame?
- **Good team behaviors:** Do the team members demonstrate active listening? Do they appear relaxed with one another? Do they divide speaking time appropriately? Do they ask open questions?

If you found yourself answering "No" or "Not as much as we/they should" to any of these questions, you've identified some deficiencies in psychological safety. Keep a note of any areas of weakness to tackle in the next stage. You can also ask other team members what they think.

In Logan's team, the India-based team members did not trust those in the UK, and vice versa. They blamed one another for mistakes and resisted asking the other half of the team for help. They did not handle problems together but rather went to Logan to solve the problems—for example, deciding which document to use when work was duplicated.

They also found that the UK team members dominated the conversation in joint meetings. This is problematic because, in their research, Google showed that good teams tended to have well-dispersed turns at talking. You can see why this might be the case, as there are no dominant characters, everyone feels as though they have an equal say, and they are able to make sure that their contributions count.[2]

Does your team lack clarity and trust about who does what?

If you have a team or are a part of a team that is unclear about who does what or has a sense that they can't rely on one another practically to deliver what they have said they will, they will struggle to function.

Identify if this is an issue by observing:

- Do people avoid detailed conversations about who is going to do what and how, meaning that there is a lack of clarity regarding roles?
- Is there a regular sense of task overlap, stepping on toes, or deliverables not being done?
- Do team members grumble to you or one another about others not pulling their weight or having to pick up the slack for others?

This last point can lead to big problems, because when a team member feels that they are doing an unfair amount of work compared to others, they can start to feel demotivated or cut back their own productivity as a result to try to even the balance, and you end up in a vicious cycle. This kind of complaint may not make it all the way up to you if an employee doesn't want to be seen as a complainer or not a team player, so it may be helpful to specifically ask other team members what they think about their workload as compared to others.

In Logan's team, because the UK half of the team was slow to deliver their work, the Indian half would step in and do the work. This would create a lack of clarity on who was responsible, created because one half did not trust the other to get their work done on time.

Does the team lack a sense that their work matters?

Teams work best when they feel that their collective work matters and can get behind the goals and objectives they have.

Signs that the work isn't firing individuals up include:

- a sense of slowness or apathy with task completion;
- a lack of projected enthusiasm over the task; and
- the team not seeming to band together in the face of a new, potentially interesting task or a thorny challenge.

There could be other reasons for these, though—like overwork, stresses at home, or a team conflict. But if you feel that a lack of meaning or impact could be to blame, a spot test can help to clarify things.

You could try, at a team meeting, to ask everyone to write down what they think is the most impactful element of the work the team does, read these out, and gauge reactions. You could ask individuals to talk to you about where they find a sense of joy, purpose, or meaning in their work. And just see what they say. And then reflect, using your own sense of how they've answered, and what you've picked up on, as to whether there are issues with meaning and impact or not.

I was recently asked to work with a team in the financial services sector who were seen by their seniors to have weak performance and to be slow at delivering. I asked them to write down the most impactful part of their work, and they really struggled. A couple said, "Providing recommendations," another couple said, "I'm not sure," and one sarcastically wrote, "Lunch." They said that they were slow and unenthusiastic because it felt as though everything they delivered to their seniors was questioned and adapted. Very few of their plans were implemented. The reason for this was because the industry was changing a lot due to new regulations and new market opportunities, and so what was relevant one quarter was not the next. The team knew this, but found it demotivating, struggling to find collective enthusiasm for tasks that may be rendered irrelevant in a few months.

Is your team too homogeneous?

When teams are comprised of members who are too similar or who act too similarly, they lose opportunities to explore topics from a range of viewpoints. This may reduce their creativity and weaken their decision-making and problem-solving.[3] Team members who are too similar and hold similar views may make blind decisions as a result. If you are in product development, for example, and all your team members are similar, you are less likely to come up with a high number of novel ideas if they are all seeing the project through a very similar lens.

Team members could be very different but putting on an act to try to fit in. When team members are actually different but do not feel psychologically safe to be themselves, they can avoid debate and discussion, worried it will turn into conflict. Teams that rush to a solution rather than discussing issues thoroughly arrive at weaker solutions. They can avoid talking about their differences or showing their differing perspectives because they are concerned that people will not like them as a result. In a thirst to be liked, to stay together, and not to conflict as a team, team members can convey an artificial sense of homogeneity, agreeing to safe decisions rather than challenging one another with their diverse perspectives so that they can come up with something better.

Or teams can be diverse in just a few ways, and then the team can divide along visible, demographic, or professional lines into sub-teams—perhaps based on geographical location, or cultural heritage, or whether you are a doctor or nurse, or if you are a cardiac specialist versus a psychiatric specialist in a multidisciplinary medical team. These sorts of divides can create fault lines in teams, where teams work in small, homogeneous subgroups, split by these fault lines, and team performance breaks down as a result.[4]

As a leader, you can ascertain if there are potentially problematic fault lines in your team by observing the way that people act.

- Do they repeatedly split into the same subgroups for projects or activities?
- Are they in subgroups clustered around easily discernible differences in culture, heritage, age, gender, role, or another aspect of their lives?
- Do these groupings create tensions or observable differences between the work style, views, or behaviors of the different group members?

If you are noticing these patterns and they seem to be causing team problems, this is important to note, as we will look at ways in the later sections to reduce or resolve these splits.

Is your team in the conflict danger zone?

Healthy conflict is an important feature of high performance. Perhaps better categorized as "healthy debate," this is when there is healthy disagreement over work elements with the intention of improvement. This might be around how to do a task, how to best serve a client, or how to organize a process, usually with the shared intention between the debating parties of making the output better. It's what's lacking when a team is too homogeneous (as above).

The key challenge for you as a leader is identifying early when a small and productive challenge, debate, or disagreement threatens to spill over into unhealthy conflict. Watch out for the following signs.

- Debates that return, meeting after meeting or email after email. Ask: Why are they rumbling on?
- A lack of action from team members because they have not resolved what they will do. Ask: What is slowing this decision-making down?
- Discussions where one or more team members appear to be dominating, trying to force through their way of doing things. Ask: Is everyone with something useful to say being listened to?
- Situations that some people are trying to portray as "healthy discussion" or "positive debate" or similar, intentionally putting a positive spin on it. Ask: Does everyone perceive this discussion or debate as good?

If you find evidence of these behaviors, commit to taking action before the situation escalates. What starts as a "healthy debate" in one person's eyes can escalate into toxic team relationships, poor psychological safety, and a team that cannot perform together. Tensions can often occur between those who are from country cultures that are quite comfortable with expressing disagreement outwardly but don't see it as conflict, such as France, Spain, Italy, Mexico, or Russia, and those from country cultures where it is frowned upon to express negative emotions in public, such as China, Japan, Korea, or Singapore. To these latter country cultures, disagreement will more quickly feel conflictual and unhealthy.

Bad conflict comes in many varieties—outward arguments, public disagreements, loud complaints, or the subtler ostracizing of someone from a group, unspoken tensions between people, harbored annoyance, or resentment. It can be hard for leaders to discern the subtler forms of conflict, so it's important to be sharply alert to anything you do notice that feels off or spiky, and to ask team members what is going on. Try to gather as much information as you can. Who's involved? What's happened so far? Where did the problem spring from? How bad has it gotten?

Remember to seek a range of viewpoints—ideally those inside and outside the conflict, as there are likely to be a number of perspectives on what's going on and what has caused the conflict. You may find it helpful to draw a diagram of the different players, the issues at stake, and how it's developing, so that when you start to put a solution together you can make sure it reflects the full extent of the problem.

FIT THE CONTEXT: IS YOUR ORGANIZATION ENCOURAGING CONFLICT?

In some industries or functions, a strong appetite for competition can create a workspace that is more conflictual. In others, a serious lack of resources can create lots of infighting. Performance targets, challenges with resource allocation, and competitive organizational cultures can all create environments where competition is high and people or teams are pitted against one another. These environments may, in turn, attract and retain people who are more comfortable in working in a highly competitive environment and be a turnoff for those who do not like such a setting.

- Heavy performance targets can be found in sales and production settings, where output can easily be measured.
- Competition over resources is particularly common in sectors that are cash-strapped, such as the public sector (schools, universities, government departments) and those companies that are low-cost leaders in their market (such as Ryanair in the airline industry).
- Cultures that set themselves up to be internally competitive include professional service firms, where only a few will make it to the very top; Amazon also encourages high

performance in a culture that has been described as "aggressive" and "bruising," pitting employees against one another.

In these settings, leaders will need to invest extra effort in making sure that the competition does not spill into conflict. There may be a higher appetite for debate and competition, so it will be important not to jump in at the first sign of debate. We will look at strategies in the next section, but a heightened awareness of where competition appears to be turning sour and increased efforts to build psychological safety, show empathy, and reward cooperation will all be beneficial.

When you speak to those directly involved in the conflict, meet them separately to build up a clear understanding of the situation from all perspectives without the risk of immediate escalation. It'll also be easier for you as a leader to demonstrate empathy this way, without it looking as though you are taking sides. You should only meet them together later in the process (which we'll talk about in the next section) once you have a clear picture of what's going on. However, if at this early stage anything is revealed that is truly concerning—accusations of harassment or bullying, for example—then you may need to get HR involved.

BEFORE MOVING ON:

- What problems are your team members facing with working together?
- Have you confirmed your suspicions with research?
- If it's a conflict issue:
    - Have you talked to all the relevant parties?
    - If it's quite complicated, have you mapped it out?

LAY OUT YOUR SOLUTION

In this section, I've deviated from the order that the problems are presented in during the "Open the Box" section because there's a pressing need to deal with unhealthy conflict first. And then it's important to work on the foundation of psychological safety and ensure that team practices are clear (which further reinforces psychological safety). Everything else this section covers can be implemented more easily after the problems of conflict are dealt with and the foundations of psychological safety are laid.

Mediate and fix unhealthy conflict

If you've identified any unhealthy conflict, early resolution is best. Leaders have a growing habit of using formal mechanisms to solve conflict, perhaps fearful of things blowing up and making them and the organization look bad or leading to costly legal action. However, unless it's really serious (and we've already identified what types of conflicts these might be in the earlier section), I would strongly advocate trying to resolve it yourself. It's often a lot easier and quicker than you think and can avoid months of messing around.

If this scares you, try not to let it. Relationship management is a key element of your leadership role, and the sooner you can be comfortable in helping people tackle the trickier aspects of their work relationships, the more effective you will become as a boss. But how? *Learning mediation skills and applying them is the best step a leader can take to becoming skilled in conflict management.*

Mediation is about creating a space for people to resolve their problems, but with you there to create a safe space in which to do so and to structure the conversation so that it is fair, so that everyone feels heard, and so that there is an outside party who has heard what has been promised and can help the participants to commit to their actions if needed.

At the heart of mediation are mediation meetings. In these, you, as their mediating manager, set rules to help them understand how each feels and to try to reach a resolution they are both happy with. You have already conducted individual meetings in the Observe phase of the problem-solving process. Now you are going to bring them together. You should find a private space and schedule the meeting in a place and at a time that is equally convenient for them both. You can choose the degree to which you follow this process or whether you are more informal. The more serious the conflict appears to be or has the propensity to be, the more purposeful you should be about following a mediation process, and so scale it up or down based on what you have observed.

MEDIATION MEETING: BEST PRACTICES

At the top of the meeting, you should set clear rules on the following:

- That this is **not about trying to convince you** of who's in the right so you can judge—you are there to mediate, not decide.
- That they should **devote their energy to resolution** between themselves, reaching an agreement by the end.
- That they should **own the outcome**—and be prepared to take any actions they agree on in good faith.
- That **timings are important**, and you should all be keeping an eye on not overrunning and not dominating the talk.
- That there should be **no interrupting**.
- That **you will ask questions to draw them out** if needed—for example, why they see this as a problem or why they are not happy.

You should also reiterate these rules and principles at the beginning of each subsequent meeting if more meetings are needed.

In terms of reaching an agreement, if they are both reticent to make big promises until they see how things go, or do not trust the other party to follow through, mediation researchers[5] advocate using one or more of these elements in the agreement:

- **Limited duration:** Revisit the agreement after a set period of time to see how things are going and adjust if necessary. If they opt for this, make sure they do revisit the agreement at the set point.
- **Contingent:** Based on a future event happening or not happening. If these contingencies occur, a different agreement takes effect (you may wish to get them to specify the agreement or the process by which the agreement will be reached at this stage).
- **Non-precedent setting:** If there's a similar conflict in the future, they are not committing to following this same agreement again.

I find that, when I work with teams where there is some conflict, what they need most of all is a sense that they are going to be treated as equals and that I have not prejudged the situation. So if you take just one element or principle from the above, being scrupulously fair on who gets to speak and when, and making sure that both parties feel equally well treated in the agreement at the end, is the essence you should seek to preserve. Jessica Tamsedge, CEO of Dentsu UK, reinforced this, saying that she finds conflict resolution is most successful when both parties really feel as though they've had a proper, fair chance to be heard.

Improve the team's psychological safety

Psychological safety is, you'll remember, the foundation stone of great team performance, and so if you've found it lacking on your team, you should look to build it up.

You can improve psychological safety by creating an environment where it's okay to speak out about issues that threaten the usual way of doing things or that risk showing knowledge gaps or highlighting mistakes. Do this by encouraging people to share these sorts of challenges or observations and then thanking them for their contribution and respecting what they have said. Where they've shared a mistake or spotted a problem, make sure it's not seen to be an opportunity to cast blame but rather an opportunity for learning. For example, any problems with delivering the quality or quantity of work promised, or delivering to the time frame promised, should be addressed early on, and actions should be put in place to solve the problems, rather than turning it into a big issue.

Step by step, each time you and your team members choose to act this way in the face of a problem or challenge, you create a norm where people feel they can make mistakes. These measures will allow learning and growth, as well as helping people to seize relevant opportunities and take appropriate risks.

Anthony Julius, deputy chairman and former managing partner at Mishcon de Reya, as well as first chairman and former vice president of the Diana, Princess of Wales Memorial Fund, shared a story with me that illustrates brilliantly how seriously a leader should take the need not to blame. Someone reminded him recently that back when he was head of Mishcon's litigation department in the 1990s, they had come to him telling him that they had taken home a crucial client file and accidentally left it on the train. Anthony did not recall this at all, but at the time, he had apparently said, "Right, that's fine. Let's fix the problem." They managed to retrieve it from lost property and never spoke of it again, to the extent that Anthony had actually forgotten it. He raised it in my interview with him to illustrate the point that the person in question is now very senior and an exceptional lawyer and leader. If there had not been the safety to own up to the mistake and the support with learning from it, his career could have been ruined as a result of this very human error.

It's also about removing the idea that to disagree is to be difficult or unkind. Actually, as long as a different opinion is shared respectfully,

Liane Davey's work on team performance shows that people are usually willing to hear it.[6] It can also be the source of significant innovation, as it can challenge a team to think about something in a braver or different way. If you think that you should pitch to a new client in one way and a team member thinks about another, and you're brave enough to have a conversation about it, you can arrive in a better place than just blindly going with the first suggested option. Decision-making expert Ed Smith reminds us that good psychological safety is *not* about being a big, happy family—teams that are great have an "unsentimental focus on performance, which would be terrifying in a family!"[7]

Ensuring that your team's practices are clear

Make sure the team's goals and approaches to working together are crystal clear, and encourage the team to take responsibility for this, too. They need to be communicating with one another regularly and clearly about who will do what and how they will work together. A great way of doing this is through a team charter. This is a document that usually outlines key responsibilities, preferred modes, times, and styles of communication for different elements of the teamwork, how team decisions will be made, and how they will deal with problems and conflict. Sometimes team charters also cover how the team will interact with the rest of the business, how they will deal with their customer interactions, and how they will work toward their values, vision, and/or objectives.

They can vary massively in length and style. I recently worked with the EMEA (Europe, Middle East, and Africa) office of a small but rapidly growing private equity firm who wanted to create a team charter. Theirs was very straightforward—it contained only five bullet points, and they said they would try this one and experiment with it, adding to it if they really needed to. The brevity reflected their culture of wanting to be straightforward and brief in their interactions with one another and their clients.

On the other end of the scale can be a team charter that runs to many, many pages with various appendices laying out document templates, how to liaise with seniors, juniors, customers, and others, and incorporating instructions for how to choose whom to delegate team tasks to. I recently worked with a very large team in a financial technology company whose first draft ran to seven very packed pages, and it only got longer thereon in.

I would recommend trying to go for brevity initially and experimenting, as it's less burdensome and easier to follow. You can always add more if you need to.

I would also encourage a bullet point about assuming positive intent of others and making the assumption that they are assuming the same about you! In other words, I should be able to trust you *and* believe that you are placing your trust in me. This means that if anything goes wrong, people's initial stance should be that no malice was intended and they should be able to find a way through it by assuming everyone's positive intent.

And key to having policies for how the team will work together and who will do what is keeping them front and center. Return to them regularly to recap on what you've promised, and hold one another accountable for working in the way that's been agreed. If it's not working, adjust the rules; don't just ignore the approach you've signed up to.

FIT THE CONTEXT: THE ADDED DIFFICULTIES OF PSYCHOLOGICAL SAFETY FOR VIRTUAL-ONLY TEAMS

Lived experience and research both show that virtual-only teams have a number of additional challenges to building psychological safety. Reaching out for help is more complicated, and tasks take more explaining when someone is not in the same room. People are more inclined to form bubbles, communicating repeatedly in twos and threes rather than in the wider group, creating feelings of exclusion and reduced psychological safety in interactions with others. Building trust, reading emotions, and having general conversations are all harder in virtual working environments.

I worked with the exec team from a consultancy firm specializing in helping governments with big projects. They were a team of seven, located across the globe, and as they only met up twice yearly, they saw themselves as a virtual team. When I was asked in to help, they were struggling with performance and had received feedback from their juniors in a recent 360-degree exercise that they were not joined up enough and were too quiet in their wants and needs. They were doing what we often do when people are harder to reach—not reaching them. And as such, communication was too low relative to what was needed in this type of team-based knowledge work. And because they were busy and working across time zones, they felt that their juniors—and one another—would rather have the time back than engage in small talk.

To work on the problem, we decided they should create a document that mandated small talk with juniors and with one another, and that created the expectation that they should ask more clearly for what they wanted from others. They also completed an exercise in which they shared how they each liked to work and made a promise to one another that they would try to honor these preferences going forward. These actions have already, just six weeks later (this is a very fresh example!) transformed how they engage with one another—a lot more conversation and honesty—and they have scheduled check-ins to keep themselves on track.

Improve the sense of meaning and impact

If your team members are struggling to see the value of their work, then it's important for you, as a leader, to help the team to draw a clear link between what they are doing and the purpose of the team to the wider vision, mission, and strategic objectives of the organization. In other chapters, I talk about the importance of this for individuals, but here it's about the role of the team as a whole and how, by working together, the team members can help to deliver on these elements that are critical for the functioning, survival, and success of the organization.

Rather than just saying, "Do this more," I think it's good to have a target. I suggest to the leaders I work with that they should be reaching most team members with a message focused on the connection between the work that the whole team is doing and the wider organizational mission or strategy, at least twice a week. For example, you might make a link in the whole team briefing, or you might mention it to most team members in their weekly catch-ups.

Some templates or approaches you could think about:

- "You know, the work we're doing really matters, because it helps the organization to deliver on its mission of... In particular, the activities we've been undertaking in... have a really big impact because..."
- "Thanks so much for the work you're doing on this team. It's really helping the function as a whole to deliver against the company's plan to..."
- "Without your work this week, we couldn't have... which would mean the company couldn't..."
- "You know, without our work, our customers would not be able to..."

Create a diverse and inclusive team

Great teams should be comprised of individuals with meaningful differences, which can widen innovation and reduce blind spots. Creating diverse teams and then welcoming the people on them to act in a way that is unique and diverse makes it more likely that we have people who will balance out one another, that we can spot a wider range of risks and opportunities, and that we can solve problems and make decisions with more options in the mix. Bear this in mind when you are given a say over team composition or when you are compiling ad hoc project teams. Try to get a good balance of any factors that might matter to the project, and bring in as many actively different voices as is feasible.

However, diversity alone is not enough—you then need inclusion. For example, it's one thing to have older members on a project team; it's another to listen to them rather than dismissing them as being "out of touch." In fact, just to think about this example, older people tend to have higher "crystallized intelligence," making them great teachers and useful for projects that need high levels of prior knowledge.[8] Inclusive teams willingly and usefully work with their differences (not in spite of them). If you want to move from diversity to genuine inclusion, concentrate on these five measures:

1. **Encourage open dialogue and feedback between team members.** This could be about feelings, about practical work matters, or about anything else that feels important. This should create empathy, which can build understanding and trust.
2. **Establish clear expectations that this is an inclusive team.** Emphasize how important it is to respect differences and to foster an environment that is supportive of a range of views and approaches.
3. **Celebrate diversity.** Highlight how the differences between people are what allows great ideas to emerge, risks to be spotted, and high-quality decisions to be made. For example, telling the team that the reason the latest project was so successful was because there were contributions from everyone and that these contributions were meaningfully different. Give examples if you can.

4. **Encourage collaboration across potential divides.** If you have previously spotted that there may be some fault lines in the team, look to reduce them by bringing together people from across the divides.
5. **Lead by example.** Show unfailing respect for all team members and expect the same from others, holding them accountable.

Samantha Hawkins, a coach who works with "rebel leaders" who are interested in driving meaningful organizational change, talked about how important it is for leaders to drive for inclusion. It is their strong modeling of showing respect for all team members, and driving the organization to create strong expectations that nothing else will be tolerated, that pushes through meaningful change. But it can be very hard if you are working in an organization or sector that is less good at inclusivity. If there is a culture of exclusion or sidelining people who are different, but you do want your team to flourish due to its differences, you will need to be good at creating a subculture in your own part of the company and protecting it fiercely.

Step away sometimes

If it's a team that you lead, as opposed to a team that you are a part of, and things start to improve, it can be tempting to helicopter over them, trying to make sure that they get along and that things continue to work. However, as you are not in the team but are instead managing them, they need to ensure their continued functioning, as you cannot and will not be there all the time. As such, it's important to encourage team members to embrace the norms, the charter, the objectives, and to feel a sense of ownership over them. Encouraging them to bond away from you can be important, too.

In her interview, former head teacher Dame Mary Marsh said that she felt leaders were most successful when they recognized that they were not just regular members of the team and stepped away early from social events to give team members the chance to interact without the leader there, so they could relax and talk freely among themselves. Mary said that stepping away also reflected a sense of trust in her team and a wish to grow them in a way that meant that she, as the leader, could move on and away because they were able to do it without her. Think about giving your team members space to spend time together without you there. This will show your trust in them and allow them to get to know one another and forge good relationships. It will ultimately make them more likely to act in one another's and the team's best interests.

If you would like to know how things are going in more detail than you appear to be able to glean organically, ask team members for honest feedback on how they think they're doing as a team. You can also drop in occasionally unannounced to online or face-to-face meetings to see that things are running as they should be. Be clear with the team that this isn't about trust—it's about getting an unvarnished view of the way things are running.

BEFORE MOVING ON:

- What do you plan to do to solve your team problems?
- What's your time frame?
- How will you know you've been successful?

VENTURE FORTH!

This is where you'll start to tackle your team problems. I'd start with any conflict you've spotted and then move on to the other elements. Some will be quite quick—establishing a team charter can be done over the course of an afternoon and then refined in the days following. Others will be much longer term—establishing psychological safety on a team that has lacked it can be a three-month project or more. But that's not to say you won't see results before that—as soon as the trust begins to grow, you should notice a change in practice and atmosphere.

Here are a couple of common problems that leaders run into when enacting team process changes. If you do, here's what to do about them.

If the team won't let a conflict go…

If a team has been split by conflict and you've tried all you can to fix it, but you've still got people who won't drop it, you may need to pivot a little. Rather than trying to ignore or discipline the refusal to drop the conflict, start by trying to understand, from a point of empathy and curiosity, why that might be.

You may find that there is an area they genuinely feel has not been resolved, which needs further work, and which you (or they) were not aware of until now. Or you may find that they crumble quickly, expressing regret or guilt for not allowing everyone to move on.

Empathy and curiosity remain key, just as they were in the earlier stages. You do not want this person to feel judged, turn defensive, and leave the conversation with even more to gossip about and even less desire to change.

You want a genuine understanding of what, if anything, is needed to bring it to a resolution. And then you can look at ways to act on what they have said, whether it's a mediated conversation, or more work on increasing psychological safety, or a shift in team, or something else.

If they still won't let it go…

At some stage, you may decide it is beyond you to be able to resolve it. Perhaps they see you as a part of the problem or everyone is too entrenched in their views. Perhaps one person is threatening to leave, or to speak to HR, or take some other potentially problematic route. This is the time to bring in HR yourself, to see if they feel you need a qualified mediator (who will have more tricks up their sleeve) or to explore other avenues (such as relocating a particularly difficult team member or invoke disciplinary action).

This is not a failure. This is a realistic route to take when you've tried what you are able to, and if it feels as though the problem is not going to go away, then this is absolutely the right route to take. Make sure that you share with HR all the key details that you have, including any notes you've taken, dates, key parties, and so on. They may ask you to stay involved or to step away—at this point, I would default to their expertise and let them handle it as they think best.

ELEVATE YOUR LEARNING

If you've seen the value of increased psychological safety… consider slowing down meetings

If you've found it really helpful to work on psychological safety and you're looking for yet more ways to improve it, focusing on meeting speed can give huge benefits once the other major elements are in place.

To create more psychologically safe meetings, you should try to remove a sense of urgency or rush—provide space to speak up, get to know one another more deeply, and stop the feeling that there are secrets lurking, when actually it's just that there hasn't been enough time to discuss everything. Everyone is always asking for fewer and shorter meetings, so this can be a hard one to execute. But if you can promise people that this slower, more deliberate pace will come alongside discussing fewer issues—moving things that are less important to email or team chat apps—you may well win them around. It should lead to better-quality meetings that people feel are more worthwhile than the one-hundred-miles-per-hour ones where nothing is ever really discussed properly, and a better sense of team purpose, too.

To make the discussion deeper, you can think about asking questions like "Why is this important?" "What is at stake here?" "How do we feel about this?" "Is there anything we're forgetting?" and "How can we make this 10 percent better?" Each of these should move the dial on the quality of the conversation and, on balance, justify the extra time spent.

If you want your team to get even better . . . celebrate success in a results-focused way

Teams that have improved deserve to celebrate their success—but make the celebration mean more than just a chance to eat food together! Pick an event that allows you to further enhance the team's functioning.

TO DEVELOP A SENSE OF IMPACT

Organize a team outing to meet customers, clients, or the people who ultimately benefit from the work that you do.

TO DEVELOP A CLEAR SENSE OF WHAT EACH PERSON DOES

Create a "pub" quiz (but in the office, or a café, or a private function room) with at least two rounds on the work itself. If you want to improve team bonding and knowledge, include a round where people submit unusual facts about themselves and you have to work out who it's about.

TO DEVELOP PSYCHOLOGICAL SAFETY

Play a game of "just like me" in person or over Zoom (if your team has not been able to meet in person for a while). Each person says, or types, a fact about themselves, and then people hold up a card (or type in the chat) "Just like me." After each round, pause for a moment to see if anyone wants to say something (don't announce this, just pause and see what happens). If budget allows, send everyone a snack box in advance that they can open on the call, so there is a sense of sharing a social space, too.

TO DEVELOP A SENSE OF INCLUSION

Make sure you choose an activity that no one will be excluded from as a result of their religion, gender, age, or ability. Throw an informal lunch and ask people to bring a dish from some aspect of their heritage, childhood, or culture and to share it with a story about why it's important to them. If you don't expect people to cook, give them the option of bringing something ready-made or a story to tell instead.

To return to the team in the opening chapter: instead of continuing to ignore the problems that they had run into with bonding across the team, they started having virtual coffee meet-ups where all team members regularly attended and shared a little of their interests and the like. They started to talk about how much harder it can be to establish trust, and to ask for help, and so on, which helped them to then have a dialogue about how to overcome these issues. And they also created much clearer processes for interaction and standardized which technologies they would use across the team to reduce the formation of subgroups and bubbles across the multiple platforms they had access to.

Logan was lucky; his team's weak performance had not degenerated into full conflict, and through the online coffee breaks and standardizing team processes, they were able to move past the team division and the fault line that had opened up between the UK-based and India-based workers. However, Logan kept an eye on the situation, ready to handle any disagreements should he need to, while the team grappled with their new collective approach. Logan found that his natural empathy was very helpful in continuing to listen to how the team members felt, and whenever they appeared to be struggling with the divide again, he would look to understand why and try to put solutions in place. He also encouraged team members to try to talk to one another about any challenges they were feeling and for them to be empathic with one another, further building a sense of psychological safety. The session that I ran for them on how to have conversations about process and performance was something they regularly referred to, seeing it as a shared experience they could use to safely discuss subjects such as work coordination and trust, which might otherwise feel undiscussable.

REMEMBER:

- Team performance generally goes wrong when the team isn't taking care of itself—to improve team functioning, check that the team has good psychological safety, a clear sense of who's doing what, trust in one another to do what's needed, and a sense of why the work they're doing is important. A team charter can help.
- Healthy debate can be great for creativity, decision-making, and problem-solving, but needs watching to make sure it doesn't become unhealthy conflict. Unhealthy conflict needs handling quickly, with skills aligned to those used by mediators.
- Inclusion can also help team functioning, which you will need to generate through insisting on particular team behaviors and modeling them, too.
- Encouraging the team members to maintain the processes themselves, and to work on their relationships, can help with improving the team and reduce reliance on you.

PROBLEM 7

Hybrid and Remote Working

"I thought remote working would go away after COVID, but it looks as though it's here to stay. I think my team are working far less well than they were before they allowed people to work remotely, but the company is insistent we need to keep allowing remote work to retain staff."

"Our hybrid working policy is a total mess. Everyone seems to think everyone else has it better than they do. Those who are in the office think they have the bad end of the deal—those at home say they feel left out of projects a lot of the time."

"Our work environment is rubbish for hybrid! Our meeting rooms, our tech, our offices—none of it seems to work for the hybrid approach!"

TIM IS A MIDDLE LEADER IN THE HR FUNCTION OF A MEDIUM-SIZE LAW firm. He wrote into Dear Katie in 2023, frustrated that his team wasn't getting on very well with hybrid working.

As there was no company-wide policy, employees were largely free to choose which days they came into the office and if they came in at all. Some were choosing to work primarily from the office—mainly those in house shares who wanted to escape noisy roommates. Others chose to work mainly from home—typically those with long commutes and parenting responsibilities.

Tim disliked the rivalry that had built between the office-based and the home-based workers. The office workers envied the freedom of those at home to choose when and how to work, with Tim less involved in the detail. The remote workers felt they were missing out on the juicier projects. Tim admitted giving important work to office workers because he could oversee their work more easily and had an easier, more trusting relationship with them, as he felt he knew them better.

Tim felt as though he was at an impasse. He couldn't instigate a hybrid policy single-handedly in a firm that had rejected having one. He couldn't force anyone to come in or stay at home more. And he couldn't publicly admit his tendencies to favor those in the office. He voiced his frustration in his letter that, post-COVID, team members had high expectations around being allowed to work remotely and not being penalized as a result.

The very different expectations and requirements that team members can bring to their desires to work remotely or in hybrid form make this area stressful for leaders like Tim, who are trying to marshal the problem into something manageable. And wow, are there differing desires! While 98 percent of the US workforce would like at least some of their work to be remote,[1] the variety after this is astounding, with some preferring to be fully remote, others preferring to be at home just once or twice a month. To clarify, remote work refers to people performing part or all of their role out of the office; hybrid work refers to the combination of remote and in-person work, often where team members are trying to interact between the office and a remote working space as a result.

Even though there are headaches for leaders that come with hybrid and remote working, which we'll dig into further in this chapter, in sectors where remote work is common, they cannot sidestep the discussion and just insist on staff coming in. Or if they do, they may need to be prepared to lose the war on talent to competitors who are more progressive in this regard.

STATE THE PROBLEM

Try to state the problems with working in hybrid or remote form using the following question prompts to help you:

- **How would you describe your hybrid working arrangement?** Who is on a fully remote contract? Are you able to ask them to come into the office if you need them to? Who is on a fully in-office contract? Who is on a hybrid contract, and can you stipulate when they come in?
- **Which of the following problems are some or all of your team facing** with regard to hybrid/remote working?
    - They're unhappy with their working arrangements.
    - They feel as though they're getting a bad deal compared to others.
    - They are seemingly happy, but you notice a negative impact on their work or their well-being.
- **Which of the following problems are you, as a leader, facing** with regard to leading a hybrid/remote team?
    - You feel that hybrid/remote work is weakening the team/organizational culture.
    - It's harder to onboard and upskill team members in an online environment.
    - You are struggling to establish a hybrid or remote working policy that feels fair and appropriate.

Use these and your experiences to summarize the problems you face with hybrid and/or remote work. As you read, you may refine your understanding of the problem, but identifying the issue is a good starting point.

OPEN THE BOX

Hybrid/remote can be messy and create an array of problems for leaders and their teams, including the ultimate contradiction: employees strongly desire hybrid work, despite there being considerable evidence that, done wrong, it can have negative impacts on mental health[2] and career progression.[3]

Remote and hybrid work can make taken-for-granted things harder

There are a range of elements that we previously took for granted at work that hybrid and remote work means we can no longer take for granted. When we work at a distance from one another, there a number of ways the work can become harder as a result. Which of these do you think are affecting your team?

IS IT HARDER TO TALK?

Not only is it harder to talk—there's less ability for us to perceive when someone wants to talk or to check they've really heard and understood you. We accidentally interrupt them, or talk over them, or the line drops and we're not sure we've heard properly. And if we widen this to other forms of communication, we just tend to "say" less when we have to write it down. If you're relying on chat functions or emails, you're likely to tell someone less about a situation than if you were speaking to them face-to-face.

ARE YOU UNDER-SHARING?

When it's harder to talk, we share only what we see as "the most important things," which can lead to under-sharing. In a "Better Collaboration" workshop I ran for a financial sales team, participants lamented that online working had made their team interactions too brief. They felt that they lacked the context that had previously allowed them to make more sales and serve their clients better, because they had broader knowledge of the clients and their needs, accumulated from longer, less focused conversations.

IS THE TEAM MORE EASILY DISTRACTED?

It's also much easier to be distracted without others noticing. Online working can have a tedious texture, not standing up to switch meeting locations or being able to turn to talk to a colleague. This monotony can bore some of us quickly. Because the work feels flat, we can welcome distractions! The washing machine beeping or the *bing* to signal a new message can feel very tempting in preference to listening to Ryan drone on. The sense that we are less monitored may make checking one's phone or trying to answer an email while having a creative discussion all the more likely.

ARE THEY FINDING IT HARDER TO CREATE AND INNOVATE?

Tech has become better at supporting "parallel creation," meaning two or more people being creative asynchronously and then feeding the results into a clearly structured process.[4] However, where creativity requires natural, free-flowing conversations from which ideas emerge, this remains very hard in a hybrid or fully remote setting. This could be project work, brainstorming, or intentional innovation or creative exercises. The factors above—interruptions, boredom, and difficulty conversing—all play into it. You may have seen this with your team members: they're very good at these tasks in the office, but get them to perform them at home and the process somehow destroys the quality of the output. It's particularly true for initiating projects, where a lack of space for unstructured creativity and discussion can reduce the quality of ideas and output.[5]

Ad hoc opportunities for innovation and creation also disappear, because those spontaneous moments to bond with someone in the cafeteria—because you both ordered the same weirdly specific coffee and end up talking about work—disappear. You can't switch from riffing on coffee to finding out more about the other person and their work, which might, immediately or in the longer term, lead to opportunities for collaboration and innovation as you put your unique views of the world together to create something novel. Even overhearing a conversation that gets you to think differently about a client or a piece of work is lost. You lose the information you didn't know you needed.

DOES THERE SEEM TO BE LESS TRUST?

We have less trust for people we meet online than those we meet face-to-face, with it being harder to build knowledge of the other person and to try to read their intentions.[6] The secondary impacts for work quality can be large.[7] Team success hinges on psychological safety, and you can't have it without trust. One interviewee, who leads a team that spends a reasonable amount of time working remotely, told me she had seen how easy it could be for those people to build a personal narrative of being disliked or being an outsider. It is as though, when they can't pick up on social cues or get to know colleagues properly, they fill the gap with a negative take on the situation. Evidence backs this up: we take the absence of interaction as a mark that we are being excluded or are disliked, and it reduces our sense of belonging and trust.[8]

IS IT HARDER TO OBSERVE WHAT OTHERS ARE DOING?

Learning from colleagues is much harder when we can't observe them in the wild or interact with them casually. Of particular significance for leaders is that mentoring, coaching, and developing staff who are working remotely is much harder, with some tasks much harder to teach online without both staring at the same bank of computer screens or laying out documents on a desk to show how different processes relate to one another. The difficulties with remote observation also make it hard for leaders to monitor how much work is being done and how well. Online work often lacks visible inputs and measurable outputs. In the opening case of this chapter, Tim was suffering from this problem, struggling to trust his remote team members because it was harder to keep an eye on the quality and quantity of their work.

IS IT HARDER TO BUILD CAREERS?

Social capital is harder to boost on days when you are at home, with fewer ad hoc conversations, fewer opportunities to network or share information, and fewer relationship-building opportunities. It takes longer to establish bonds and for people to build a picture of your strengths. This can reduce chances to progress. This is not a universal picture—women, for example, report that they feel their opportunities of progression are greater when they are at home—possibly because they are doing less "office housework" when they are at home (making the tea, typing up the notes, arranging the conference room—they do 29 percent more of this work when they are in the office than men do).[9] However, junior workers report that they worry they will find it harder to be seen—and promoted—when they are at home.[10]

ARE YOU FINDING THAT THE CULTURE AND VALUES ARE WEAKER?

You are not working in an office space dripping with the artifacts of a culture or surrounded by people having conversations and interacting in a way that is culturally aligned. Online, this sort of informal cultural development is restricted, and for new employees, this is particularly tough. Going in one or two days a week—and not on the same days as organizational role models—may not be enough to pick up on all the social and cultural cues needed to understand and act in line with the culture.

You're missing out on the benefits of home working

While there are lots of challenges associated with allowing home working, as above, there are benefits, too. If you are a leader who's dismissed working from home out of hand, your team may be at a disadvantage compared to other teams or organizations that are using working from home to their benefit.

ARE YOU MISSING OUT ON THE BENEFITS OF AUTONOMY AND FLEXIBILITY?

Most significantly, many people like home working, feeling it gives them more autonomy and flexibility than fitting into the monitored schedules of days in the office. This comparative sense of freedom can have a positive impact on their work quality, job satisfaction, and motivation, and make it easier for you to retain talent. If you have ruled against people working remotely for some or all of the time, and you are seeing people who are dissatisfied or leaving as a result, you may need to reconsider.

ARE YOU REDUCING THE CHANCES OF DEEP WORK?

Another benefit is that, without the constant interruptions that come from being in a busy office, deep work is easier. Staff who are able to undertake deep work benefit from the higher task satisfaction deep work brings,[11] and you as their leader benefit from the higher productivity and work quality. If you're not allowing home working, you're reducing the chances of the high-quality output that can come from deep work and the chances of your employees feeling a deep sense of satisfaction with their work.

ARE YOU MISSING OPPORTUNITIES TO REDUCE THE TIME, MONEY, AND CARBON FOOTPRINT IMPACTS OF COMMUTING?

Another benefit that team members who are not allowed to work remotely miss out on are the time and money savings that home workers get when they do not have to commute. The time saving can give opportunities for better work-life balance, as well as providing the opportunity to complete more work in the time saved if they choose to. The money saved could also represent a big personal benefit. There's also the potential for a reduced carbon footprint, although the extent of this depends on how big the carbon saving is from not commuting versus the carbon spend of powering and heating the remote workspace. As workers place higher expectations on employers regarding environmental impact and the impact it has on their work-life balance, there are opportunities here to please employees with a good approach.

You don't have a good remote working policy

Not having a decent remote working policy means that your company has not discussed the benefits relative to the problems of remote working in their context and therefore isn't able to say with certainty what the best approach is. Should people be at home all the time, or just some of it, or not at all?

By not taking a strategic view on what the best approach is for them, a company is allowing employees to take matters into their own hands, working in ways that benefit them, rather than the organization.[12] Employees may push to work from home more, which may not mean that they are able to collaborate as well or as often as when they are all in the office. Your boss may realize this and push you to get them in more, but this is hard to do without a policy. As a middle leader, you may thus end up feeling wedged between the expectations of your employees and your bosses.

If there isn't a good hybrid working policy, this is something to pay careful attention to and which you should certainly be looking to address, either for your team or more generally, in the "Lay Out Your Solution" section.

FIT THE CONTEXT: BEING REQUIRED TO CROSS-SELL WHEN YOU'RE HYBRID

We've already thought about how in-person working helps with chance encounters, networking, and building trust and goodwill. These skills are critical in organizations that rely on selling additional products and services from across the business to existing clients. Perhaps you are a lawyer providing property conveyancing services to a corporate client, and you realize, as a result of this new building acquisition, they will need more staff, and as such, refer the client to the firm's employment law function.

For this business model to work, staff need to be able to identify other relevant services and be willing to recommend them to clients they already have strong relationships with and who trust them to treat them well.

If you don't know others in the business so well, you won't know what they are selling, nor will you trust them so strongly to do well by your client.

This is a big problem with remote and hybrid working for those in organizations that rely on cross-selling, such as law, accounting, consultancy, and computer service companies. Without these good relationships, there's the potential to lose out on a great deal of business.

One interviewee, Anthony Julius (former managing partner of the law firm Mishcon de Reya), spoke on this: "I have a valuable client. He means a great deal to me. He's somebody who I have worked with for a number of years. He has great instrumental value to me, but I also very much care about him and want to ensure that everything that the firm does for him is of the same standard that I try myself to meet when I'm working for him. If I'm five days a week at the firm and the firm is not of an impossible size, I'm going to know many of the lawyers in other departments. So when that client comes to me with a problem that, on my profile, I'm not able to address, I'm going to know who to recommend him to. Now with hybrid working post-COVID, that knowledge has been radically diluted. I see fewer people for less time."

It's worth reflecting on whether, as a result of more remote working, you and your team have been hampered in their ability to sell other services or to have their services sold by others in the business. This could have a big impact on your company and your career, and so it's important to take action.

BEFORE MOVING ON:

- What is undermining your organization's ability to perform well when working remotely?
- Have you identified problems with your communication, ability to trust, work monitoring, or other aspects of your hybrid or remote work situation?
- Have you ascertained if your hybrid policy is fit for the purpose? If not, how is it falling short?
- What initial thoughts do you have about how to solve your hybrid and remote working problems?

LAY OUT YOUR SOLUTION

For most organizations, abandoning work from home is not desirable. Employees want some home or remote working to be part of the job offer, and being able to work off-site brings benefits for focus and efficiency. So how to make it work?

Create a hybrid or remote working policy that is justifiable on the basis of the data

Leaders need policies that fit their teams' needs and that they can justify on the basis of robust data. If you have any control over the process, aim to follow (or encourage others to follow) these steps:

1. BE CLEAR ON WHAT YOUR POLICY SHOULD DELIVER

You should be clear on what you want to gain from remote and hybrid working. Is it to increase or protect productivity? To attract or retain talent? Enhance relationships and social fabric? Think about what your team or organization wants to achieve. (And remember to make sure this is in line with the organization's mission and values and any broader policies.)

2. CONDUCT RESEARCH THAT WILL ALLOW YOU TO DELIVER ON WHAT YOU WANT

Now research how your policy can help you achieve your aims. Start with your staff's wants and needs. What working patterns would they like? What are their biggest struggles with office working? With remote working? How can you find the right balance for the type of work they are doing? Consider researching best practices in your industry, country, or function. Ask others who do similar roles, and check in with HR to see if they are aware of the latest facts and figures. Other figures that may be useful to consider when designing the policy are as follows:

- **Productivity stats:** Does the revenue and/or profit per employee go up or down when remote working increases? Are any other factors affecting this?
- **Building usage:** Is the building well utilized? Do you have too much or too little space on any days of the week? Which types of workspaces are used the most? By whom?
- **Wants and needs:** What working patterns would staff like?

What are their biggest struggles with office working? With remote working?

You are aiming to build up a picture of what might maximize your organization's key metrics, such as productivity, employee satisfaction, and customer feedback. If you can build up a picture of what is going to optimize your metrics, you can arrive at a well-designed policy.

3. DECIDE HOW PRESCRIPTIVE YOU WANT THE POLICY TO BE

Some companies' policies have only a few simple guardrails, such as "Everyone should be in three days per week, unless they have a good reason not to. Core hours on the three days are 10:00–3:00. Please feel free to arrive any time before 10:00 and leave any time after 3:00 to reduce the cost or length of commute. Please try to coordinate your in-office days with others who are working on the same projects and arrange any meetings that require creative thinking to be in person between 10:00 and 3:00 on those days." Others have much more detailed hybrid and/or remote working policy documents that run to many pages to create a clear sense of fairness and to deal with any exceptions to rules and so on.

Vague policies run the risk of being exploited. Overly prescriptive policies risk inhibiting good work. For example, research shows that half of all workers prefer a clear separation between work and leisure, while the other half of the workforce prefers to blend work and leisure in smaller chunks throughout the day. Forcing workers to act like the other group leads to burnout and job hunting.[13] Instead, if you don't need to be prescriptive on this point, you can satisfy a higher number of staff. Jessica Tamsedge, CEO of Dentsu UK, uses the lovely expression "freedom within a framework" to talk about her approach to setting those guardrails, making sure they're there to guide the organization to be able to be creative without forcing anyone to have to do horrible unnecessary commutes, sitting in the office for eighty-five hours a week, or missing their kids' bedtimes on a daily basis.

4. FOCUS THE POLICY ON THREE KEY AREAS

You should channel your attention toward the three key areas that your working policy will want to consider:[14]

- **Communication:** How will people communicate with one another to ensure that fairness is being maintained, that sufficient knowledge and information are being passed around, and that problems are being flagged? If you have no choice but to perform creative tasks remotely, how will you organize your communication so that sufficient information and ideas are being fielded to help innovation and good decision-making?
- **Coordination:** How will you coordinate work efforts to make sure that colleagues are aware of what the others are doing and that they don't duplicate efforts or leave tasks out? This sort of clarity is important for all teams—but whereas it's technically easier to achieve when everyone is colocated, the details of who/what/how can go missing when communicating online. Specifying how you'll organize this leaves nothing to chance.
- **Culture:** How will you talk about the culture, bring the culture into being, or reflect your values in the work that you do? What specific actions will you undertake to keep the culture front of mind? How will you live it—and show that you're living it—at a distance? If your culture is one of empathy, listening hard on calls rather than allowing yourself to be distracted would be critical for cultural reinforcement. GitLab, a famously remote company, has a handbook that lays out details of how to do just about everything, as they do not expect people to gain this information through in-office osmosis.[15] What can you do in the online environment to make it clear what the expectations, rules, and behaviors are that are expected around here and that build into the culture?

5. RESPECT THE IMPACT ON TEAM MEMBERS

Any sort of change to working arrangements can be hard for some team members to adjust to, whether it's more days in the office or more from home. A change in working relationships, working patterns, costs of commuting, and ability to provide ad hoc care to family at home can all create misgivings. You should actively listen to and empathize with their concerns and frustrations. Providing a stepped approach from one style of working to another—for example, moving from four days at home to three and finally two over the course of a year—may make the transition easier. It's important not to make permanent concessions for one team member, because the policy needs to be about fairness. Once you start to make exceptions for one person and then another, you'll undermine the policy you've spent so long arriving at.

However, if over the long term, you find there are still problems, you can absolutely iterate. I'll look at this in the "Venture Forth!" section.

Provide good solutions for all modes of working

Here are some actions you should take to optimize the three main elements of working hybrid: remote work, in-office work, and colleagues working across the home/office divide.

OPTIMIZE WORKING FROM HOME

If you have team members who are working remotely, either permanently or a few days a week, look at how to optimize their performance when at home:

Get them thinking about in-person versus remote

If you are going to use a hybrid policy, you can increase the chances of success by encouraging workers to break their role into tasks and thinking about which of them are better suited to office work versus remote work.

Tasks most suited to home working have:

- Minimal physical requirements, so you don't need to take equipment home.
- Well-defined deliverables, so there's less need for complex communication.
- High need for individual focus, as most workers may find it easier to focus away from a busy office.

Coders, UX mappers, data analysts, customer service agents, account managers, solo animators, bookkeepers/accountants, and graphic designers are all organizational roles that are regularly recruited for as fully remote roles because of the high level of solo work and the benefit of being able to focus.

Have regular check-ins

Regular check-ins can prevent a lack of oversight at home. Clearly set expectations and check in weekly to assess and adjust performance. It's a good idea to be honest with workers about the need for this—don't try to surreptitiously see what they're up to, as it can look like spying. Explain that you need reassurance, as their projects are business critical. As your trust in a team member grows, you can step away from the detail, but weekly check-ins should be maintained to check they're getting on okay and don't need help.

Reduce threats to well-being

The biggest threats to well-being from working at home include feeling lonely, not being able to unplug, working more, staying focused or motivated, and getting out.

Checking in with staff about the negative impacts they feel concerning the remote elements of their work (and especially if they are remote the whole time, as the downsides could well be amplified) is very important. Focus on dealing with the following three situations, which are particularly problematic:

- **If you have remote workers who are struggling to switch off**, help them find strategies to close down. This may be blocking their email after a certain time at night or sending them a reminder to log off. Set a good example by not sending emails to those staff members in antisocial hours.
- **If they are struggling with motivation, feeling lonely, or not getting out**, encourage them to leave their desk at lunchtime and go for a walk. Building in a regular stop at a local coffee shop or the library or at the park will embed them more in their community, which can prevent loneliness.
- **If fully remote workers are struggling to connect with colleagues who are in the office**, encourage more social time online that is compulsory for everyone to attend, fostering conversations that aren't just about work. Some of the better methods I've seen are compulsory online coffee mornings; starting all team meetings with "getting to know you" questions that have a focus on finding shared interests or views; and walking chats, where team members go for a walk while having phone conversations and catch-ups, to encourage freer-flowing dialogue. Remember, if you have some remote workers and some who are in the office, it's not just about remote workers knowing remote workers. You need everyone to know everyone, so make sure your in-office workers are putting in the effort so that *everyone* feels a part of the same team.

FIT THE CONTEXT: USING REMOTE WORKING TO BOOST DIVERSITY

Another benefit of going hybrid—or remote—is that it can be a way to increase diversity and improve inclusion. Here are three upsides of remote working for increasing workplace diversity:

- **Remote working can reduce the sense of having to "fit in."** In a workplace where an individual is in the minority and is trying to learn the "culture" of the majority, it can make work feel incredibly stressful. What should they wear? How should they act? And so, as well as doing the day job, on days in the office, they are working hard to fit in, in a way that they should not have to, hiding trips to the prayer room or wondering why everyone else's sneakers are okay for a client meeting but they've been told theirs aren't. This is not to skim over the toxic workplaces that create these problems but rather to say that if you are unfortunate enough to be a leader in one, you may find it easier to recruit diverse team members if a decent proportion of their work can take place online.[16]
- **Remote working can work for people normally shut out of the workplace due to caring responsibilities.** If you have caring responsibilities or are fitting in this role around other commitments, it can be more feasible to undertake remote work, particularly if the hours are flexible and it's acceptable to spread the hours over a longer day around other personal commitments.
- **Remote working can open up a global talent pool.** If you adopt fully remote working, you can recruit globally, meaning you can open the recruitment pool and look outside the typical candidates for someone who's really well suited to the role.

OPTIMIZE IN-OFFICE WORK

The other half of a hybrid working policy is recognizing when in-person, in-office work is going to be beneficial.

Get team members to think about which tasks are better suited to office work

Increase chances of success by encouraging workers to break their role into tasks and identifying those that work best in an office. Tasks that best suit office work have:

- Elements of complex communication, which is hard to undertake online. You need to be working in the same space to share information, pick up on subtleties, or share complex resources.
- Collaborative creativity at their heart. This could be anything from brainstorming, to starting on a new project, to solving a tricky client problem. A large number of participants, free-ranging conversations, situations where emotions and social bonds are important, all make tasks a better fit for in-person time.

To optimize the value of in-office days, try to get people to come in the same days as one another. Create spaces for collaboration and creativity, which increase the chances of "bumping into" colleagues, building networks and innovation. Breakout seating spaces to encourage discussion, open-plan offices, long communal tables, and warm, domestic colors that mimic a café or private space can all enhance the possibilities of collaboration and creativity. LinkedIn is just one company who have radically redesigned their offices to include all these elements, actively experimenting with furniture to see what encourages collaboration and keeping those configurations, such as conversational spaces, that work best.[17]

Create spaces for focus work

Despite most people wanting to use their remote working days for focus work, there will be some workers who need quiet sanctuaries at work to get their heads down and avoid noise and disruption at home. Therefore, in any new office design, creating some space where people can get their heads down is important. Cubbyholes, telephone rooms, and quiet-focused workspaces all do this job and should be a design feature of even the most collaborative cultures.

Make office time feel meaningful and worthwhile

If you are asking people to come into the office more, reinforce the benefits for their social relationships, creativity, and career development. Schedule valuable creative sessions, organize team lunches, and hold one-to-one development meetings in these face-to-face settings. Show genuine appreciation for their having reorganized their lives so they can come in more regularly. Avoid attracting people with pizza, well-being zones, or dog hotels! While common, these initiatives can seem tone-deaf, designed by wealthy leaders who don't understand the costs of being present in the office and what team members lose out on (money, family time) by coming in.

OPTIMIZE COLLABORATION ACROSS THE DIVIDE

Even if people know the optimal balance of remote versus in-person working, it won't always follow that they can be in the right place at the right time. And when they find themselves needing to attend a meeting when at home or need to collaborate creatively with colleagues who are located in different offices, you'll need to think about how to support colleagues across the digital divide.

Get the best tech you can for the challenges you face

Each team and each project will have its own requirements in terms of collaboration and making sure that you have tools that can help can make a big difference to your success. Find what is going to work for you all, within the constraints of what's allowed by the organization. If you find that what they prescribe is not suited to your team, you can try to adapt (e.g., how can you make the tools work for you?), or you can lobby for the company to offer tools that will work for your context. You'll find this latter argument easier if you are the only team doing this type of work, and if you can suggest software, an app, or other tool that is *affordable* and *secure*. Complex isn't always better—some teams just find it easier to work off shared spreadsheets and documents in preference to using tricky scheduling and coordination software. Whatever you opt for, encourage your teams to use the chosen approach until it becomes a habit.

Prioritize making sure everyone feels equal

Whatever works for you and your team, whether it's a complex color-coded project plan or a basic spreadsheet, make sure you're all aligned and that everyone knows how to use the relevant features. It's critical that, when collaboration is remote, everyone is given the chance to feel on equal footing, not being held back by nervousness or cynicism about the tech.

Nowhere is this more important than in hybrid meetings. Do the best you can to create meeting spaces in the office that make everyone equal—whether they are in the office or at home. High-quality meeting rooms allow a layout that makes remote participants appear human-size and to all "sit around the table" so that everyone has an equal footing. It's also critical to make sure that the sound quality is good, because if it's hard to hear the people at home, it's harder for them to interject with useful comments, and you lose the full value of having them in the conversation.

BEFORE MOVING ON:

- If you're going to write a hybrid or remote working policy, what will it contain?

- How will you optimize:
    - Remote work?
    - In-office work?
    - Connecting those who are working across the digital divide?
- Is there anything else you now plan to do to improve hybrid and remote work?

VENTURE FORTH!

You should find that, as you structure your remote or hybrid working approach, you'll see positive changes in attitude and approach. However, here are some further issues that your actions may trigger and suggestions to tackle them.

If the policy's working as well as it could... don't be afraid to iterate

It's important not to react to complaints about new policies or remote or in-office working requirements by making exceptions for individuals or rewriting the policy in a panic because no one is happy. However, as you start to apply your policy, you may find it needs adapting. LinkedIn decided to embrace this uncertainty about what was going to work for them by using their office as a testing ground. They tried out conference rooms with long tables, sofas and chairs, and stadium-style seating to see which worked. They realized that having the conference space flexible so it could accommodate face-to-face and hybrid meetings of all scales required lightweight chairs so they could reconfigure the seating arrangements easily. They also invested in improving AV to make hybrid meetings easier, having seen that they were going to be a useful approach for them.[18]

Alongside trial and error, there will be other potential reasons why you find you need a new policy. As research on hybrid and remote working continues to grow, the advice changes on best practice. Next month, or next year, there may be a groundbreaking study on what remote work should look like in your industry, and you'll want to change your approach to take this into account. Additionally, new technologies will also develop, senior leaders will increasingly come from younger age groups who are more comfortable with online working, and companies will move into offices more able to cope with hybrid.

If you think people are using remote working as an opportunity to slack... build performance criteria into your policy

In any typical organization, there will be some staff who take days working from home as an opportunity to slack. If you find that remote working policy appears to be leading to a slackening of effort, first check your data: it may be your managerial assumption rather than "a fact." You may also want to iterate the policy to make remote working a benefit that is contingent on work quality and quantity.

This gives you the bandwidth to rescind on their ability to work from home until you are convinced that their performance is to the right standard. To avoid falling foul of employment and equality laws in some countries, you will need to evidence their performance drop-off.

It is also common for organizations to tell staff that they will not formally enter the hybrid working pattern of other staff until they have completed their probation period, and you may want to include this in your policy, too (or specify it during the job offer phase). It can mean then that you can keep a closer eye on performance until you are confident of both their skill and will, providing you with opportunities not only to monitor but also to align the staff member with what is culturally expected in terms of performance by your organization and the subculture of your team.

ELEVATE YOUR LEARNING

If you are prepared to offer fully remote contracts... take advantage of the global job market

One of the great advantages, once companies offer fully remote contracts, is that they can take advantage of the global job market, looking globally for recruits and therefore literally being able to recruit the best in the world![19] If this describes the direction that your company or even just your team is going in, then you could look to take advantage of this.

There are two primary approaches to be considered. The first is to offer the usual full-time contracts but remotely. Remember that time zone differences and whether they are working in the same hours as your domiciled team are important. It'll also be important to think about whether, and if so how, they should be seen as part of the team and how you'll make sure that they get to know the others in your team (who may still be on hybrid or face-to-face contracts) and not feel left out.

The second is to break jobs down into tasks and look to recruit freelance specialists to perform a more limited set of tasks, but to the highest standard and possibly at a cheaper rate. For some organizations, this seems a very long way from their current way of doing things. But for those who have already taken up this way of operating and are finding the benefits, they would not look back. The marketing, PR, and consultancy industries are all very savvy at this way of working and gain real advantages from doing so. They can tap into leading experts to contribute on particular projects or tasks and use them as and when required. Before discounting this, even if it's not common in your sector, spend a moment thinking about whether you could break jobs down into tasks and whether there may, from the perspective of recruiting the best in the business, be a good reason to do so.

If you saw the value of evidence-based policy... stay up to date

Data—reports and internal data—are very valuable for justifying policy, but the research and best practices on hybrid work shift regularly as it continues to be researched heavily and perceptions change.

If you want to continue to harness the benefits of a good hybrid working policy that staff support, keep up to date in terms of:

- their expectations,
- company performance with regard to remote working, and
- best practices according to external research.

Remember, share the rationale of any policy updates with team members, making use of the data. The best appeals for change of a hybrid working policy, in my experience, work on the head and heart simultaneously. For example, "Switching to set days is a good idea for us now, because 72 percent of employers in our sector are requiring set days in the office and we want to be competitive when we are trying to recruit. It's also been shown in multiple studies to enhance creativity, and this is central to our organization's mission."

This chapter opened with Tim, a middle leader in a hybrid team where disparate working patterns were splitting the team into warring factions, with Tim struggling to trust those working remotely with the more exciting tasks.

After Tim and I spoke, he sought permission from his company to establish a hybrid working policy for his team and was told this was fine as long as it was not too prescriptive. He put up a few guardrails—that he would like the team members to all come in on Wednesdays and, on most weeks, at least one other day. He asked them, where possible, to save Wednesdays for the work that they needed to do as a team (e.g., team meetings, as well as multi-person internal meetings that could happen with other teams) in the office.

He also worked hard to correct his view that those working remotely could not be trusted with the interesting work, sharing honestly his concerns with the team members and finding ways for them to check in with him, and vice versa, to establish his confidence that most of the work of the team could be done by both those who were mainly in the office and those who were mainly at home. His confidence in their abilities grew, and they all started using a wider range of collaboration tools available on Teams, such as collaborative document editing, real-time messaging, and having a shared WhatsApp group for sociable team chat, such as photos of team members running races, going on vacations with family and friends, or even just relaxing on their sofa with their pets!

Not all the problems went away—Tim still had one team member who really didn't want to come into the office at all, who had accepted the job during COVID when she didn't need to come in and hadn't thought that it would return to a face-to-face setting at all. Tim worked with her and HR to try to identify another role in the firm for her to switch to, and she is looking around for other roles.

REMEMBER:

- Online and face-to-face are not the same—each has different opportunities and challenges, and trying to make both perform in the same way is doomed to fail! Instead, remember that collaborative, creative work is easier performed face-to-face, and individual focus work is often best performed remotely or in a setting where a worker can "get their head down."

- Keeping people happy with hybrid work is about it seeming fair, the approach being well evidenced and transparent, and the organization iterating as requirements change and best-practice guidance moves on.
- Office work and offices should be designed to maximize chance encounters, networking, and creative and collaborative work. Spaces will still be needed to provide quiet focus for those who need to do this sort of work while nonetheless being in the office.

PROBLEM 8

Delivering on the Strategy

"We've got a strategy, and it's pretty good, but translating it from the page to the work that my team is doing is difficult. How can my facilities and catering team feel as though they're a part of the strategy for this auditing firm, which is all about high-quality client assurance? What does the staff cafeteria or the room bookings desk have to do with that?"

"I tell my team what they need to do to work in line with the company's mission and strategy, but they seem to just ignore me! I think they just don't get it. All the key strategic aims like 'streamline processes' and 'beat our rivals' feel very abstract. And now it's a problem I don't know how to fix."

"As a middle manager, I just feel like the exec team's lapdog. They say we have to deliver the strategy in a particular way, but it's not right for me and my team. I hate it. I feel as though I have no power at all."

I RECENTLY RAN A WORKSHOP FOR A FAST-GROWING GLOBAL FINANCIAL technology company, SinTech. Their newly formed senior leadership team—the leaders one level down from the executives—attended the workshop with the intention of bonding as a group and creating their own operating charter. However, the task was more of a challenge than any of us (the course designers, the senior leadership team, or the exec team) had perceived.

In particular, the members of senior leadership team felt that they were expected to deliver on the company's strategy but were rarely clear on precisely what it was. As a company in scale-up mode, the strategy regularly changed. It perhaps needed to, they conceded, to enable the company to meet changing market needs as it carved out a space for itself, but it didn't make it very easy to deliver on it. It also meant that it was hard to understand it in depth, as they would just gain this level of understanding and devolve it to their team so they could get them onside when the strategy would change again.

And even where the strategy *was* clear, the company-level OKRs (objectives and key results) did not always resonate with their work. Some functions, such as learning and development and the specialist financial modeling functions, failed to see their work in the OKRs at all.

However, as middle managers, they recognized they had an important role to play in ensuring that the company delivered against the strategy by aligning the team members' objectives to the strategy. Moreover, their team members below them would only be exposed to it if they integrated it.

The problem was exacerbated by an executive team member's reluctance to share data, with the perception being that they enjoyed controlling the flow of information. The lack of transparency made it difficult for senior leaders to track their progress against the OKRs. And there was a sense in the senior leadership team that the execs could not stomach negative feedback. If the senior leaders had problems with—or criticisms of—the strategy, they felt that voicing them to the execs did not sit well and could lead to some form of formal or informal sanction (being let go; being given the cold shoulder by the founder for a few weeks).

Whether you are, like SinTech's senior leadership team, part of a team of middle leaders struggling with the strategy that's flowing from above, or are an individual leader facing these sorts of problems, it can be hard! Not fully understanding the strategy or how it affects your function or team, not being able to work out how to implement it, and battling to recognize when it's not working... these all threaten to derail strategic delivery and alignment and reduce your efficacy as a leader.

STATE THE PROBLEM

You should work out what sort of strategy delivery problem you are looking to solve before you start to examine the details. When it's a problem with delivering against the strategy you think you're facing, answering the following questions before you start to "Open the Box" will help:

- **Which levels are struggling to deliver against the strategy?** Your level? Those above you? Those below?
- **What is the nature of the problem as you see it?** One of the problems below, or something else?
    - We don't understand the strategy.
    - We understand it but don't know how to implement it.
    - It feels like the wrong strategy.
    - There isn't a clear strategy—it's just chaos!
- **How far-reaching are the problems?** Is it just with a team or two, or the whole company? Do you think the customers are being impacted by the problems, too?

OPEN THE BOX

The strategy lacks clarity

If the strategy lacks clarity, you may be unable to work out how to deliver on it. This lack of clarity can happen for a host of reasons: too many voices make the document chaotic; a rushed process has left a messy strategy; the strategy is too short or vague to be helpful; or the objectives it includes aren't clear or measurable. If the strategy lacks clarity for any or all of these reasons, your work as a leader can be much harder as you try to discern what it needs you, and your team, to do.

FIT THE CONTEXT: SETTINGS WHERE YOU MAY BE MORE LIKELY TO ENCOUNTER UNCLEAR STRATEGIES

While any organization can have an under-executed strategy document, I see it commonly in:

- **Family businesses:** Because of the dysfunctions that can occur in family businesses, with the relationship politics being on a different scale compared to other businesses, the document can represent a wide range of views and not bring them together particularly successfully. As such, due to the lack of one dominant voice, the strategy does not provide clear direction.
- **Small businesses with founder-owners:** These businesses will often be new to the strategy-creation process, with the owner perhaps being more used to formulating a strategy in their heads and pivoting on a regular basis based on market demand. This means that the strategy-creation process can be a little chaotic, and the document, if not created by a team but rather just by the founder, can be idiosyncratic and have large gaps.
- **Large businesses without a dominant voice:** As with family businesses, large businesses that do not give primacy to one voice or have a CEO who prefers to rule by committee may have a document that is too long and where all voices have a say, meaning some objectives clash and it is hard to work out what to prioritize.
- **Scale-up businesses in rapidly moving markets:** Where companies are looking to create or dominate a market and are

growing rapidly to do so, they may need to change their strategic approach regularly, meaning that what is produced can feel quite roughshod. It can be hard for a leader to take this and know what to do with it, particularly when it stands in contrast to what they have seen before.

- **Small organizations that are looking to stay the same:** Often, small organizations do not need a long strategy document. They wish to stay the same size and do the same sorts of things, so there is no need for an elaborate strategy. One interviewee, Caroline Barlow, who runs the charity Arts for All (a fantastic charity that holds art classes for local children and vulnerable adults), talked about how they don't need a full-blown, multipage strategy document because the focus is entirely on securing enough funding to keep going (at time of writing, around £110,000 per year (around $140,000). It's not about growing, it's not about changing, or metrics, or growth goals, or anything else you might typically see in a strategy document. It's just about being able to continue doing what they do. It could all be summarized in just a few sentences focused on knowing whom to ask to raise the money that they need to keep going and how to ask them.

As a leader, you are reliant on all the leaders above you sharing the strategy well so that it is clear when it reaches you. Ideally, you want access to the actual strategy plan, with a clear interpretation by your manager. However, if the plan is bad or the communicator is weak, then by the time it reaches you, it can be very hard to follow.

If you are a frontline manager in a largish hierarchy, by the time the strategy reaches you, it may have been through six levels of hierarchy. If each leader only reshares about 80 percent accurately, with seven layers and six reporting points, it will only be 26 percent accurate by the time it reaches the front line. That's a pretty frightening stat! Leaders are nearly ten times more likely to be criticized for under-communicating than for overcommunicating.[1] Are you and other managers communicating or discussing strategy sufficiently with the levels above and below you?

The C-suite themselves can represent the biggest problem here. Their brains—and conversations—may be chock-full of strategy and the way forward. However, if they don't communicate this well, their good intentions can be left on the boardroom table.

Your team can't see itself in the strategy

As a leader, you may find it difficult to spot the link between the organization-level strategy and the work your team does, and also to translate it. The strategy can be exceptionally clear, but you can still struggle to translate these broader expectations to your team. Jessica Tamsedge, CEO of Dentsu UK, felt that many people battle with this, as strategy feels oblique or people just can't see themselves and the type of work they do in a broad strategy document, particularly when it has been designed to encompass the work of hundreds or even thousands of people.

Any manager who is not talking strategy to their team in a way that locates that team member in the strategy risks having a team that works without the organization's intentions in mind. If, for example, an HR manager in a law firm does not recognize that their recruitment and training policies will be key to delivering on the strategy of "being a tech-forward firm," their team may misuse the training budget and recruit lawyers who are tech-reticent, undermining the company's strategic aims. In organizations that are highly attuned to the strategy up and down the hierarchy, strategy, mission, vision, and OKRs drip out of every document, conversation, and decision, showing the way forward. You should consider, with your team, how far off this mark are you? And is this coming from you, or the layers above, or a bit of both?

I/we feel constrained by the strategy

Your team (and you) may be able to see yourselves in the strategy but not like what you see. And if the strategy feels wrong or uncomfortable, it can be very hard to deliver on it. Team members usually feel constrained by a strategy when it has a negative impact on them or someone they care about. For example, it might create more work for them, betray their values or create a sense of threat, or make them feel as though they have no sense of autonomy or agency.

Often, middle managers feel this lack of autonomy keenly. A promotion to (middle) management has been sold to them as a way to gain more power and control. However, when it comes to strategic implementation, they are often expected to feed down the strategy from the senior leaders to team members who may not be too keen on enacting it. Rather than feeling like a powerful strategic actor, they end up feeling like a lapdog to the senior leaders, doing their bidding and protecting them from the complaining staff members below. Some commentators unkindly see middle managers as ineffectual, or "permafrost," which nothing gets through.[2] But this is a mean portrayal of what can be a very difficult role—trying to balance the demands of those above and those below, aligning them toward the achievement of a strategy that they themselves have not had a large hand in crafting but are expected to have a large hand in executing.

Feeling constrained by the strategy may not have adverse effects, with people carrying on despite their misgivings, either because they are on board with a "disagree and commit" policy (more of this in the next section) or because they mask their feelings. However, it can lead to a full or partial refusal to engage with the strategy by team members. A team that will not enact the strategy or push back on your requests or those that come from your boss undermine your role as their manager and can make you look weak to your peers, boss, and other seniors. As a middle manager, you need the strategy to flow from the top of your company, through you, to your team. If your team is a stumbling block to the instigation of initiatives, you will not be popular. You will look like a middle manager who is powerless.

In all cases, not agreeing with a strategy but having to put up with it, whether you voice it or not, can lead to a feeling that you have no power or agency within the organization and ultimately reduce motivation. Reflecting on your own role, if *you're* not in agreement with the strategy, you may feel that your efforts to fit in are a self-betrayal and make you feel deeply inauthentic.

Pete Thornton, former pricing manager at an international pharmaceutical firm, said that he would send his proposed sales targets for his UK team for the year up to the bosses in the European HQ. These would come back significantly larger than he had proposed, and there was an expectation that he would just "go along with it." He hated it, feeling like a fraud. Quite quickly, he realized that there would be no repercussions if he told his team he didn't buy into the strategy that he was expected to promote, as it was too ambitious. But this didn't remove the feeling that the strategy itself was problematic, impossible to achieve against, and Pete still had to pretend to his senior managers that he was on board with it, feeling inauthentic and as though he could have been stronger.

Putting on an act by pretending to support a strategy is a form of emotional labor.[3] Psychologist Arlie Hochschild's term describes scenarios where workers are expected to shape emotions as part of the job. You as a leader are expected to appear supportive, happy, and compliant. We can all tolerate some emotional labor, but too much can lead to stress, burnout, and a performance drop. Looking down the hierarchy, leaders should live and breathe what they expect of others. If you are not embracing the strategy in your own work and actions, you cannot expect others to, and if you're not feeling it, then this acting can be exhausting, too. If you feel that you are having to do a lot of acting in supporting the initiatives from above and it is making you feel stressed or burned out, you should be mindful of this.

The senior leaders ignore our problems with the strategy

Information should flow upward from bottom to top, including market observations and external factors. Generally, the more junior a manager, the more important their feedback is, as they will be closer to the ground. Staff closer to where the work is done will gather all sorts of data, intelligence, and ideas that should be fed into the strategic conversation. However, this does not always happen. In a study of over twenty-seven thousand workers, Leadership IQ found that only a quarter of them believed that their feedback regularly led to important changes.[4] But why?

Management may not have the time or will to listen, leaving your team feeling unheard. At SinTech, the senior leadership team was reluctant to share thoughts on strategy issues with the execs, for fear of reprisals. As an outsider, I could act as a go-between to create a mechanism for the exec team to receive regular feedback from senior leadership. It is not easy. But if there isn't a mechanism to feed up on strategic problems in your organization, then you and your team may be facing similar frustrations, too.

And if employees have been ignored previously or felt punished for speaking up, they may feel dissatisfied with the company, reduce their commitment, or even quit. A feeling of lack of control can lead employees to act against their company—for example, through sabotage. I noted in the workshop I ran for SinTech that, during a creative exercise where they were asked to build a tool to help the senior leaders achieve their work, there was a collective sense of "getting their own back" by building imaginary tools that had overtones of destruction directed at the company failing under its own inertia or the exec team not having a sense of what was going on from the lofty heights they were working at. A gentle form of sabotage, but it was possible to see the exercise as the releasing of some sort of pressure valve for the participants who'd been bottling up their feelings.

From a distance, it may be easy to believe that those at the top of the organization are in a comfortable state of hubris and ego, but research shows that these are not the only reasons why they ignore upward feedback. It is often because they are expected to adopt a short-term outlook that doesn't allow for the sort of reflection and process change that bottom-up feedback can require. It's also because there may not be a mechanism in the strategic process that easily facilitates them integrating and acting on input from below.[5] It may seem as though they are in control, but often they are at the behest of a large strategic process that has been that way for years, and if that process doesn't seek upward feedback, then what should they do with that information?

You should also consider, however, whether you as a manager create a further divide between those above you and those below by filtering out less palatable messages from your juniors. Protecting your bosses from what they may need to hear may protect you, but it may not be in the best interests of your team or the company. It's worth thinking about whether you have withheld or are in the process of withholding any critical messages and why you are doing so. Is it fear? Hubris? Ego? No process in place? And if your seniors are doing the same, then why?

Trying to understand your motivations, and theirs, will help you to work out what to prioritize as you move on to solving the problems.

BEFORE MOVING ON:

- Where are the problems with delivering against the strategy coming from?
- Who is playing a role in the problems?
- Do you have any initial thoughts about how to solve the problems?

LAY OUT YOUR SOLUTION

You've identified problems with delivering the strategy—and here are some appropriate solutions to help fix them.

Send feedback up (and receive it)

First and most important is to create a mechanism within your team, but hopefully more broadly than this, for feedback to flow from the lowest levels of the firm to the CEO. There should be formal feedback mechanisms within all organizations that solicit employee feedback and have ways to integrate it into current and future strategic planning. Leaders at all levels should be encouraged to be comfortable with receiving strategic feedback, and you can play a powerful role in this by creating a great process in your team and advocating for it across the firm. The justification for this is strong; leaders do not know what's going on in any real sense, and they need to admit it. The workflow interdependencies and the complexities of how work is done pass them by and can make their strategy somewhat naïve.[6] By having good feedback mechanisms, you're helping the company to do better.

In companies where I've seen upward feedback work well, it's where it's possible to give it both on an ad hoc, informal basis and on a formal, regularly scheduled basis. This means that the company captures those fleeting thoughts from employees on the train on the way home, as well as the more structured proposals and ideas that may take a few weeks or months to gather data on and to work up into something more robust.

Possible formal mechanisms

You could look at a school council–type model at the team, function, or company level. Here, nominated reps gather views from the staff and feed them back at regular intervals. In this case, you will want to choose workers who are good at standing up to their seniors but who are cognitively flexible and will not become wedded to one issue for their tenure on the council. The other formal mechanism that works nicely is running regular feedback meetings with senior leaders where anyone can book in to come and present an idea or give feedback.

Possible informal mechanisms

The best way to give feedback is, simply, to feed back. Take the opportunity in your one-to-ones with team members to find out how things are with them and then funnel their feedback up to your own managers through your check-ins with them. If this hasn't been happening before, there may be a good reason why not, or it may just be because you, or others, haven't thought to do it. If it's the case that it's just not a part of the current process, you can change this by starting these conversations immediately.

If you would like a mechanism where team members can give feedback in a slightly more structured (yet still informal) way, a simple online form that people can fill in—anonymously or attributable to them, depending on if they want the credit for the idea or would rather remain anonymous—can work brilliantly. If you'd like all ideas to be attached to a specific person, using a Slack channel, a Teams chat, or a WhatsApp or Notion thread can be great ways to gather this information.

How to deliver better feedback

In most leader-team relationships, there is room for improvement in how strategic feedback is delivered and received. Where the receiving party has not been directly involved in the creation of the strategy, it is easier to deliver this in a very honest fashion. We are far less bothered, as leaders and humans, by feedback that does not feel personal.

However, if you feel that the person you are talking to has a personal stake in the strategy as it stands, you or your team should be sure to seek permission to share the feedback and ascertain when would be the most appropriate time to share it. Unsolicited feedback is often perceived as criticism, so seeking permission makes sure that you are checking that this person is ready to hear it and giving them the space not to hear it right now. However, you should also be ready to share immediately if they say, "Now is as good a time as any!" In preparing to share, you should be thinking about examples or data that you have that justify or illustrate your feedback, but hold these back unless you think you need them. Adding them in at too early a stage can feel a little like an onslaught!

Prepare to commit

Once there is a good feedback mechanism, you should then encourage the principle of "disagree and commit." This means that people have a space to voice their concerns, and there is a promise that they will be taken seriously. However, whatever emerges after this process, you promise to commit to it. Of course, this can be hard if you are still not in agreement, but your salary is paid on the basis that you work for the organization, not that you work against it. The same is true for any of your team members who disagree heavily with what they're being asked to do. If they cannot come onside, they may need to be encouraged to move on.

You may be able to help yourself with this commitment by regularly reminding yourself of the upside of your compliance. If you are heading for a promotion or a bonus, and following the strategy is a key part of that, then the reward at the end may be sufficient to justify the pain on the way there. I've seen leaders place coded Post-it notes on the edge of their computer screens: XXV (Roman numerals for that £25,000 bonus) or a simple upward arrow to remind them that their compliance will likely bring a promotion.

Can you also find those areas of your work or the work of your team where you and/or they can exercise more autonomy and control? Perhaps a new project that they've been asked to deliver where they have a lot more creative freedom, or even being responsible for organizing the team social calendar for the year? People can often cope a lot better with a lack of autonomy in one area of their role or doing work that they don't hugely agree with if other areas bring more freedom and opportunity to shape into something they do agree with. If this is a way to affect your commitment or that of your team, then it is worth exploring.

(NB: You should look in the "Venture Forth!" section as to what to do if you really cannot commit to the strategy. I signpost this in case you are screaming inside at what I'm asking you to do. I am only suggesting this if you think it is possible. For some of you, it may not be. And then there are other steps you can take. But I want you to consider your ability to commit and try to find a way to do it before you consider other more drastic options!)

Create better strategy communications

If you have found that your team is struggling to work with the strategy because it is unclear, then you need to play a role in improving quality and quantity of communications. You should work on taking what you are given by your boss, fully understanding it, and translating it into something that will work for your team. You should then concentrate on communicating it as clearly, and as frequently, as you possibly can. These three actions tend to help massively:

PROACTIVELY TELLING THEM WHAT THE STRATEGY IS

It is the job of managers, from the top to the bottom of an organization, to communicate with their team members about the strategy. What is it? What's important at the moment, based on the strategy? Where is the organization focusing its attention?

When people join the law firm Lewis Silkin, they spend the first hour with one of the two managing partners, Jo Farmer or Richard Miskella. From their first moments at the firm, the senior leaders are looking to create a clear message about what the strategy is for everyone—lawyers, paralegals, HR, IT, marketing and finance staff, and anyone else who joins. They start how they mean for people to go on—with a very clear view of what the strategy is. And Jo, in her interview, said how she would hope this is reinforced at all stages, with the strategy built into the language and actions of leaders across the firm. I witness this firsthand when I deliver their partner transition program each year—each year, we adapt it to bring it in line with the strategic elements that are of particular importance that year and that the new partners can play a significant role in helping with and communicating to their teams.

HELPING THEM TO UNDERSTAND THE IMPLICATIONS OF STRATEGY FOR THEIR ROLE

Once the strategy is set, the work begins in translating it for your function or team. As you work with the strategy and explore which elements are relevant for you and your team, you should be setting OKRs based on it, and you should be explaining how your expectations on and hopes for your team members are centered around the impact you would like them to have on the organization's achievement of its strategy.

A couple of years ago, I coached the collections director of a national museum. He was facing the substantial challenge of ensuring that everyone on his team fully understood what they were doing and why they were doing it, rather than viewing things as a series of tasks or projects. In his own telling, he had wrongly assumed that the relationship between people's tasks and the longer-term strategy was apparent. However, they were telling him that it was not and that they felt as though their work was unimportant. Considering that his team was doing the critical work of preserving and displaying objects in the museum, he needed to communicate to them how each of their tasks were intricately linked to strategic outcomes of widening audiences, increasing visitor numbers, and appropriately interpreting and sharing the collections of the museum.

To overcome this problem, he was very proactive. He took the opportunity to link his team's tasks to the museum's strategic objectives at every available opportunity. This took place in individual staff catch-ups, team sprint meetings, and wider meetings where different teams came together. The difference was almost immediate, and astounding—he found his team was much more engaged and thanked him for taking the time to explain why their work mattered. When I spoke to some of his team members as part of a follow-up project, they also praised his efforts, not knowing that I was the person who was coaching him when he undertook this big change!

Consider how you can use every opportunity to talk strategy and link it to team members' work. Can you, like the collections director above, bring it up in multiple meetings, one-to-ones, and email and other written communication? Consider, too, whether managers that you in turn manage are doing enough to talk strategy to their own teams and help them to see and follow through on opportunities to do so.

FIT THE CONTEXT: EVEN JUNIORS SHOULD UNDERSTAND STRATEGIC ALIGNMENT

In service of bringing team members in line with strategy, I think the concept of strategic alignment is very powerful and something that should be talked about at all levels. *Strategic alignment is when every level, function, department, and employee is organized according to and works in a way that is aligned to the main organizational strategy.* If they have functional or departmental strategies or objectives, these are focused on helping to meet the organization-wide strategy.

Often, strategy is a term that is reserved for the upper echelons of a firm: the senior leaders "do strategy," and everyone else falls in line. I have been surprised at how many middle managers and emerging leaders—as well as nonmanagerial staff—I have met who have absolutely no concept of what strategic alignment is because they have not been asked to align themselves to the strategic journey of the company, or it's being organized for them through function-level objectives that they have no comprehension are based on the main organizational strategy.

I think that finding a way to talk to everyone about strategic alignment, and their need to be strategically aligned if they want to be working in the best interests of the organization, is critical for success.

To explain the idea of strategic alignment to those who are new to it, I often use the metaphor of matryoshka dolls, the wooden nesting dolls from Russia. Each doll looks almost identical but is a little smaller than the last and has a slightly different set of flowers or patterns painted on it. Think of the biggest doll as the corporate strategy in its full form, and then each level down the sub-strategy that comes next, then the one below that, and the one below that. In the case of a leader I worked with recently, the strategic alignment matryoshka dolls looked like this:

ALIGN OBJECTIVES AND DEVELOPMENT CONVERSATIONS TO STRATEGIC AIMS

At moments where you are guiding a team member on their future objectives or OKRs, you should look to align them to the strategy, with each performing a role in helping the organization to achieve it.

Sometimes these will be direct—so if, for example, your company's strategy this time around includes "Develop relationships with fifty new clients," a clearly related objective for someone in sales could be "Develop relationships with two new clients." Someone in marketing could be asked to "Develop advertising that reaches new markets." Someone in IT could be asked to "Ensure the customer relationship management database is fully functioning and debug where necessary." Someone in finance could be tasked with "Identify ways to save costs." While this may not appear directly related to strategy, the team member would know (because their manager would have told them) that cost-saving could free up enough money to recruit another member of the sales team—an expert at selling to an industry where the company knows it can find many new clients.

No matter what the task is, you should look for a way to link it to the organization's strategy, vision, or mission. At first, this may seem odd, but the more experienced you become at showing how the work of IT, for example, builds the customer base or how the work in HR allows the organization to serve a wider range of stakeholders, the easier it will become. As Jessica Tamsedge, CEO of Dentsu UK, shared with me, "You have to help your direct reports deeply understand what they are expected to do and show how it links to the company's aims, because then they can start to translate a slightly oblique but ambitious strategy into what good would look like in their world."

You will find it helpful for those off-the-cuff conversations to have a short summary of the strategy that you are able to hold in your mind. This enables you to communicate the headlines clearly and to find ways to weave the big-picture strategy into your talk, actions, and requirements on and feedback to others.[7]

Then when you are giving feedback to your team members, appraising them, or providing development points, you can focus on where there's a gap between their OKRs and what they are doing or have done. You can provide recommendations of how they can improve their future performance—through skills development, training, and the like—so that they are able to reach it in the near future.

Again, by creating this clear link between their work and the organization's strategy, there's a further opportunity to make tasks feel highly significant to the individuals conducting them. It's another way of saying, "You know that little task that you do? You can trace that all the way up to the strategic aims, the mission, the vision of the organization."

BEFORE MOVING ON:

- How will you improve your ability to deliver against the strategy and that of your team?
- How will you measure your success?

VENTURE FORTH!

As you work on improving your ability to deliver against the strategy, you'll likely find that the impact of better strategic communication, and recognizing the role you play in ensuring that the strategy is a success no matter your level, will pay off with clarity of work and outcomes for your team.

However, this is not to say that stepping up your efforts to be a better strategic implementer will be without challenges. Some of the more common challenges I have been consulted on as leaders have made moves to be more strategic are detailed below, with some ideas on how to overcome them.

If you still feel stuck in the middle... encourage skip-level relationships

A common feeling for a middle leader involved in the strategy process is that they are being pulled in different directions by subordinates and their bosses. Your team resists the strategy, your boss expects perfect alignment. Work on this by encouraging them to talk directly. Developing skip-level relationships can seem odd if your organization is quite hierarchical. However, you can sell their benefits to your boss to enable them to get closer to what's happening on the front line, to build trust with their juniors to increase engagement and performance, and to demonstrate that they value everyone, irrespective of their level. And you can sell the benefits to your team members as having the ability to share their feedback with seniors to improve work, to get to know someone more senior—which may be useful career-wise—and to give them a voice in the organization.

The simplest format to improve skip-level relationships is a simple, occasional meeting between your boss and one or more of your team. If you want to turn up the access senior leaders have to the work being undertaken in your team, you could suggest a few hours of reverse work shadowing or a team member showing your boss the project they are working on or the detail of what they do.

The benefit to you in these relationships can be that your team member can express the challenges that they keep coming to you with directly to your boss. Your boss, hearing them directly, may be more inclined to act on them or at least give them a response. Your team member, on being given access to your boss, may reduce their view that you are the only conduit for their ideas and that therefore you are a blocker to their ideas. Increasing empathy for someone two levels up or two levels down can reduce the friction that you have to handle in the middle of the two parties, potentially reducing the amount of indirect translation and mediation that you need to do.

If you can't get behind the strategy... consider other jobs

I've already encouraged you to use your company's feedback mechanism to disagree with the aim that you then commit. However, this will not always be possible. You may fundamentally disagree with your organization's strategic choices, or they may cause you too much personal loss. We often say "disagree and commit" and see this as a management principle, but to put it in the context of the original line, from Scott McNealy, cofounder of Sun Microsystems, it's "agree and commit, disagree and commit, or get out of the way."[8] So if you find you really can't get behind what you're being asked to do, and this is likely to be a problem that is ongoing, or you're likely to face lots of future problems like this one, then maybe it's time to get out of the way. Perhaps you need to question if your current role is for you. It may be time to think about either a sideways move to another company (if you feel what they will be asking you to do will be sufficiently different) or a shift in role or industry altogether.

This may seem like strange and potentially quite harsh advice from a leadership book, but I see it as a valid response to a situation that doesn't suit you. I have seen plenty of people who've stayed in organizations with strategies that they do not agree with, and it has slowly chipped away at them and their sense of self. I have seen people made redundant after years of playing along feel such a sense of relief that, finally, they can look for a job that suits them more. I have also seen people who have made a leap into something more aligned with who they are and who have skipped into work in the morning, full of a sense of achievement and purpose, able to comfortably do what the organization is asking of them.

But if you do decide that you need to leave, consider keeping your current job while you hunt for a new one. This is because the sort of playacting required from supporting a strategy you don't agree with often becomes a lot easier when you know it is likely to be only for the short term and that, as soon as you've found another role, you will be out of there.

ELEVATE YOUR LEARNING

If you've seen the value of getting your team to deliver the strategy... teach your customers to do the same

You'll hopefully have found that getting your team to operate in line with the strategy reaps significant rewards in terms of their engagement with and passion for their role. Surprisingly, the same can be true for customers. In *Uncommon Service*, Frances Frei and Anne Morriss examine companies that construct exceptional service encounters with the idea of sharing the lessons. Among the many gems, one of their fantastic but perhaps counterintuitive observations is that, if you want a customer to be really impressed by your company, you can "train them" to help you to deliver to your strategy so you can show your company off to its best advantage.[9]

They talk about how, at Starbucks, one of their key strategic aims is to serve good-quality coffee quickly. They train you, as the customer, to help them to deliver this aim. So if you go into Starbucks and order your coffee all wrong, baristas will repeat your order back to you, as if just confirming it, but they will switch the language and order of the words. You say: "I'll have a big hot coffee with some milk, please." They come back to you with, "Venti white americano. And would you like the milk hot or cold?"

Eventually, through their prompts, you'll learn how to order "correctly," which will increase the chances of them serving you the correct order and them being able to serve you speedily, reducing queuing time and improving quality delivery of what you ordered.

Can you find ways to train your customers to help you deliver your strategy? If your strategy is to improve profit, or improve customer service speed, or expand to a new city, how can you use your customers to reduce costs (self-service checkouts or automated invoicing?), or increase speed (ask them to have their order number ready before phoning or use AI to answer basic questions?), or spread the word to their friends in

Houston (through a social media competition?). Once you start to see customers as coconspirators in strategy delivery, the possibilities are huge and the potential rewards significant.

If you have seen the value of strategic alignment... take it to the next level

As part of the plan above, you'll likely have injected strategy into more of your communications with your team. But what happens if you start to take this to another level, looking for ways to build strategy into all that you and your team do? Again, back to Starbucks, the way they talk to customers, every single word, is oriented to the achievement of the strategy. The way the coffee machines are designed to allow multiple coffees to be made at once. The way the tables and chairs are organized to allow some chance encounters and other people to get their heads down to work, supporting the whole community. How can you design your workspace, your documents, your talk, your online workspace, your team nights out, and your marking of special occasions with activities that fit with your strategy?

Lewis Silkin, the law firm where the managing partners, Richard and Jo, greet every employee with a talk about strategy from day one, has used an office move to reorganize its space to suit its strategic aims. It wants to be a law firm that serves each of their clients across their multiple legal needs (rather than them going to separate firms) and that trains exceptional lawyers. By moving to an approach that is open plan, different types of lawyers mix, and junior lawyers can overhear the conversations of more senior lawyers and learn from them.

In the opening example, SinTech's senior leadership team was struggling with the expectation that they should act more strategically, delivering on a strategy that they were not clear on and that they had not had a hand in crafting. Over the course of the workshop and for a number of weeks afterward, I worked with members of the senior leadership team to help them to develop their understanding of what the exec team expected of them in terms of delivering on the strategy. I talked to the exec team and asked them to create a forum for receiving feedback from the senior leadership team (which they did), and I encouraged them to be transparent about how they had arrived at the strategy to encourage buy-in.

For those members of the senior leadership team who were not able to see themselves in the strategy and could not go along with a "disagree and commit" approach, the move toward a more structured strategic delivery process and higher, clearer expectations around the strategy placed on them helped them to realize that perhaps this was not the best environment for them. There were some resignations, but this was not seen to be a problem by the exec—rather, it would allow them to recruit new senior leaders who were more aligned to where the company wanted to go.

REMEMBER:

- Strategic delivery needs every layer of the hierarchy involved. Find ways to understand the strategy from above and translate it for those below—as well as infusing it in your own work—to ensure that you are a key player in the strategic delivery.
- Emphasize strategic alignment whenever you can and remind your team how their work relates to the strategy. From documents to conversations, ensure that your managerial and leadership work reiterates what the strategy is and how your team's work is achieving it.

- Recognize that it can be frustrating and stressful to be asked to go along with a strategy you don't necessarily agree with. Sometimes it's necessary to give space for dissenting views and encourage bravery in yourself and team members to voice concerns. Create and make use of good feedback channels.
- When you've spoken out enough, remember to be a good follower and encourage the same in your team. The principle of "disagree and commit" is central here. If you find that you can't bring yourself to commit, consider a job move.

PROBLEM 9
Culture and Values

"The culture around here is toxic. Something must change or we're going to get ourselves in serious trouble. People are already leaving."

"There's someone nice in my team, but they're just not in line with the culture. We're risk-seeking, they're risk-averse. We're passionate, they're passive. But what can I do about this, as they're not a bad person—they're just not the right person?"

"Our culture is strong, which should be great, but it doesn't leave any space for individuality. How can we be creative if we're all the same as one another?"

SOPHIE IS A TEAM LEADER IN A SMALL ACCOUNTING FIRM. SHE WROTE to Dear Katie, facing problems with her team culture. The team had been used to following a set process for years, using the same software and following the system to the letter. As such, their culture was quite rigid and safe. They all liked this—it felt comforting and meant that they could easily switch off in the evening, never worrying about work, because it was very straightforward.

However, after a recent merger with a larger firm, they were being encouraged to come into line with the more dynamic and entrepreneurial sales culture of that firm. The company they had merged with had a system with a lot more features, meaning that rather than just offering bookkeeping services to their clients, they could sell various tax advisory and business improvement solutions to their clients, too. The team didn't like this—it felt at odds with their culture of serving their clients well and providing them with a reliable, safe service that they could trust. Suddenly, Sophie and other members of her team were lying awake at night, worrying about whether they were delivering on the company's expectations and concerned that they were betraying their clients by trying to sell them services that they may not need.

Sophie wanted to know, as team leader, what should she do? Try to drag her team into the new way of doing things? Be content to have a subculture at odds with the rest of the company (even though this could get them into trouble)? Leave? Because the culture of a company affects so much—its processes, its decisions, the way that people interact with one another—cultural problems can feel particularly unpleasant if you are a leader. And they're often made worse because of the very nature of organizational or team culture. The culture of a place, or a team, is the sum of its shared values and assumptions, coupled with the history of the organization, the composition, and backgrounds of the people in the organization or on the team in question, and the function or occupation it reflects. Because it's a sum of so many parts, which impact in ways that we cannot as yet predict, how a culture ends up is only partly the work of the leader.[1] And this in turn means that, when leaders try to solve cultural problems, because their influence is limited no matter how senior they are, it can be frustrating.

Whether, like Sophie, you're struggling to align with the organization's values, or you're having an issue with a single team member who's not in line, or you take issue with a culture that is toxic, or stifling, or weak, this chapter will teach you how to identify the source of the problem and how to have a positive impact, even if you can't always solve the problem entirely.

STATE THE PROBLEM

You need to work out the headline problem you think you need to solve before getting stuck in the details. In the case of value and culture problems, answering the following questions can be particularly helpful for getting an overview of what's happening before digging into the details:

- **What appears to be the problem?** Some of the more common problems are below, but you may have spotted something that I haven't listed, so feel free to add something totally different:
    - We have a toxic culture, or I've heard others describe it as a toxic culture.
    - We have a problematic individual or subculture that is pulling the main culture out of shape.
    - Our culture is really unclear—no one knows what we stand for!
    - Everyone is too similar—we don't have any cultural diversity in our company, meaning we have massive blind spots and we exclude important voices.
- **Who appears to be facing the problem with culture and/or values?** Is it you, a team member, a colleague, or a whole team? Cultural problems can affect individuals or whole groups, so don't be surprised if you find yourself writing down, "My entire team."
- **When/where does the problem show itself?** All the time? When the person or team is under pressure? When they're working with others who are very different from them?

Remember: What you capture here are just your initial thoughts to help you have more focus when you now read the "Open the Box" section, so it doesn't matter too much if your answers don't feel very certain—by the end of the next section, you'll have a much better sense of what's going on.

OPEN THE BOX

Leaders can run into a variety of cultural problems when managing organizations or teams, and many that I'll highlight below can happen at once, worsening one another.

Is the culture too weak?

A weak culture is one that doesn't have clear rules, behaviors, or attitudes, and it's uncertain what the organization stands for. This lack of substance can lead to feelings of ambiguity, confusion, and apathy—as we seek meaning from companies and brands, there is a sense that all organizations should stand for something.

A BLAND, MEANINGLESS CULTURE

A culture that, when stated, is very generic does not provide a template to work by. For example, if a company states that its culture is to "be successful" or "compete in the market" or "work well," what is that actually saying? Surely, that's what all companies do? A good way to determine if your culture is too generic is the opposite test: select a cultural value, and then ask yourself whether an organization may want the opposite value.[2] No company would want to work badly or be unsuccessful! But if a value was to "be brave," it *would* be feasible for some companies to want to be cautious. If your values don't represent a meaningful choice, they can do better than that.

MORE DOMINANT SUBCULTURES

Another sign of a weak organizational culture is when a firm's subcultures are more dominant. Subcultures are cultures held by a smaller group—maybe a function or a team. They are usually helpful, setting up more specific shared values, assumptions, and processes. But if the subculture isn't in line with a clear organizational culture, they can run wild.

In a group coaching session, a cardiac doctor brought the following problem. He worked at a private hospital in mainland Europe that prides itself on high survival rates, and as such, its culture should be risk-avoiding, leaving potentially groundbreaking but risky surgical procedures to other hospitals. However, it rarely talks about its culture, and it's assumed that everyone will just act in this way. But because it's not something they talk about, the head of department had recently recruited a cardiac surgeon and his team who are pushing cardiac surgery into exciting and potentially lifesaving new territory but not without some risk to individual patients along the way. There is nothing unethical in the practice, as he is only offering these surgeries to seriously ill patients. However, it is riskier than the hospital is comfortable with, but because the hospital's culture is weak and not discussed, these procedures are continuing, and this more risk-seeking approach to surgery is creeping into other departments that want to recruit similar sorts of doctors. This goes against the hospital's culture and the way it markets itself to patients. Where there is a cultural weakness, the subculture is beginning to dominate in a way that may undermine the main culture of the organization.

Consider whether your culture is too weak:

- Do employees struggle to understand what is expected of them by the culture? Would they struggle to give examples of what the culture encourages them to do?
- Are the subcultures of each team more dominant, or becoming more dominant than the main organizational culture?
- Do team members act in erratic ways or very differently from one another because there's not a standardized way of doing things?

- Do people struggle to talk about the culture or values of the organization in any meaningful way?
- Are teams and subcultures pulling away from one another?

Positive answers to any or all of the questions above may suggest that your culture is weak and you may wish to tackle this.

Is the culture too homogeneous?

Homogeneous organizational cultures were historically seen as good for companies. When men turned up in practically identical suits to do standardized work at the same company for years on end, it was very easy to coordinate and control.[3] However, now we know that if workers are too similar, they lack diverse ideas, don't reflect client bases, may exclude those who don't fit the mold,[4] and could even face legal action.

Samantha Hawkins, a fellow coach who works with leaders who are proud to be different, nonetheless sees these leaders often battle against cultures that exclude them for their differences. Samantha told me how they often end up feeling "burned out from sticking out or from sticking their necks out." And so there is a risk that they leave and the culture continues to exclude, to its own detriment and that of society.

Unfortunately, you may find it hard to spot if your culture is too homogeneous, particularly if you are part of the dominant group.[5] Try to take a critical view on your workplace as you answer the following questions:

- Do you or team members feel shocked if someone suggests a different way of doing things? Do you stick to old processes or behaviors even if good evidence suggests a new, potentially better way?
- Does your team look, act, dress, or speak the same, more than the setting requires (e.g., not for health and safety reasons, or because there is a customer-facing uniform)?

- Is the culture quite exclusive, restricting access to some sociodemographic groups through its rules?
- Are they tracking below average on diversity stats (e.g., the gender pay gap, staff identifying as being from a background other than the Western majority)?
- Does the company emphasize looking for people the "same as us" when recruiting?

If the answers suggest high cultural homogeneity, it could be a problem that holds your team or organization back.

FIT THE CONTEXT: WHEN SUBCULTURES ARE CRITICAL

Sometimes as part of your work, you will identify a subculture that appears anathema to the organization's main culture and feel that you need to "handle" it. However, sometimes subcultures are business critical.

For example, Nick Rice, CEO of Consolite, talked about the importance of subculture in their company, which manufactures highly controlled precision products for naval ships and military aircraft. The culture in Consolite more generally is entrepreneurial and big picture, as the company focuses on winning innovative contracts for work with big clients. However, in the in-house workshops that actually do the building, the culture must necessarily be around attention to detail, because for them to achieve their work, they should minimize errors and maximize quality. Here, the subculture is critical for protecting the company's reputation for quality.

In an advertising firm that is focused on creativity, the accounting function may have quite a different culture. And in an accounting firm, the advertising function may have quite a different culture. To ascertain if a subculture is a problem, it's about questioning whether this subculture is dragging the main culture down or whether it's helpful to achieving business success.

Is your culture toxic?

A toxic work culture is when a company has practices and policies that cause conflicts and unhealthy habits among team members. This could be through a culture of overwork, being overly negative, or personal conflict. It could also include workplace bullying, employee exclusion, or other abuses of power. Toxic cultures reduce work quality while increasing dissatisfaction and employee turnover.[6]

If a company deals swiftly and decisively with problems, then it's not permitting a toxic culture, because the bad behavior is being tackled. But if problems are ignored, encouraged, or allowed to run on, then over time, this builds into a toxic culture.

In 2022, I provided coaching to the C-suite of a company selling Microsoft services. During my first one-to-one coaching sessions with each of the C-suite, it was clear that I was dealing with a CEO who was mean to his staff, didn't respect their work-life boundaries, talked dismissively about the women on the senior leadership team, and wanted me to convince the senior leadership team, through coaching, that he was correct in his approach. When he saw that the coaching may give the team members stronger voices, rather than silencing them, the relationship ended. This was such a toxic culture, I was pleased to be out of it, but I still wonder how it turned out for the C-suite.

If you are a leader in a company with a toxic culture, reflect critically on whether you are proliferating it. Even if you're not directly involved, casting a blind eye on bullying, exclusion, or conflict is allowing the habit to remain.[7] The C-suite were allowing his bad behavior to infect all levels of the company by allowing him to talk to them like that and to their team members, too.

To ascertain if you're likely to be working within a toxic culture, consider:

- Does your company have a culture of overwork, exclusion, bullying, nasty talk, conflict, or power abuse that is not addressed?
- Do people discuss the culture in a negative way, seeing it as being a destructive force for the company because of the behaviors it tolerates or even encourages?

If your answers to the questions above suggest cultural toxicity, you will need to look at what you can do to resolve or reduce the impacts on your team.

Is someone pulling the culture out of shape?

Whatever form your culture takes—whether it's to be collaborative or individualistic, competitive or consensual, creative or fastidious, big picture or detail-oriented, and so forth—there will be people who struggle to align. Sometimes these people stick out massively, as they act in ways that are anathema to everyone else. Sometimes they mask their behavior, as they are worried about sticking out but end up feeling dislocated from the rest of the firm or exhausted by all the masking they have to do. Their actions have a negative impact on the culture as well as possibly creating personal feelings of disengagement and discontent, which manifest in lower job satisfaction, worse work quality, and increased chances that they will leave.

- Can you point to ways that this person is unhelpfully different from the culture? Perhaps they pull rank when the culture is egalitarian or are too influenced in a culture that values independent thinking?
- Do they express frustration at the culture and what it expects of them?
- Is it hard, even with inclusive attitudes, to reconcile this person's behavior with the culture? For example, do they

consistently turn up late in a culture that values promptness or act individually when they're part of a team with a strong cohesive culture?

- Do they seem to have to put on an act at work, which perhaps slips when they are tired or under pressure?

This can happen at a group or team level, too. I recently ran a workshop for a Dublin-based sales team in a global software company. Their organization had gone through a large change process to shift from being an inbound business (where clients came to them as they needed the software) to an outbound business (where they needed to do more active selling, as they had a higher number of competitors). It meant that the culture needed to shift from reactive and responsive to being entrepreneurial and risk-seeking. However, a subculture formed in one team where they did not want to change and were continuing to wait for business to come to them and then responding to it. The workshop that I ran was to try to demonstrate the need for the culture change and to get them to move, as nothing else seemed to be working and they were pulling the culture out of shape with their actions.

FIT THE CONTEXT: SHIFTING FROM A SMALL-FIRM CULTURE

Companies usually begin with one or two founders who have a strong vision. The culture comes from them—in many ways, they are the culture. Nothing really needs to be written down, and if people need a sense of how to do things, they often just think, *What would the founder do?* But as the company grows, fewer people have direct experience of working with the founders, and there often needs to be more formality around what the culture will be. And this is where problems can arise—because the founder can want to maintain the flexible, speedy, easy-to-pivot small firm culture that reflects them and their entrepreneurial spirit. But this culture can be totally out of line with what is required in a rapidly scaling company.

As such, scale-up companies can have quite a messy culture, with lots of subcultures, lots of infighting around "how we do things here," and quite a few senior staff members who seem to be out of line with the main culture. Stenn is a real success story—it has grown rapidly in the past few years, making it one of the fastest-growing firms in the financial technology space. However, because of the speed of growth, it can be hard to always execute on the firm's values. Fozia Raja, chief people and culture officer, told me there was one cultural value, "elevate together," that leaders deeply believed, but in their rush to make progress, they sometimes overlooked it. Instead of acting together, they had occasionally pulled in their own directions, resulting in conflicting ideas further down the line. Although elevating together was recognized as an important cultural value, in the heat of the moment, with the pressure of scaling up, it could be momentarily forgotten.

If you work in a scale-up, it's important to recognize that these complexities and tensions among different cultural forces may exist and to see that it's a product of this moment in time. Hopefully, you will have a C-suite who are keen, like those at Stenn, to iron out differences in cultural application.

BEFORE MOVING ON:

- What problems with culture have you identified?
- How far-reaching are they (i.e., are they a problem at organizational level, team level, or individual level)?
- Have you worked out where you think the problems are coming from?

LAY OUT YOUR SOLUTION

As an individual leader, solving cultural problems can be tough, as culture is much bigger than we are. As such, I'm focusing suggestions below on those that you as an individual leader could stand a reasonable chance of achieving.

Identify the culture or subculture you're aiming for and share it

If you've identified problems with your culture that you need to correct, you should start by stating what culture you need instead. This only works if you have enough control over the culture in question that you are able to prescribe how it should be. If you're in the C-suite, this could be the whole firm culture (following discussion with other C-suite members). If you are a team leader, it will likely be restricted to the subculture of your team.

The culture you need may be a previous culture or one you've been aiming for but haven't achieved. Or you may not have a statement of culture at all, in which case you'll have to create one. This could be a paragraph laying out your cultural vision, or a set of values, or a combination of both. You are aiming for a cultural description that is clear, realistic, and distinct. You may want to get others involved in the process of creating it, asking them how they think it should be and working hard to create a statement that others can get behind.

You then need to find ways to share it with your team, clearly and directly.

Talking the talk and walking the walk

Writing down your desired culture is the easy part! Enacting it is so much harder, and it must be done well; otherwise, it will be weak. The key is to talk culture constantly and consistently. The way you speak and what you say should be influenced by the culture that you are trying to create because words create—and change—cultures.[8]

If you want your company to be collaborative, regularly using *we* instead of *I* would be a way to use language to signal it. One interviewee, who is not a part of but works closely with her company's C-suite, said that there has been a recent intention to shift the bank's culture from quiet and formal to collaborative and informal. As such, the C-suite have been trying to leave their doors open, create more noise, and have more conversations in the open-plan space to increase the buzz and sense of informality. Here, the act of talking in a specific place (the open-plan office) and in a particular way (loudly and chattily and not just about work) is a signal of the more informal and collaborative culture that they know they want to have going forward.

You should also talk directly about the culture. On a regular basis, when you are justifying your choice of action, or debating what to do, you should talk about what the culture and its values require you to do. Is it checking documents more carefully because you want to promote the culture as having an eye for detail, or having more lunch-and-learns to reinforce the culture's emphasis on knowledgeability?

This isn't just about what you say—it's your broader actions, too. If you want others to work flexibly, you need to do so, too. If you want others to be brave when presenting new ideas, you must do the same. And if you want your team to greet customers with a smile, then guess what? Yep. Get that grin ready! Of all the common themes, this was one that my interviewees repeated time and again, from Dame Mary Marsh, the former head teacher, to Jessica Tamsedge, CEO of Dentsu UK: to be a good leader, you must live the values you are expecting of others. Otherwise, everything fails. Because how can they be expected to do what the culture asks of them if you, as a leader, are not doing it? Thinking about what you say and how you say it, as well as talking about culture, will elevate its importance, signal your commitment, and infuse it in the day-to-day actions of the organization.

WORK ON THE SPACE

Just as you can inject the culture into your behaviors, you should look at how you can inject it into the workspace. This isn't about writing the values on a big glass wall (although do that, too—every little bit helps!). Instead, this is about finding ways to shape the space that allow people to live the culture more easily. The bank's C-suite leaving their office doors open allowed the right kinds of talk to happen. It physically changed the space to change the way it was used and therefore changed the culture.

As a leader, you should consider whether the tangible elements of what you have a say over—from the offices to the pens, to the food in the cafeteria—signify the culture that the organization wants to have. If you want a culture that's dynamic and collaborative, create hot-desking spaces, open the office doors, get everyone talking. If you want a culture that's private and secure, close those doors and create lots of spaces to huddle and guard information.[9] If the organization is focused on employee well-being, pay attention to the food the cafeteria serves and ensure lots of light and air. Some organizations became famous for matching their workspaces to their culture. For example, the smoothies-and-juices company Innocent carpeted their office with Astroturf to make it feel fun and creative and filled it with furniture that could be moved around to allow for collaboration.[10] Having been to their offices, I can confirm that the atmosphere feels informal and fun, signaling quickly to an outsider that things are done differently around here and it's okay to have fun while working.

And Ryanair, the budget airline whose CEO goes to great lengths to remind everyone just how cheap it is to fly with them, infamously told staff to steal their own pens from hotels and legal offices, as it didn't want to foot the bill of pens. Shaping the contents of their space and boasting about it underlined its proudly "cost-conscious" culture.[11]

Use these examples as inspiration—how can you influence your workspaces to reflect and reinforce your desired culture? Can you remove or change elements of the workspace that stop you achieving your desired culture?

INSISTING ON BEHAVIOR MORE IN LINE WITH THE CULTURE FROM OTHERS

Once you are acting in line with the culture—and aligning the workspace, too—you can justify holding others responsible for pro-cultural behavior. I advocate rewarding great cultural behavior as the most useful approach, but there is also a place for holding people to account.

Rewarding great cultural behavior

People are much better at replicating good activities than trying to stop or change bad ones. We can use the same skills to repeat something we've done well or mimic good behavior in others very effectively. As such, praising people for being in line with the culture and letting others see what you consider to be great cultural behavior can be very helpful. Actions that may help:

- **Providing discretionary rewards or bonuses when you see someone acting in line with the culture:** This might be done through formal approaches, such as appraisals and yearly bonuses. Or it can be done on a more ad hoc basis, through prizes or rewards that are given out publicly to mark someone's strong adherence to the culture. The prize can even be symbolic as opposed to valuable. Joey Coleman, in his work on creating great customer cultures, talks about Roma Moulding, a frame company that makes museum-quality frames and that hands out "values cards" as a reward when someone hits a value brilliantly.[12] People see these on others' desks or see them being handed out, and they become a marker that this person is helping the company do great work.
- **Highlighting great cultural actions through public praise:** Now that you see someone acting in line with the culture in a very positive way, turn it into a lesson. "Thanks,

Barb, for showing great collaboration. You know that's important to us culturally, and I think when you asked Toni to input and listened carefully to her answer, then asked others what they thought about incorporating it into the solution, you were really collaborating. Even more so because I know you were nervous about this idea, but you could see that the group largely backed it." If you would like to know more about how to give positive feedback, read the "Lay Out Your Solution" section in Problem 4: Individual Performance.

- **Linking promotions to good cultural behavior:** In many organizations that work hard to proliferate their organizational culture, they link promotions to someone's ability to align to it. The more senior they become, the higher the expectations become. So a junior manager may be expected to be a role model for the broader culture and help team members to display the culture to clients. A C-suite leader may be required to help shape and guide the culture, acting as a role model both to their team and to the broader organization.

Holding people to account for bad cultural behavior

If you find individuals who are pulling the culture out of shape, you should address their behavior before it becomes contagious! Often, people are not pulling the culture out of shape on purpose, and being called out is all that's needed. Talk to them, highlighting the cultural mismatch and being as specific as possible about the problematic behaviors you're noticing and why they're a problem. Present them with suggestions of how to correct their behavior. For example:

"The culture is one where we respect one another, but in turning up late to most meetings, you are not respecting others' time. Last week,

of the seven meetings I was in with you, you were late to four of them by five to ten minutes, and for the facilities and IT team meeting, you were fifteen minutes late. Can you share your reasoning with me, and let me know how you plan to address this?"

Or:

"I think you're aware, because we've talked about it before, that one of the key values here is that we collaborate to accelerate. However, when you're working on a new project, your team has let me know that you tend to hoard work for the first few weeks, thinking you can do it all. This means that they end up having to stay late toward the end of a project to meet deadlines and that they aren't learning as much as they would if they were given more access earlier on. How can we solve this?"

Mark Etherington, project manager in the UK Civil Service, was given feedback early in his career that he was amazingly analytical but that he was not speaking up as much as expected. This was a collaborative culture and one that expected him, no matter how junior he was, to contribute. He was nervous to start with, as the meetings would often have some very senior people in them.

He had to find the courage to speak, to become a collaborative thought partner in a culture that valued all voices. And as he leaned into what he was being asked to do, he found he liked it and could see the value of it. He was successfully socialized into the behavior by being called out on this shortcoming. And he saw the value of it quickly, making an impact on the conversation a number of times, even in the first few months. Now, he is culturally aligned, and rather than thinking good work is individual, analytical work, he sees good work as everyone having the confidence to share great analysis in a meeting and getting to a better place together.

FIT THE CONTEXT: CHOOSE YOUR ACTIONS BASED ON YOUR SENIORITY

Leaders at different levels need to focus attention at different aspects of culture change to lean into their influence and to avoid frustration. These guidelines should help you work out where to concentrate your efforts.

If you are in the C-suite: You will guide culture change efforts and will be seen as a role model, so you need to talk about culture a lot and be seen to live it. Make sure that you link your talk back to the culture and values on a regular basis: "We are doing this because we value *x* around here." "We're taking this action because it's in line with our caring culture." "We're stopping our relationship with supplier *y* because they are heavy polluters and not aligned with our cultural value of sustainability."

Your actions will be taken as a cultural marker whether you like it or not. One CEO I interviewed said he felt as though he was constantly watched, with his actions signaling how others should act. He felt the pressure of this, but knew that whatever he did would still be taken as a signal, so he'd better be a good reflection of the culture.

If you are a middle leader: You play a critical role in the day-to-day of the company culture, acting as a role model and influencing the behavior of more junior leaders and frontline workers. However, your control over the culture is likely more limited, and you'll be less involved in culture-change conversations than more senior leaders. Make a positive impact by trying to live the culture and talking about it, so it trickles down the organization. You should also build a positive subculture within your own team that 1) is aligned with the broader organizational culture, 2) is inclusive, and 3) facilitates great work.

If you are a first-level / junior leader: You play a critical role in ensuring that frontline workers embody your organization's cultural values in their interactions with customers and in their performance of their daily work.. Encourage cultural alignment in your team members' talk and actions so that the client can palpably feel the culture. There's also value in working on your team's subculture, again making sure it 1) is aligned with the broader culture, 2) is inclusive, and 3) facilitates great work.

Create an inclusive culture

Research shows that companies benefit from cultures that are *strong but inclusive*, meaning that their values and beliefs allow for difference and promote inclusion. As a leader, you need to find ways to encourage inclusion, as it's to the benefit of work quality and equality. Create an inclusive culture by making sure that you have one or more values that speak to being inclusive and then living them. The law firm Lewis Silkin pairs the two values of being kind and being brave, looking for employees to be kind to one another and to have the bravery to speak out when they don't agree with something. Comanaging partner Jo Farmer feels that this pair encourages inclusion, as it creates safe spaces where all colleagues and their views are welcome, and she works hard to live this value herself. Having worked with her for a number of years, I've really seen her actively work to be braver at tackling difficult subjects, and she sees this in herself, having had to make some tough calls recently.

You should also ensure that your culture and its values do not read as being exclusionary. For example, a value of being "refined" or "worldly" might privilege a particular WASPish socioeconomic background and disadvantage many other backgrounds.

If you see someone being culturally excluded in a way that is problematic, take action, or flag those who have the ability to do so that they need to take action. It's never been more important to take a stand against issues of exclusion. No one in a position of authority should be comfortable with being a bystander.

BEFORE MOVING ON:

- What changes to the culture will you make?
- What's your time frame?
- How will you know you're making progress?

VENTURE FORTH!

Changing a culture is hard and slow. Remember it will take time, and the more people you can enlist to the mission, the better. Where you can make changes yourself or ask your team to take practical steps, you'll fare better, but if you are more ambitious in your scope, then well done and keep going! Here are three problems you may run into and what you can do about them.

If new behaviors are hard... keep at it

Cultural change is best seen as a series of small actions that over time add up. When you change the way you talk, your office layout, what you praise your team for, and the like, you are gradually shifting the culture. But because it's all-encompassing, it will sometimes feel tiring and overwhelming, and it can be easier to default to how you've always done it. But don't! Instead, find ways to make the changes easier. Build in diary reminders, standard slides, and standing agenda points that speak to the new behaviors you're looking for. Prompt yourself to talk about the culture each time you see team members. Come up with stock phrases you can use that reflect the culture and values you're trying to promote. And ask those you want to see the changes in to do similarly, finding ways to prompt themselves to enact new behaviors until it's an unthinking part of their routine. You're looking to establish new paths in the brain, and that takes work to move it from the conscious to the unconscious. These methods will help you get there.[13]

For example, if you want a creative culture, send regular emails saying, "Now that we're focusing on being creative, I'd like us to…"; introduce a "curious questions" section into the team's weekly meeting; ask, "Why do we do it that way?" more frequently; talk to clients about the creative approach; and keep going until people start to respond. And even then keep going, rewarding good cultural behavior throughout.

If you've accidentally changed the culture… work with it

Trying to change one element of a culture often changes others you didn't want to change, too. Nick Rice, the CEO of Consolite, said that after receiving feedback that the company's culture was too mistrusting, he tried to correct it by giving people more autonomy, asking the whole C-suite to check up on their staff a bit less and pushing back on employees to make independent decisions. The culture was seen to be more trusting, but also more hands-off, as though the C-suite didn't care.

Do not be surprised if, as you try to get one element of culture right, another goes awry. Work quickly to correct misunderstandings and work out how to get back the bits of culture that you've lost or at least get close to them again.

Nick moved to a model that had more delegation and assumed trust but added back in some check-in points. Managers also offered to help where team members were stuck, reducing the perception of a hierarchical culture. It took work to move things once and then move them again, but eventually, Nick ended up with the more autonomous and trusting culture people had been asking for.

If you can't shift attitudes... consider letting staff go

If a team member questions their will or skill to be able to come into line with the culture, you may want to remind them that, for career success, sometimes it's important to stick to what they believe and that sometimes it's important to be able to "merge into traffic."[14] In this particular case, merging into traffic is the appropriate response, as what you're asking is positive and culturally important. You are there to support them, but it's important that they give it a go. If you still face problems, we'll cover what to do in the "Venture Forth!" section.

If someone is still pulling the culture out of shape despite your efforts to change it, you should consider if it's time to sever the relationship. Sad, but it could be important to protect the culture, particularly because their behavior could be contagious! A law firm I worked with had accidentally hired someone at the most senior level who turned out to be far more authoritarian and exacting than the firm's culture. They asked me to coach him to try to effect change, and while he initially tried to change, or at least pretended to try to change, ultimately it was too much of a mismatch, and they had to let him go.

If you find that you can't turn them around, you should consult HR to check the correct process within your country and to see who you need involved in the offboarding process (or whatever euphemism you prefer for sacking, decruiting, or letting someone go). Certainly in Europe, you will need to prove their performance is lacking rather than relying on values misalignment as a justification, as this is a little too abstract to stand up in court! You will find, however, plenty of examples where their work is not in line with expectations precisely because they are not fundamentally aligned to the values.

ELEVATE YOUR LEARNING

If you've seen the value of knowing the culture . . . learn to describe it well

Throughout this chapter, I've used a variety of words to talk about culture, such as *collaborative*, *individualistic*, *dynamic*, *creative*, and so on. You'll also have noticed I've talked about your intended culture and your real culture, to differentiate between what you want versus what you have.

I recommend, if you are keen to keep working with culture, that you build up a good lexicon that you could use to describe the culture of your organization and to keep adjusting and adding to it. Ask others how they see the culture and compare it to what you have.

And one of the very best ways you can access a fresh view on the culture is to ask a new member of staff. When they have been with you for two to three months—long enough to know your culture but still see the difference between it and other places they have worked—ask them to describe the culture to you and how it differs from other places. You can use their fresh lens as a way of seeing the culture from someone else's perspective and build your own understanding as a result.

If you see the benefits of having an aligned team . . . socialize them well

Organizational socialization is "the process through which an employee's pattern of behavior, attitudes and motives is influenced to conform to that of the organization."[15] You will want to encourage them to act and think in a way that is commensurate with the culture and values of the organization. Practical training around processes, showing them the organization's expectations in terms of behaviors and actions, and providing mentors who are in line with the cultural values of the organization can all help.

Think of what you can do to give someone a good flavor of your culture. How can you socialize them into your organization in a way that works? Remember to focus on the areas that are within your control.

If you want to protect your culture further... have a long probation period

Socialization can take a while, and as such, it can be good to take advantage of the option of a long probation period, if your organization is prepared to write one into the contract for your recruit. It gives you more time to see if someone is a good cultural fit. It is easy to do surface acting for a few months for most people—whether they are doing so on purpose or by accident—but the longer the probation, the likelier you are to see the "real them" in stressful situations or in moments where they are too engaged in their work to be able to act. Barry Sheerman, former Labour MP, talked of the benefits of being able to see how someone does in the role, having been stung by people who've performed brilliantly in their interview but then never quite delivered the performance or alignment with the culture that they seemed to promise. When you're working on projects that are of high social significance, such as Barry's work to pass the UK smoking ban and his ongoing campaigns for clean, safe cities, it is critical to have people who believe in the organization's values and are prepared to get behind them.

Employees can be unhappy about long probation periods, feeling that it puts control in the hands of employers, but I have heard many senior leaders say that they ask for their probation periods to be longer, because they want to try out the company, too. If a new hire expresses concern about this long probation period, assure them that the longer period will help them determine if the organization is a fit for them as well.

In the opening example, Sophie had written to me asking what to do about the new culture her team had been asked to adopt—more dynamic and entrepreneurial. I advised that, seeing as the merger was very new, she should give it time to see what happened to the culture after a few months. She told me after three months that there had been a bit more meeting in the middle and less emphasis on her team selling, but also that her team was more willing to come in line with the culture that was emerging, as they had seen that clients actually liked the new products.

However, there were still doubts in a couple of her team members, and she found that they were not prepared to sell these products to the clients. They felt it went against their personal values of providing high-quality service. She started to take notes to address their behavior in the coming months, but one handed in their notice. She talked to the remaining team member, using the evidence to present specific times she had seen the team member act counter to the new culture—for example, criticizing the new systems to a client. She asked the team member to address their behavior, and while the team member does still struggle with this approach, they are now doing a better job of "merging into traffic," recognizing that this attitude is critical to their career.

REMEMBER:

- Organizational cultures can go wrong in all kinds of ways, including being too homogeneous, too weak, or toxic. Individuals and subcultures can also pull a culture out of shape, particularly if the culture is weak. Understanding the problems with the culture will provide pointers on how to improve matters.
- However, culture can be very hard for an individual leader to change, so focus on areas that you can influence and control, such as your own behaviors or trying to help your team members to change and "merge into traffic."

- It is particularly important for organizational effectiveness and ethics to create cultures that are inclusive. You should focus on having some values that are focused on inclusion, while ensuring that all values do not exclude. If you don't have a clear view on this, ask others.
- Where you cannot directly effect change, but you think change urgently needs to happen, you should share your thoughts and ideas with those who have more of an influence. This is to avoid being a bystander to a culture that is exclusionary or toxic.

PROBLEM 10
Leading Change

"My team doesn't seem to be able to change. It's like they're too lazy, or they don't believe in it or something. But they have to change. I have to get them to change. And I don't know what to do."

"This doesn't feel like change, it feels like chaos! I think we bit off more than we can chew. We don't seem to have the processes or support in place to be able to drive it through, and I think it's just going to fail."

"I hate change! But as a leader, I'm expected to be a role model. I would so much rather things just stay as they are."

ELWOOD WAS THE NEW CHIEF OPERATING OFFICER FOR NARRATIVELOOM, a brand narrative consultancy practice. He'd been brought in to improve operations with an eye to the company being sold by the founders within the next two years.

Elwood knew he needed to streamline and standardize processes to align with other similar consultancy practices. As things stood, there were duplicates of almost every document template, used haphazardly. It added a level of chaos, which brought unseen costs to each project.

But getting the change through proved extremely tough, with widespread resistance in the consultants and the support staff. Resistance was greatest from those who had not been asked to get involved in document and process redesign—they were on the outside, looking in on a process they'd had no hand in shaping.

The consultants were petrified that the new process would be too time-consuming—when they were already working sixty- or seventy-hour weeks for a salary much lower than they would get in a bigger consultancy firm. And they were cynical as to how necessary it was, because the chief consulting officer, who still worked directly with lots of clients, was not using the new process at all. When we spoke over Zoom, about two months into his new role, I could hear his frustration and disappointment. He felt he had been tasked with something impossible and, like many leaders,[1] felt he lacked the skills to achieve it.

Change is not, and never has been, easy. It keeps leaders awake at night and makes team members sad, angry, and fearful, making them extra hard to lead. And as the pace and quantity of change continue to increase, our need to be able to lead through it only grows. Elwood was experiencing this firsthand, fearful that this would become one of the 70 percent of change programs that fail.[2] Turning it around was certainly going to take some time, some resources, and some changes from senior stakeholders to demonstrate the importance of this change and encourage others to get on board. But it was not impossible.

This chapter discusses common issues with change leadership and ways to improve your leadership of it. This includes developing your individual skill at leading change and improving the organizational change environment. Let's go!

STATE THE PROBLEM

If you're having problems with leading change, you should try to work out roughly what is going on before going further into the details. This will help you to focus on solving the major problem. Answer these questions before you go further:

- **To what extent are you struggling to lead change?** With just one or two team members or with a whole team or wider group?
- **What appears to be the problem?** Some possibilities follow, but here, you should be looking to describe what is going on at a headline level.
  - The team is resisting or refusing to change.
  - The team is changing, but too slowly.
  - I feel scared of this change, as it's going to have a big, negative impact on me.
  - This change feels chaotic.
- **When does this change need to happen by?** Understanding how pressing the problem is may be important for working out just how severe the problem is and, later, in figuring out how decisively you may need to act.

OPEN THE BOX

Change is all about people, and so a problem with change universally comes back to a problem with people. Perhaps they are feeling sad, scared, afraid, bored, frustrated, or confused. Perhaps they have underbudgeted a project and so they can't initiate the change. Perhaps they are battling on with a change that clearly isn't working. There are a heap of reasons why change can't happen, but people lie at the bottom of all of them.

This does not mean that people are being intentionally difficult when they slow, block, or moan about change. It does not mean that they can just stop resisting and go with the flow. As you'll see, they are often scared, sad, or stressed by the changes that are being suggested and cannot see the benefits of them past their self-defensiveness or fear.

To move past these feelings and on to successful change leadership, you need to try to understand where their resistance is coming from, and this is what this section will work through.

They don't perceive the change to be necessary

While the change may be important and necessary, a staff member may not see it this way. Either they have not given it any prior thought, or they have discounted the need based on their experience and evidence. I have seen this regularly with team members who do not see the benefits of a new piece of technology—a new program, a new feature on Teams, a new system for logging invoices, a new way to get in touch with other colleagues. They may not be right, but they have not been shown persuasive evidence to the contrary.

If you have not explained why this change is needed, what it will help with, and what might happen without it, this could be a big part of the problem. The more information you can gather to work out why they don't perceive the change to be necessary, the easier it will be to counter it at the next stage, when you are laying out a solution.

The change will cause personal losses

During change, we often focus on losses rather than gains. This focus on protecting what we have has strong biological roots in protecting our food, our children, our living quarters. We can turn down great opportunities to work abroad, take a promotion, or switch functions because we are worried about quite minor losses (*I've got the best desk in the office! That won't be mine anymore*).[3] I worked with someone who wanted to turn down a really exciting career move that would have taken them to the countryside (with a huge garden) because they didn't want to leave behind their allotment in London! If a team member focuses on the personal losses that may arise from a change, then it is not a surprise that they may back away from that change.

A common fear is that a change will mean that they will lose respect or status. One interviewee talked of how she knew an organizational restructure needed to happen but that it would reduce her status significantly. She was okay with it because she could see the bigger picture, but some of her colleagues could not and acted as a barrier to the change by not handing in paperwork on time and not contributing to conversations about how to redistribute work under the new structure.

And another type of loss that causes resistance to change is that the change widens the perceived gap between a person's values and the values of the organization. Collaboration may be a key value for a team member, and they may feel that the new sales system places more of an emphasis on intra-team competition and individual merit. If their values feel threatened, it may lead to resistance.

Other losses that people may be scared of are loss of job, change of job title, reduction in pay and/or benefits, lowered status, loss of preferred tasks, reduced autonomy, fewer opportunities for career advancement, less access to senior leaders, reduced sense of community, and less free time.

Keep this section in mind as you try to figure out what team members are worried about losing. Working out what a team member feels they are going to lose in light of a change will be important to improving matters later in this chapter.

Individuals don't rate their ability to cope with this change

Workers often lack confidence in their own abilities to cope with change. This can come in two main forms: they can feel incapable of the new job requirements and/or they can feel that the change process itself is too much for them to handle.

It is common for people to feel that what the change requires is beyond them. Requirements to gain fresh knowledge, engage with unfamiliar technology, or move into a new team as part of a restructure can certainly place team members out of their comfort zone, which can cause resistance before, during, and after a change is implemented. In our conversation, Pete Thornton (former pricing manager at an international pharmaceutical firm) talked about a colleague who believed she would never be able to learn the technology that was being integrated into her work as part of the change and chose to leave instead of staying to see whether it was right for her.

It is also common for people to fear the process of change itself. The health and safety executive has identified that the process of organizational change, with all the uncertainty it brings, is one of the leading causes of stress at work.[4] It can feel better not to try to go through with the change than to try and fail, and then be held accountable for the potential mess that results. In the opening example of Elwood trying to get NarrativeLoom to standardize their processes, he told me how even very senior consultants seemed stressed with the process of change, worrying that learning the new systems alongside the juniors would make them seem less expert. Their fear was exacerbated because this was such an important project: the stakes were very high, as it was seen as a key action to enable the company to grow and to be bought by a larger consultancy practice. They did not want to be responsible for failure of the new process, so they just tried not to change at all![5]

Team members don't trust you (and the other leaders)

At times of change, team members need to trust leaders along three dimensions: They need to trust that the leader is competent at leading the change that is required. They need to believe that they have the required knowledge and skill to drive the change forward. They also need to feel that the leader has their backs and will not throw them under the bus if the change goes wrong. Leaders who have, in the past, blamed others for mistakes and not been supportive during difficult times will usually have more of a struggle to get their team onside with change.

If you are a new leader, you may also be starting from a disadvantage, as people have not seen your competence and support in play and so may not be prepared to hand over their trust as readily as you would like them to.

To understand if a lack of trust may be an issue, you should reflect on whether your team may lack trust in you or the other change leaders to drive the change forward. Do they perceive that you have the competence to drive this change through? Do they trust that you will look after them during the process in the ways that they feel they need? Warning signs will include questioning your decisions, looking cynical when you suggest a path, and turning to others for change guidance and support instead of you.

They're okay with the change, but the way isn't clear

Team members may be fine with change but be unclear *how* to change, being unsure of what's required of them. If a change initiative lacks clear direction, of course change will be hard! Does your team have clear objectives as to what is expected and a sense of why? And you may think it is clear, but check again—is it really? I've seen so often leaders who think they have been really clear, but when they take a critical look at what they've shared with their team, there is a lack of detail, a lack of achievable objectives, no timeline, or no sense of what it's all for.

And even if all of the above is clear, if you are saying that something needs to change, don't change yourself—this can be extremely confusing! Consider this: Tammi, a senior manager in sales at a software-as-a-service (SaaS) firm, was upset when her effort to encourage collaboration among sales teams for cross-selling failed. She thought her clear meeting updates, new appraisal process, and set objectives would be enough to drive the change. But no one was changing. I asked her to talk me through her day. She said that she typically greeted her team, then headed to her office to talk to her clients, have meetings with them, and deepen relationships and sell more products. I asked how often she brought team members into the conversations, and she paused. "They're well-established relationships. They should be working on new relationships." As she said it, the penny dropped. She realized that her actions must be confusing to her team. They were expected to work together while she carried on working alone. Moreover, almost all of them had come from very individualistic sales roles and probably didn't have the first clue how to collaborate. They needed clarity from her on what it looked like in practice. But she wasn't giving it—she was working solo.

Are you expecting your team to change without making the way clear? Have you neglected to give them a good change process or objectives, or have you failed to model the behaviors that you want to see from them as a result of the change?

The processes and/or systems aren't in place for change to happen

In contrast to our biases against many changes, if we do buy into a change, we are almost endearingly optimistic about it. Our biases lead us, repeatedly, to underestimate the costs of a project and the time it will take, and to overestimate how great the change will be.[6] This significantly reduces the chances of the change succeeding, as people run out of enthusiasm, or budget, before the change is completed.

A common complaint from leaders I've coached is that IT, HR, marketing, and the other support functions don't have the capacity to support the short-term workload change from implementing and training on a new system, or the longer-term change. If you haven't brought these stakeholders into your conversations about the change and the impacts it may have on them, this could be problematic.

Consider whether you or other leaders have been overly optimistic about the change and if this has led or will lead to problems. Is the budget right, is the timescale right, will the change really be able to achieve what you have claimed, and are the support functions able to support during the change and after?

BEFORE MOVING ON:

- What is holding up the change you're hoping for?
- Do you have any initial thoughts about how to get the change moving?

FIT THE CONTEXT: CHANGE IN PUBLIC BUREAUCRACIES

If you work in a large public bureaucracy, such as government or public administration, you may find change even harder to instigate. There are potentially very good reasons for this: despite serving an audience that may be as diverse as the country they operate in, with varying levels of literacy, computer access, and cynicism of the government, they have to be seen to be scrupulously fair.

The onerous paperwork and processes that come with this—to safeguard and demonstrate fair access and consideration for all—can slow down change enormously. Any attempts to suggest or undertake a large-scale change require such extensive consideration to make sure no one is unfairly discriminated against and that the process is followed that it becomes too cumbersome for a mere mortal to take on. And so things stay the same.

What starts as a suggestion that the box on a housing form should be changed from a free text box into a checklist becomes a six-month debate over whether this change would remove a sense of choice from those looking for housing in a way that might lead to them feeling less heard. This is despite the form currently running to thirty-two pages and the team having to skim the answers anyway, as there is too much to read if they are to stay on top of the paperwork!

By the time someone is brave enough (or cross enough) to drive a bigger change forward, such as a new IT system, the change is so overdue because no one has made smaller changes along the way that the process is huge and totally overwhelming. If someone had been brave enough to shave down the thirty-two-page housing form a few years earlier, then there wouldn't be a need to streamline it simultaneously to launching the new online system, which can't handle data as complicated as the form contains. And so the big change, coming way later than it should have, creates lots of unintended consequences along the way.

We can see why people in public bureaucracies are often cast as disliking change: they see it as ugly, drawn out, chaotic, and adding a heavy additional workload.

Being aware of the added challenges and pressures of change in large bureaucracies can be important for a leader in these settings, wondering why the change process is so hard. You may well have it harder than others, and the barriers to change are likely much higher than average. As you start to think through solutions, you will want to pay particular attention to the elements that relate to process change.

LAY OUT YOUR SOLUTION

Now is the time to formulate a plan for improvement, focused on two main areas: developing your skills as a change leader and creating better circumstances for change.

Grow your transformational leadership skills

Of all the change factors, the one most in your control is how you, as a change leader, act.

Research has shown repeatedly that adopting particular change leadership behaviors—together labeled the *transformational leadership approach*—can help. We'll use Bernard Bass's version,[7] the efficacy of which is well researched. It comprises four easy-to-remember elements: inspirational motivation, individualized consideration, idealized influence, and intellectual stimulation (the four *i*'s):

Inspirational motivation	*Individualized consideration*
• *Tapping into the emotions and values of team members to drive the change* • *Encouraging, motivating, and supporting change*	• *Listening to and working with the individual wants, needs, and concerns of team members*
Idealized influence	***Intellectual stimulation***
• *Walking the talk* • *Acting as a role model for the change*	• *Encouraging team members to challenge their views, to innovate, and to think creatively*

Improving the four *i*'s will improve the quality of your change leadership and increases employee acceptance of and satisfaction with change.[8]

To work on developing your transformational leadership:

ENHANCE YOUR *INSPIRATIONAL MOTIVATION*

This means engaging team members emotionally with the change. It can be useful to perceive this element of leadership as being a "persuasion campaign,"[9] doing what you can to show that, without change, the organization will collapse, but with it, it can survive and thrive. You are essentially looking to tell a story that contains some or all of the following parts:

- What the company stands for (make it the hero of the story).
- The problem it faces (what monster does it have to slay or hill does it have to climb?).
- What might happen if it does not succeed against the problem (likely death or exhaustion from monster fighting or hill climbing).

- How it can overcome its problems (how will it kill the monster or climb the hill?).
- The positive future that will exist when the problems are overcome (what will the victory be like?).

You can also enhance inspirational motivation by celebrating small points of success along the change path, especially if the path is long. Using regular check-ins to mark and celebrate successes can be extremely motivating, as it encourages the flow of positive emotions and gets people happy and excited about success so far. With bigger milestones, celebrate in bigger ways—for example, a team lunch, a thank-you note, or a small well-done gift on everyone's desk. Celebrating wins provides a helpful confidence boost for those who are worried about their abilities to change.

ENHANCE YOUR *INDIVIDUALIZED CONSIDERATION*

It's so important not to make the assumption that everyone will be feeling the same way about the change. Ellie Mulcahy, a former employee of the Centre for Education and Youth (CfEY), a think tank focused on improving education for young people, said that during her tenure, she saw staff members perceived and reacted to a change in CEO in very different ways from one another. Some were instantly okay with it, and others needed warming up to this new person, who had different aspirations for the organization.

Ellie noticed that the team leaders who listened to their team members and understood how they individually felt about the change were quicker to regain the engagement of their team. Part of this was simply the listening—with the team member feeling heard and as though someone had taken the time to listen to their concerns. But it also meant that opportunities presented themselves for those team leaders who listened to their team members to help them come to terms with the change. For example, if a team member was reticent because they were worried that there was going to be a big change from the new CEO, the team leader could allay their concerns, showing how for the most part processes were going to remain the same. And for those that were going to change, the team leader was able to ask for support for her team as they learned the new process, as well as sharing with them why she thought the process was changing, so they could be more comfortable with the shift. The individualized consideration that they showed—and which you should look to show—can prompt greater team acceptance of change through feeling validated.

Showing individualized consideration is about treating your team members as individuals during the change process, learning what they need by listening carefully to them. You can then find ways, within what is realistic, to factor in their needs and to improve the change or the change process for them. You don't need to take action on everything they need, but you can factor them in where possible, increasing their trust in you and their ability to get behind the change.

ENHANCE YOUR *IDEALIZED INFLUENCE*

Do what you expect others to. Tammi, the sales director in the SaaS firm I mentioned earlier, realized her error in not modeling the change and moved out of her solo office into the open-plan space. She gave her office over to be a team meeting room and committed to bringing others to client meetings. This prompted other team members to share clients and cross-sell, and cross-selling increased by around a fifth in the first year. This leader moved from being an obstacle to change to walking the talk brilliantly and showing what others should do.

Your seniors (if you are not in the C-suite) can help, too, by modeling behaviors and showing public support for the initiative. In Honeywell, the engineering firm, the chair was not directly involved in every step of the digital transformation program. However, by running the monthly meetings and operating reviews, he found a powerful way to show that he cared about the digital transformation sufficiently to sponsor it in a significant way and to clarify the process on a regular basis and thus smooth the transition.[10]

ENHANCE YOUR *INTELLECTUAL STIMULATION*

Change leaders need to prompt team members to challenge old ways of doing things and explore the possibilities of innovation and trying something new. This can be as simple as asking, "What if we were to do this in a different way?" all the way up to running large-scale workshops getting team members involved in exploring and planning change.

McKinsey research advocates spreading responsibility for change initiatives widely across the organization, up, down, and across the hierarchy. This means the change doesn't get stuck with a few people who are too busy to drive it. It spreads the seeds of change further and makes them harder to ignore.[11] Ellie Mulcahy has seen how beneficial it can be to give people a role in driving a change process forward. When she was at CfEY, she divided out tasks such as researching alternatives and found the team was more motivated to change because they had meaningfully contributed to the process.

Spread the responsibility for change around your team. Give someone responsibility for the new documentation, give someone else responsibility for keeping track of the OKRs, divide out the task of keeping stakeholders informed, get someone else to form a project team with IT and HR to figure out how they'll integrate the change, and keep asking questions that you don't have the answers to. In particular, there's value in these three, at all stages of change:

- How could we improve this process/thing/department/task?
- What do you think we need to do to get this change moving?
- How do you think we're succeeding? What else is needed?

FIT THE CONTEXT: BEING A NEW LEADER WHO'S TASKED WITH MAJOR CHANGE

Often, senior leaders are recruited because they have the skill set to handle a change that the company believes is needed. However, because staff do not know them very well, they are often greeted with cynicism and change resistance. This is because there is low trust in their abilities.

At NarrativeLoom, one of Elwood's major challenges was that he was new and people did not have a sense of his competence or that he was going to protect them if anything was difficult or went wrong.

If you are a new leader charged with change, you may want to consider requesting a slowdown on the change process until you can establish trust. I think it's one of the major reasons why the idea of not doing anything much for your first ninety days in a senior leadership role has been embraced. This approach encourages you to do lots of listening, getting to know the company, building relationships, and establishing your expertise.

I would add to this that it can be helpful to undertake a few small, low-stakes changes and show that you care about people during these and that you follow through to a successful result.

These elements paired—relationship building and demonstrating competence at change—will create a much better platform for the major change you've been asked to deliver, meaning it's more successful and actually takes less time overall, as you've had to deal with much less resistance.

Alongside improving your change leadership, you should focus on the broader change context and what else you can do to enable successful change. I think there are three major areas on which to focus your attention.

Conduct change premortems

A well-organized change is one that comes in on time and on budget. Reduce the chances of coming in over time and over budget by conducting a change premortem.

Prior to green-lighting a change program, you should assemble a small team of diverse people who see the organizational context from a different perspective from yours. That might be people from different functions, different levels of seniority, and with different views of the world. Together, you should imagine yourselves at a point in the future where this change has not worked out as planned. It is as though you are assembled around the cadaver of this change program. You are looking down at its lifeless body and trying to work out what went wrong. You should ask yourself the following questions:

- What went wrong?
- What caused it to go wrong?
- Could we have done anything to stop it from going wrong?

You can repeat this exercise, looking at many ways the change could go wrong. You may need lots of coffee and cake to handle the gloom (both key tools in a leader's arsenal!), but it'll be worth it, because then you can consider what you can do to prevent project failure. Is it waiting until you have better processes? Or do you need to plan for the change to take longer, or to take up more of people's time? Do you need to find the budget for a new system to support the change? Do you need to rewrite people's employment contracts before you begin the change process? What else needs to be done to grow your confidence that the change can work? A change that is well planned has much better chances of success, and a premortem can help significantly with this.

Help good habits form

Change is often about breaking habits and starting new ones, which can be very hard. According to change-making experts Chip and Dan Heath, you can make it easier by "scripting the critical moves." This way everyone is crystal clear on what behavior is expected and when. If you want people to spend less time in internal meetings, don't tell them, "Have fewer internal meetings," which can be hard to implement. How? What should they cut? Instead, say, "Don't book internal meetings on Fridays"; "Make sure internal meetings are twenty minutes [instead of half an hour] or forty-five minutes [instead of an hour]"; and "Every meeting needs an agenda circulated at least one hour before the meeting, or the meeting is canceled." The critical moves are scripted so that there is no room to wiggle out of this new way of doing things, and it's clear what needs to be done to create the new behavior.

Now you can reflect: Which elements of your change process can be scripted? How can you create a clear script that prompts behavior change and makes what needs to be done crystal clear?

Be okay to iterate

Despite premortems, careful planning, and great leadership, change rarely goes entirely according to plan. As this is almost inevitable, seeing change as iterative prepares you to monitor and improve on change implementation, continually finding ways to pivot where things aren't working.

Address this from the earliest stages in language and planning. Introduce measurements and feedback on the change process. Have regular scheduled review points, and be aware of the data points you can use to inform your decision. This will help to reassure your team that even the unplanned elements of change are, as much as they can be, a part of your plan!

I recently ran a workshop for the twenty-five-strong senior leadership team of one of the fastest-growing financial technology companies. Less than a handful of the team had started a year earlier. They had been tasked with creating a team charter by the exec team as to how they would work together. They wanted to create a perfect blueprint of how and to change exactly in line with it, but due to the enormous change and growth expected in the company, and the senior leadership team size, over the coming year, I encouraged them to think about it as a document and change process, which would need to be iterative. They could start on the journey toward working that way, but they may well need to pivot as the situation changed and expectations shifted. It's important to be ready to iterate as the situation shifts. In the time since I last saw them, the structure of the company has changed again, but rather than being sent back to square one, they are able to carry on with adapting and iterating their documents, their processes, and their view of themselves as a team in a way that is in keeping with where they are now expected to be.

Rather than seeing change as a straight line from start to finish, instead seeing it as a wiggly line, and understanding that sometimes the end point you're heading for will move, too, will help to increase bravery and lower tension.

FIT THE CONTEXT: PIVOTING AGAIN IN AN ORGANIZATION WITH CHANGE FATIGUE

Some companies and industries are in a constant state of flux and feel as though they are constantly pivoting from one change initiative to the next. One training company I used to be an associate lecturer for went through three significantly different organizational structures, lean management, kaizen, and three different managing directors in the course of three years. When they suggested another structural change to the training team, many of them rolled their eyes and said, "Oh, really?" But it turned out to be the big one—the one that the training provider stuck with after all those previous abortive attempts to improve. But it took them so long to get everyone around to seeing it as the big one because they were fed up! It could have turned out to be just another thing.

If you are in a company that has been through a lot of change, how can you help your employees get behind the latest initiative or pivot?

- Start by acknowledging your employees' concerns about "another change"—explain that you see it from their perspective and that you know there has been a lot going on.
- Try to remove or minimize any other changes that are still rumbling on—can they be rolled into this change program, mothballed, or downgraded in importance? If so, make sure that you show respect for what has already been done, and if possible, find ways of showing how that important work needed to be done to get to this place and the effort has not been in vain.
- Provide well-being services not as a direct response to the change but as part of the landscape to help build employees' resilience and coping mechanisms for dealing with the stress of constant change. Signal through these initiatives that you know it has taken a toll and these are there not to apply more pressure but hopefully to help with and relieve some of the stress.

BEFORE MOVING ON:

- How will you improve your leadership of change?
- What is your time frame for improvement?
- How will you measure your success and iterate if necessary?

VENTURE FORTH!

Hopefully, your transformational leadership actions and your efforts to improve the conditions in which the change is happening will make a quick, positive difference that you can continue to work on. However, there can be further problems during the change process. Here are some common obstacles and suggestions on how to overcome them.

If the change needs to happen quicker than your efforts are allowing... consider if it's time for a little push

Wherever you can, to get people onside and keep them onside, you need change to be collaborative. But where you are not getting results, and time is critical, you may have no choice but to push the change through. To reduce the negative impacts of this, you should:

1. Continue to acknowledge peoples' wants, fears, and other emotions, even if you can't factor them into your actions. Show that they are heard.
2. Explain why you have to make the choices that you do. This is about underlining the urgency that is driving you to force through change. The company is failing. Without this change, we will not survive.
3. Show gratitude for any signs that people are trying to come on the change journey with you.
4. Resist, at all costs, showing any personal unhappiness with or resistance to the change. Showing any dissatisfaction on your part—even as a concession—will act as a justification to keep refusing to change. You can listen to their dissatisfaction (to a degree—don't take it too far), but don't suggest you share it.
5. Show an appropriate level of enthusiasm for change successes. If this change is angering, saddening, or scaring people, ululating from the top of your desk may go down badly. But you

will want to highlight that the efforts are paying off with positive results to grow confidence in the change. Acknowledge that it may still be hard for some.

If people can't find time to change... clear space

Keeping on top of day-to-day work can squeeze out the change agenda. If you need people to take on a lot of extra work or take on some extra work for a long time to enable the change, you'll need to find time for them. What, in their workload, can be paused or delegated?

This might also be a really good opportunity to look at whether elements of your team's roles can be assisted by AI. For example, can the weekly report-writing task be reduced from three hours to one by running the data through AI software, which can translate it into the standard template that is used? I suggest this here because, if you are already undergoing change, then you may be able to introduce this change that many are currently resisting (and are likely to continue resisting for a while) by fiat.

Once you are confident that they have time to do the work, give clear, realistic objectives to ensure focus on the critical elements. Again, scripting the critical moves as clearly as you can will help here. Be prepared to revisit their objectives and their workload if they still feel overwhelmed.

ELEVATE YOUR LEARNING

If you've had successes with the change process, you can now look at how to harness these to your further advantage.

If you've seen the value of transformational leadership... incorporate it into your daily conversations

Transformational leadership is effective outside of change scenarios,[12] allowing leaders to bring the best out in their staff. If you like the idea of being a more transformational leader in your daily work, I recommend looking at how you can weave transformational approaches into the way you talk to and with your team members.

To weave in inspirational motivation: Start or conclude team meetings by reminding people why you're all there. You may have a holding slide that captures the mission or vision of your team and that everyone sees as they enter or leave the meeting. In the meeting, remind people what the purpose of the team is, and link sections of the meeting to these inspirational elements. For example, if you are an IT innovation leader and an element of your team's mission is to come up with creative solutions to internal IT problems, you could ask for a summary of anything anyone has done that week to achieve it, or frame an item on the agenda, such as an update, in terms of celebrating how much closer it has gotten you to that goal. If things have gone less well, you can remind the team of the mission and why it's important to keep working toward it, because you want an organization where the IT hotline never rings.

To weave in individualized consideration: Remember to check in with individual team members and get to know them. Whether this is scheduling monthly coffees or taking a couple of minutes each day you have a call with them to ask them how they're doing, find ways to understand the world from their perspective. You may have a question that you ask everyone this week—what job did your ten-year-old self think you would do as a grown-up? What do you like most about this role? How is your family? Keep a note of important dates and key areas of interest for each employee so you can be reminded of who they are as a person when you are making decisions that affect them.

To weave in idealized influence: Show people what you care about and increase your likability (which also increases your influence, as per Problem 3: Influence) by praising team members who act in line with the way that you try to act. You can say, "I really appreciate you taking the time to run this team workshop. You know how much I care about having a cohesive, engaged team, and the effort you've put in is brilliant. Thank you." This reiterates your values, encourages people to emulate your behavior, and makes people want to follow the example that you set.

To weave in intellectual stimulation: Take a coaching approach when your team members come to you with questions. Rather than offering them the answer, ask them what they would do if you weren't around to ask, as you have faith that they could already solve this problem. If they say, "I don't know," ask this brilliant but slightly odd question: "What would you do if you did know?" While they've just told you they don't, it's amazing how, when you ask people to imagine they do know, they come up with suggestions for a solution. It's as though you are liberating them from their own self-criticism.

If you want to be more comfortable with change... get yourself out of your comfort zone more frequently

Resilience is like a muscle—you can strengthen it with exercise. If you have seen, through a change process, that you or others struggle with change, increase your capacity to cope through practice. Find opportunities to push your comfort zone. A way to script this in your life is by defaulting to say yes in the face of new or challenging experiences (rather than defaulting to no). This is the reason that many companies ask stand-up comedians to come in to teach employees improvisation skills. With improvisation, you don't ever say no—if someone presents you with a strange situation, you add to it and build on it with "Yes, and..." Try that strange sandwich filling on offer in the cafeteria, get involved in that new project, and go and try out that after-work skipping class your friend has invited you to. All these minor actions force you to take risks, and not to close down interesting avenues and opportunities. Practically, what you are looking to do with improvisation, or meeting new people, or learning a new language, or expanding your skill set is to increase your adaptability, risk-taking, and resilience. Developing the ability to cope when you are out of control can help when you find yourself in a future change situation. What activities could you seek out or say yes to in order to increase your tolerance for change?

This chapter opened with the case of Elwood, at NarrativeLoom, struggling to implement a new set of consultancy processes. As I got to know the firm Elwood was working for, and he did, too, we recognized that key to getting the change integrated was getting the senior consultants to embrace the process. They weren't trying to be difficult—they were feeling confused and scared.

First, Elwood worked with the person who had asked to head up the process change to "script the change," laying out precisely when each document should be used and how. Then he provided training in layers—with the senior consultants receiving the training away from the juniors so they could be vulnerable and show when they "didn't get it" without feeling as though they were losing face or failing.

Whenever someone subsequently ran into a problem with the process, no matter their level, Elwood asked them to come to him directly, ideally with a suggestion of what to do that could be added to the process. He used intellectual stimulation and scripting the change to increase comfort with the change and win buy-in.

It helped that Elwood was an excellent storyteller who could give impassioned off-the-cuff speeches around the office about how, if they did not follow the process, they would become less good at the core work than their competitors and fail. But if they did follow the process, he believed they would win really big work, and it would mean they could work on exciting, creative projects on a scale they rarely won at the moment. People could see what he meant, and this also helped. And he was right—within six months, they had gained three really large contracts with multinational companies, which excited them greatly. They credited the clarity that the new process had given them with this success.

REMEMBER:

- Individuals can have very different reasons for not getting behind a change—treating them as individuals and trying to understand what is happening for them is key to working out how to improve the situation.
- Change can be overwhelming and difficult, and people will look for reasons to avoid it and to keep doing things the way they are. You need to provide a context for the change that makes the change as easy as possible to implement.
- Skills of transformational leadership—inspiring people to change (inspirational motivation), treating them as individuals (individualized consideration), acting as a role model who walks the talk when it comes to change (idealized influence), and challenging them to think and act differently (intellectual stimulation)—can all increase the chances of change success.

CONCLUSION

How to SOLVE Your Other Leadership Problems

SIMON IS A LEADER YOU MET WAY BACK IN THE INTRODUCTION TO THIS book. He's a chief commercial officer in a consultancy and training firm whom I coached recently. I talked about how his company can afford me when times are good and when he least needs my help, but how when times are tough, that's when he needs me the most but isn't allowed to use any budget for coaching and how this is a common pattern I see.

At the start of this book, I promised that, by the end, you would be able to coach your way through your leadership problems yourself. And I have talked through the ten most common ones I see leaders struggle with. I have seen Simon struggle with at least half the problems I've covered here.

But he, and you, will face plenty of problems that aren't in the pages of this book. That's because leadership is complex and surprising, and it throws up all kinds of challenges that I haven't even mentioned here. Whether you've read this book cover to cover or focused on the areas you currently need help with, you'll know I chose ten major leadership problem types for this book. I picked ten that are both common and tricky to handle. But my choice still leaves plenty of other problems that leaders face and that you may be facing, too! There will be all sorts of other things that land on your desk, people who come into your office furious, situations that you do not know how to handle.

Some of the "other" problems that people have written to Dear Katie about in the past year include:

- How do I handle a boss who's a bully?
- What do I do if I hate being a leader?
- How can I still be an effective leader after a transatlantic flight?
- How do I support a team member who is terminally ill?
- How do I make four days a week work?
- How do I deal with a condescending team member?

This chapter will guide you through how to use the SOLVE method to work through problems that are not covered in this book. I'll step through each letter of the acronym, as per the other chapters, but show you what to do when you get to that stage and you haven't already got the research and guidance that I've provided in the other chapters.

STATE THE PROBLEM

You think you have a problem in a particular area, but you're not sure. What is going on?

To set out your problem, you'll know by now that you need to be able to state it in two or three sentences max. You should try to cover what the problem seems to be and whom it relates to.

If you are struggling to express it, try thinking which of these common leadership problem categories it falls in:

- **Clash/conflict:** Is it a clash or conflict between two or more ideas, teams, or areas?
- **Too little:** Is there too little of something that's needed at work? It could be something like trust or motivation, or it could be a lack of skills or knowledge.
- **Too much:** Is it that you or someone else is overdoing something (e.g., too hard, too soft, too slow, too grumpy, etc.)?

- **Mistakes being made:** Has something gone wrong and you need to do something about it?
- **Bad feelings:** You or someone else is feeling sad, bad, frustrated, anxious, troubled, or some other negative emotion about work or an element of work, which is having an impact.
- **Bad processes:** The processes you have are not right for the situation—which is a problem in itself and may be causing further problems.

OPEN THE BOX

In the observation phase, you're looking to make use of what you already know about the situation, while also deepening your understanding of the problem itself and exploring what is known—through other people's research and experiences—about these types of problems.

The biggest mistake that leaders make when trying to figure out a problem is relying only on what they already know—meaning their perspective is very limited. It is as if you were sitting at your desk and felt a twinge in your knee, and without standing up, putting pressure on it, moving it, consulting a doctor, or looking online for ideas to what it might be, you decided it was definitely a broken kneecap. Seeing a problem at work and acting based purely on your gut understanding is like diagnosing your knee without seeking to grow your knowledge base at all. There are two main ways to gather more information on a problem: carry out your own research, and look at the research that others have done.

Undertaking your own research

To try to understand the problem in more detail, you will also want to carry out some firsthand research. As a leader looking to understand what's going on quickly but effectively, you'll be best served by these methods:

- **Interviewing (or chatting):** If you want to understand what is happening with your team members, ask them! You don't have to use interviewing in a formal sense, but talk to them, ask them questions, and listen carefully to the answers. See how their answers differ from one another and start to build up a pattern of what's happening.
- **Observations (or watching):** If you're trying to understand relationships, processes, or people that aren't quite working in the way they should, use your eyes and ears to pay attention more than you normally would. Combine with asking some questions if you can't work out what is happening.
- **Using preexisting data:** Companies are increasingly becoming data houses, with our digital lives leaving traces of how we work everywhere. Additionally, we increasingly ask staff to fill in surveys and provide feedback on what this company is like to work with. There is so much data already out there that might help you to fill in the gaps in your knowledge. If you are unsure how hard a team member is working, is there a way to check their computer usage? If your team seems more disengaged than last year, can you check by comparing year-to-year data from the staff survey, isolated to your team? Worried about downsizing the office to save money? Can you use staff pass data to work out who's in when?
- **Questionnaires:** If you don't already have data on how things are for your team and want a quick, sweeping view that you can potentially take action on, it's never been easier to issue a survey. Your company will almost certainly have a subscription to surveying software, or there

are plenty of free versions you can use. Think about using scales and measures to make the data quantitative so you can look for improvements over time.

Much of this is just about dialing up your skills of observation—what can you see, what can you hear, and what can you ask or do to improve the detail and quality of what you see and hear? It's really the same skill set as is needed to be a great leader.

To be a really good leader, you need to be a psychologist, a sociologist, a behavioral scientist, a social scientist, and all the rest because you need to be able to read what's going on for your people and be able to benchmark it compared to others and across time.

If you're looking for a powerful image to remind you to listen more and talk less, think about needing to be an elephant and not a hippo! An elephant has a small mouth but big ears that are always ready to listen. In contrast, a hippo has tiny ears and a huge mouth ready to talk.[1] By thinking of the need to be an elephant, you can remember that the skills of observation will make your actions much more powerful when you take them, and this is true for leadership problem-solving especially.

All this observing will give you plenty of data, in which you can look for themes and patterns. Can it tell you what's going on and give you more detail? What is it all telling you? What does the problem seem to be?

Before moving on, you should try to rewrite your problem statement, this time being clear on what you think is causing the problem, as this is where you will want to target your efforts when you start to lay out your solution.

Looking at the research that others have done

There is a potentially bewildering amount of information available about leadership, management, and their related challenges. Search up almost any leadership problem you face and you'll find that there are many articles out there already on the topic. However, many of these are just "content," which is recycled from other content and not based on any decent evidence. If you are going to do a good job of understanding this research from someone else's perspectives, you should focus your search on the following resources:

- **Mainstream academic output:** *Harvard Business Review* (print and online), *MIT Sloan Management Review*, the Conversation, LSE Business Review.
- **Robust newspaper and magazine content:** The *Times of London*, the *Financial Times*, the *New York Times*, the *Economist*, and commercial reports: Deloitte, EY, PwC, KPMG, Bain, Gallup, CIPD, McKinsey, some Forbes content (check the profile of the author to see whether they have the authority to talk about the issue in question).
- **Academic research:** Go to Google Scholar and search the topic. This can, however, present too much of a deep dive for what you actually need.
- **Textbooks:** Undergrad and MBA textbooks on the major topics from which leadership problems emerge can be extremely helpful.

For each subject, there are some classic textbooks that are regularly updated to give you a comprehensive guide to the major topics in that field. So if you're struggling with particular problem types, here are my recommendations:

- **Human psychology/behavior:** Look for books on organizational behavior. The leading writers are David Buchanan and Andrzej Huczynski; Laurie Mullins and Gary Rees; and Stephen Robbins and Timothy Judge.

- **Leadership:** There are heaps of books out there, but you want ones with good coverage of a range of ideas and theories rather than those wedded to just one model of their own. Leading writers include Peter Northouse and Gary Yukl.
- **Practical issues of staff management:** Look for books on human resource management, where the dominant textbooks are written by Michael Armstrong, Catherine Truss, and Julie Beardwell.
- **Issues with the strategic parts of leadership:** You'll want textbooks that look at the theory and practice of strategy. You cannot go wrong with any textbook that has Richard Whittington as one of the authors (just make sure it's a textbook as opposed to a general book on strategy—you want something with six-hundred-plus pages!).
- **Issues with the change elements of leadership:** These are covered well in the strategy, organizational behavior, and leadership books above.

LAY OUT YOUR SOLUTION

You will usually find, in reading about the problem and in observing and talking to others, solutions start to emerge.

Therefore, by the time you lay out your solution, you should already have some idea of where you want to focus your attention.

As you'll have seen in the "Lay Out Your Solution" sections in the previous chapters, you'll want solutions that deal with the causes of the problem. So if you have a problem with your boss and you've worked out it's because they are too rushed in their meetings with you, you will want to help to slow them down. What could you do so that they come to your meetings less rushed? What does the research suggest? How do those ideas resonate with you? Which of them might work for your setting, possibly with some adaptions?

Match to the context: What might impact?

Throughout, I've been pointing out to you when a particular situation may require a different approach. It's very important, when you are laying out a solution, that you think about how your setting may have an impact on the solution and whether you need to adapt it to make it work.

COMPANY FACTORS

Size of company: The size of a company will generally influence how flexible they can be, how quick they are to make decisions, and also how they choose to spend money. For example, small companies will generally have more flexibility over what can be done because they are less constrained by bureaucracy. However, they may also feel that they have less "money in the pot" and so spend less per staff member on engagement initiatives because they need to use the money to safeguard their future or to grow.

Industry/profit/not-for-profit: The type of work they do, including the industry and whether it's for profit, will affect on what basis decisions are made, what is seen to be important, and what is expected of you as a leader. For example, a government body will be answerable to the general public and so may have to justify more carefully the use of money for a new initiative. A company in the IT industry may see high levels of research as business critical and as such spend far more on them than a company in the recruitment industry, where there is much less need for innovation.

Maturity of company: Whether a company is in start-up, scale-up, steady growth, maturity, or decline may impact how quickly decisions can be made, how easily they can release resources for projects, and how entrenched their culture is. If you're faced with needing to get the green light on a new way of working with clients to improve the performance of your team, you'll potentially get a quicker answer from a company that is focused on growth than from one that is mature, happy with the current way of doing things, and has a set process.

TEAM FACTORS

Size of team: Team size will impact coordination between members and your control as a leader. If you are leading a very big team, you may find it harder to check over their work, and as such, if a solution requires high levels of coaching, they may need to find additional resources to help with this, such as training a more senior team member to coach junior members.

Maturity of team: Team maturity will shape how established (or entrenched) their culture is and often how well organized they are. Newer teams may still be finding their feet and could be battling over who does what and how. Solutions that are radical may land more easily in a new team where things are less established.

Team dynamics: Whether the team has different factions, whether or not the members are good at working together, and how they make decisions will all influence the solution you choose and how specifically you apply it. For example, if a team member is known to be highly influential, you may try to win them over to the solution before rolling it out to others.

INDIVIDUAL TEAM MEMBER FACTORS

Skill/knowledge/engagement levels: Someone's skill at a job, their knowledge of relevant topics, and their enthusiasm for and therefore engagement with work will all impact the solutions that may work (or not!). For example, having low skill may mean that you cannot suggest a solution that requires them to be very independent, as they will need higher-than-average supervision.

How they feel about your leadership: If they see you as a good leader and are happy to follow you, you may have more leeway to suggest solutions than someone who is more cynical of your leadership or is less keen to follow you for another reason.

Practical job elements / contract details: Being four days a week, on a temporary contract, on pay-for-performance, a bonus structure, and the like could all impact what you can suggest for someone. For example, being on a temporary contract may mean that you do not want to invest lots of money in skills training, as you will then lose this investment when their contract ends.

LEADERSHIP FACTORS

Your experience: If you're a very experienced leader, you may be more confident in making bold decisions and have the confidence that drives your team to follow you. If you bring in experience from other roles or sectors, you may be able to find ways to make changes and implement solutions that could be good but may require more persuasion, as it's "not how things are normally done around here."

Your power: If you have a high level of power—whether formal (due to your place in the hierarchy) or informal (due to having good relationships or a lot of charisma, for example), you may be more able to apply solutions that do not initially appear popular.

Your default leadership approach: Each leader will have a style of leadership, and no matter how it can be described (consultative, delegating, dominant, paternalistic, coaching, kind, abrupt, friendly, practical, etc.), it will influence what you feel comfortable doing and what others will permit you to do. As you consider solutions, you will want to think about how you are as a leader and whether that might help or hinder what you hope to achieve.

Remember the individual

While you will often be leading a team, you should think about the impacts of solutions that you come up with on individuals, as people will react differently. Although it may take time, consider how your solution will land with each person, and in particular, think about:

WHAT MATTERS TO EACH INDIVIDUAL?

We are all motivated by different things, so consider what will drive them to want to work with or toward this solution. Winning hearts is as important (or more important?) as winning minds, so thinking about your solution through the lens of what they care about deeply will be critical to working out if this solution is likely to work for them.

WHAT WILL THEY GAIN AS A RESULT?

How will they be better off as a result of the solution? This is not about overplaying the upsides but rather explaining to them how (if at all) this solution will help them with their problems. You can also talk about how it's going to make life better for their colleagues in particular ways and how this may have a secondary benefit for them, too.

WHAT WILL THEY LOSE?

Be prepared to listen to this and explore it with them honestly if they would like to. You do not need to highlight problems they have not thought of, as they may not be important to them, but you should be okay with talking about any downsides they can see. Remember a key part of this is listening and empathizing. There may be areas that you can't help them with, but listening may help them to calm down about it and give it a try. Note the word *may*—this is not a guarantee.

PUTTING IT ALL IN BALANCE

If you are implementing a solution that has negative impacts on some and positive impacts on others, you will want to check that it's of sufficient benefit for the downsides to be okay and to think about how you might address those downsides with further elements to your solution. For example, if you realize you need a new hybrid working policy to make it fairer across the team, this may benefit some and disadvantage others. You know, overall, that you do need a new policy, but it's going to disadvantage those people who were working entirely from home. Can you help the solution to land by having a gradual adoption process over the next year, to get people used to the idea? Can you make those days in the office flexible so that people can choose which days of the week to come in for and which hours to work on those days to avoid rush hour?

VENTURE FORTH!

At this stage, your plan is being executed, and hopefully things are going well. It's normal, however, for a solution to hit some problems. So often, problem-solving methodologies focus on coming up with the perfect solution and offer little support for these later stages. But you should by now be aware that your solution may hit obstacles and be prepared to handle these as well as you can.

There are some common approaches you can take to try to head off problems as you implement your plan.

Conduct a premortem

As we discussed in Problem 10: Leading Change, a premortem is when you make the assumption that the solution has failed. As though it were a dead body on the coroner's slate, you are looking down at the failed bones and sinew of the project, trying to work out what went wrong. Except you're doing that before you even apply the solution. What could be the issues with this solution? What could you do to try to head off any problems? How could you handle these problems if they do come up?

Look for bright spots and try to replicate them

Often, a solution will work at least in part. You will have what might be called "bright spots" where the solution has really done the job. Looking for these bright spots allows you to identify where things are going well, try to ascertain why, and see if you can replicate this success in other places. It's essentially about doubling down on your solution—if it really does feel like the right thing to do—and working harder to get it to land. For example, if you had instigated a plan that everyone was going to keep Wednesday afternoons clear in their calendars and it had a positive impact, can they also keep the first Friday of every month free, too?

Diagnose the new problem

Here, research is going to be your friend, so you can work out what hasn't worked and what new problem now exists, and start to find new solutions. Essentially, it is the SOLVE process again, but often because it's a much smaller problem that pops out, it's not nearly as much work, and can usually be addressed quite quickly. When you are doing the research, if you are talking to team members, you'll need to be aware that they could be sad, fearful, or annoyed about the solution that isn't working and its potential impacts on them. Extra doses of empathy will be required in your listening exercise if this is the case.

ELEVATE YOUR LEARNING

Finally, when your solution has worked, you should be looking for ways that you can further use the skills and knowledge that you've built up as a result of your good work at solving this problem.

There are four major directions you can go in as you look to elevate your learning as a result of what you've done.

Transfer your skill to more settings

If you've developed a skill or technique that has worked really well on this particular problem, look for other problems you can use it on. For example, if you have improved the engagement and performance of a team member by learning to coach them through their problems, you could look to apply the same coaching skills with your peers or with your whole team. Or you could look at how coaching skills could help you to have better conversations with clients by using active listening, which is central to being a successful coach.

Share it

If you've discovered the benefit of a particular tool or technique, sharing it with your team members can be extremely helpful, as you can upskill your team as a whole. You may have learned how to diagnose and solve problems with a culture, but you may not have shared this with your team members who themselves lead teams. For the sake of thirty minutes of talking them through what you know, you are missing out on great opportunities for staff development that are very light on resources and stand the chance of being highly beneficial, particularly because you can shape your advice for their context, which you will know very well.

Beef up the skill / supercharge it

If you've learned a skill that has proven to be of benefit, learn more and you could replace your previous weakness with a supercharged skill. If, for example, you used to struggle with influencing other people but you have learned how to do this pretty well, you could read more and practice a wider range of techniques to improve your influencing skills. If it's a skill you've developed organically and there are development courses available in that area, you could think about formalizing your ability to do it. Many people who learn to be coaches do so because they have had to use coaching at work to help improve the functioning of their team and they discover they have a knack for it.

Embrace other, similar skills

If you have created a team charter as part of getting your team to function better, you may have discovered a skill for helping groups to make sense of what they are doing and for documenting new processes. This may mean, when an opportunity comes up to lead a steering group to develop new processes for using AI, you ask to lead this group. It's not quite the same, but it's similar—and you think you could use the skills you've developed as well as developing some new ones in the role. We can often see, when we look back at our careers, how each little side step, building on what we've done before but with the addition of new knowledge or skills, widens our skill set and improves our ability to do a wider range of roles.

Research suggests that, to be really useful at work, particularly in knowledge settings, we may want to be "T-shaped." This means we have an area (or sometimes more than one area) of deep knowledge, represented by the vertical trunk of the *T*, and we also have a wider set of less specialized knowledge, which means we can talk to others, network, and engage in a broader set of conversations, represented by the horizontal branches of the *T*. So each time we take on a task, we have the opportunity to deepen our specialist knowledge and/or broaden our wider knowledge. When we embrace other, similar skills, we're simultaneously working on both—deepening our specialist knowledge a bit and widening our more general knowledge, too.

WHAT NEXT?

If you've read this chapter and have it ready to go next time you face a problem, you should be able to SOLVE it. In your journey over the past ten chapters, you've seen how the SOLVE approach works in practice, on ten different categories of thorny leadership problems, and you've also been given a sense of how to work with these problems in particular. And now, with this chapter, you can move on to use SOLVE on your own and look to turn things around for yourself.

I realize, however, if you're really stuck, trying to fight your way out of a pile of problems that have all tumbled down on you can feel very lonely! That's why I'm also here to help.

In my newsletter, which currently comes out about once per fortnight, leaders send me their real problems and I help them with some ideas and solutions they may not have thought of before. If you feel you've tried everything and nothing is working, drop me a line!

You can contact me at katie@katiebest.com, and I'm super happy to take a look at your problem and see how I can help!

Acknowledgments

Bobbie and Patrick Connolly—I cannot believe the incredible luck of having them both in my life. They are both so unfailingly caring, brilliantly kind, and fantastically funny—this book would not have been possible without their belief and support.

Wonderful Dad, lovely Mum, and the most awesome mother-in-law, Helen, for all believing in me and offering practical help so I could get on with the writing.

Jeff Shreve, my phenomenal agent, who has worked so enthusiastically and tirelessly on this project and has shown me repeatedly what a clever and yet humble expert he is on the wonderful world of books and publishing. He is also a great person to chat with in general, and I have enjoyed getting to know him over the course of writing this book.

Emily Taber and Kimberly Meilun, my fantastic editors, who have both guided me at different times and in helpfully different ways to find the voice and structure of this book. Emily's insightful comments have made the final months of writing this book much more pleasurable than they might have been otherwise.

Sharon Wheatley, Gemma Pountney, James McSean, Alexandra Budjanovcanin, Megan Jones, Shane Balzan, Tom Keyes, Aylin Kunter, Des Felix, John Kelly, Lindsey Edwards, and Lucy Nathan, for being friends not just to me but also to this book, each of them always ready with the necessary "How's the book going?" and even listening to the answer.

Supportive colleagues and thinking partners I want to thank are Kathy Pavid, Rebecca Newton, and the rest of the CoachAdviser team, Rachael McCullough at Morgan Stanley, Nick Rice, Claudine

Menashe-Jones, and Tracey Smith as well as fellow authors Dominic Ayres and Jon Hindmarsh. Thanks to each of you for helping me on the path to book writing through feedback, friendship, and being thought partners, and for having instilled me with your confidence that I could do it.

A particular mention to Julie Keyes, who can't remember the conversation we had in a National Trust garden in Cornwall that helped me to (finally) decide on what I wanted to write about. I'm so lucky to have her as a friend, colleague, and thinking partner and am so pleased that our working worlds overlap!

My prep school English teacher, Mrs. (Jeanette) Adams, for stoking the fire that made me want to write—a fire that has changed shape a few times but has never gone out.

Jody Elphick, Ariana Dening, Lucy Smith, Karen Cromar, Nasima Hasan, Sally Oliphant, and Helen Coyle for helping with various stages of idea generation, proposal writing, chapter editing, proofreading, and all the other critical wordsmithing and business support tasks that helped the book land with all the right people at all the right times. You have all been supportive colleagues and friends in other ways, too, but I particularly want to recognize your contributions as exceptional professionals and say how fortunate I have been to have received help or counsel from each of you.

And finally, all the brilliant interviewees and leaders who gave their time generously to help with the writing of this book. Your words have informed the book, challenged my thinking in very helpful ways, and allowed the real world to shine through the pages. I want to acknowledge both the interviewees who've made it into the book as named participants and those who preferred to (or were told by their companies that they had to!) remain anonymous. You've helped to bring the pages to life with your honest and thoughtful examples and recommendations for overcoming those tough leadership problems that this book is all about.

Notes

PROBLEM 1: PERSONAL EFFECTIVENESS

1 Bryan Lufkin, "Why Do We Buy into the 'Cult' of Overwork?," BBC Worklife, May 10, 2021, https://www.bbc.com/worklife/article/20210507-why-we-glorify-the-cult-of-burnout-and-overwork.

2 Chartered Institute of Personnel and Development, *Health and Well-being at Work: Survey Report* (London: CIPD, 2023).

3 Rasmus Hougaard, Jacqueline Carter, and Gillian Coutts, *One Second Ahead: Enhance Your Performance at Work with Mindfulness* (London: Palgrave Macmillan, 2015).

4 Stephanie Neal et al., "Global Leadership Forecast," DDI, 2023, https://www.ddiworld.com/global-leadership-forecast-2023.

5 David Bawden and Lyn Robinson, "The Dark Side of Information: Overload, Anxiety and Other Paradoxes and Pathologies," *Journal of Information Science* 35, no. 2 (2008): 180–91, https://doi.org/10.1177/0165551508095781.

6 Teresa M. Amabile, Constance N. Hadley, and Steven J. Kramer, "Creativity Under the Gun," *Harvard Business Review*, August 2002.

7 Joshua S. Rubinstein, David E. Meyer, and Jeffrey E. Evans, "Executive Control of Cognitive Processes in Task Switching," *Journal of Experimental Psychology: Human Perception and Performance* 27, no. 4 (2001): 763–97, https://doi.org/10.1037//0096-1523.27.4.763.

8 Rohan Narayana Murty, Sandeep Dadlani, and Rajath B. Das, "How Much Time and Energy Do We Waste Toggling Between Applications?," *Harvard Business Review*, May 2022, https://hbr.org/2022/08/how-much-time-and-energy-do-we-waste-toggling-between-applications.

9 Gordon Tinline and Cary Cooper, *The Outstanding Middle Manager: How to Be a Healthy, Happy, High-Performing Mid-level Manager* (London: Kogan Page, 2016).

10 Jake Knapp and John Zeratsky, *Make Time: How to Focus on What Matters Every Day* (London: Bantam Press, 2018).

11 Rubinstein, Meyer, and Evans, "Executive Control."

12 B. E. Robinson, "The Work Addiction Risk Test: Development of a Tentative Measure of Workaholism," *Perceptual and Motor Skills* 88, no. 1 (1999): 199–210, https://doi.org/10.2466/pms.1999.88.1.199.

13 Cal Newport, *Slow Productivity: The Lost Art of Accomplishment Without Burnout* (London: Portfolio, 2024).

14 Patrick R. Krill et al., "Stressed, Lonely, and Overcommitted: Predictors of Lawyer Suicide Risk," *Healthcare* 11, no. 4 (2023): 536, https://doi.org/10.3390/healthcare11040536.

15 Jamie Waters, "Constant Craving: How Digital Media Turned Us into Dopamine Addicts," *Guardian*, August 22, 2021, https://www.theguardian.com/global/2021/aug/22/how-digital-media-turned-us-all-into-dopamine-addicts-and-what-we-can-do-to-break-the-cycle.

16 Anthony Klotz, Shawn McClean, and Pok Man Tang, "Research: A Little Nature in the Office Boosts Morale and Productivity," *Harvard Business Review*, July 21, 2023, https://hbr.org/2023/07/research-a-little-nature-in-the-office-boosts-morale-and-productivity.

17 Newport, *Slow Productivity*.

18 Linda Babcock et al., *The No Club: Putting a Stop to Women's Dead-End Work* (London: Little, Brown, 2022).

19 Oliver Burkeman, *Four Thousand Weeks: Time and How to Use It* (London: Bodley Head, 2021).

20 Catherine Baker, *Staying the Distance: The Lessons from Sport That Business Leaders Have Been Missing* (London: Bloomsbury, 2023).

21 Chartered Institute of Personnel and Development, *Employee Resilience: An Evidence Review* (London: CIPD, 2021).

22 Cal Newport, interviewed on I. Berwick, *Working It with Isabel Berwick*, podcast audio, "How to Slow Down but Achieve More," May 14, 2024, https://www.ft.com/content/3ddbfcbb-7fa5-492c-b7b7-67675be7bd8a.

23 Phillippa Lally et al., "How Are Habits Formed: Modelling Habit Formation in the Real World," *European Journal of Social Psychology* 40, no. 6 (2010): 998–1009, https://doi.org/10.1002/ejsp.674.

24 Barry Z. Kouzes and James M. Posner, *The Leadership Challenge: How to Make Extraordinary Things Happen in Organizations* (Hoboken, NJ: Jossey-Bass, 2022).

PROBLEM 2: DECISION-MAKING

1 Bent Flyvbjerg and Dan Gardner, *How Big Things Get Done: The Surprising Factors Behind Every Successful Project, from Home Renovations to Space Exploration* (London: Macmillan, 2023), 206.

2 Annie Duke, *How to Decide* (London: Penguin, 2020).

3 Daniel Slater, "Elements of Amazon's Day 1 Culture," AWS Executive Insights, https://aws.amazon.com/executive-insights/content/how-amazon-defines-and-operationalizes-a-day-1-culture/.

4 Duke, *How to Decide*.

5 Greg Orme, *The Human Edge: How Curiosity and Creativity Are Your Superpowers in the Digital Economy* (London: Pearson Business, 2019).

6 Adam Bryant, *The Leap to Leader: How Ambitious Managers Make the Jump to Leadership* (Harvard, MA: Harvard Business Press, 2023).

7 Ai Ito and Michelle C. Bligh, "Feeling Vulnerable? Disclosure of Vulnerability in the Charismatic Leadership Relationship," *Journal of Leadership Studies* 10, no. 3 (2016): 66–70, https://doi.org/https://doi.org/10.1002/jls.21492.

8 Susan Fiske et al., "A Model of (Often Mixed) Stereotype Content: Competence and Warmth Respectively Follow from Perceived Status and Competition," *Journal of Personality and Social Psychology* 82, no. 6 (2002): 878–902, https://doi.org/10.1037/0022-3514.82.6.878.

9 Mark Goulston, "How to Give a Meaningful Apology," *Harvard Business Review*, March 11, 2013, https://hbr.org/2013/03/how-to-give-a-meaningful-apolo.

10 Goulston, "How to Give a Meaningful Apology."

11 Orme, *The Human Edge*.

12 Duke, *How to Decide*, 21.

13 Thomas Ramge and Viktor Mayer-Schönberger, "Using ChatGPT to Make Better Decisions," *Harvard Business Review*, August 24, 2023, https://hbr.org/2023/08/using-chatgpt-to-make-better-decisions.

14 Colin W. P. Lewis and Agnieszka Dziewulska, "Improve Your Company's Use of AI with a Structured Approach to Prompts," *Harvard Business Review*, November 14, 2023, https://hbr.org/2023/11/improve-your-companys-use-of-ai-with-a-structured-approach-to-prompts.

15 Tojin T. Eapen et al., "How Generative AI Can Augment Human Creativity," *Harvard Business Review*, July–August 2023.

PROBLEM 3: INFLUENCE

1 Gary Yukl, Helen Kim, and Cecilia M. Falbe, "Antecedents of Influence Outcomes," *Journal of Applied Psychology* 81, no. 3 (1996): 309–17, https://doi.org/10.1037/0021-9010.81.3.309.

2 Harvey G. Enns and Dean B. McFarlin, "When Executives Successfully Influence Peers: The Role of Target Assessment, Preparation, and Tactics," *Human Resource Management* 44, no. 3 (2005): 257–78, https://doi.org/https://doi.org/10.1002/hrm.20070.

3 Steve Peters, *The Chimp Paradox* (London: Vermillion, 2012).

4 Cecilia M. Falbe and Gary Yukl, "Consequences for Managers of Using Single Influence Tactics and Combinations of Tactics," *Academy of Management Journal* 35, no. 3 (1992): 638–52, https://doi.org/10.2307/256490.

5 Yukl, Kim, and Falbe, "Antecedents of Influence Outcomes."

6 Falbe and Yukl, "Consequences for Managers."

7 Bertram H. Raven, "A Power/Interaction Model of Interpersonal Influence: French and Raven Thirty Years Later," *Journal of Social Behavior & Personality* 7, no. 2 (1992).

8 Sun Hyun Park, James D. Westphal, and Ithai Stern, "Set Up for a Fall: The Insidious Effects of Flattery and Opinion Conformity Toward Corporate Leaders," *Administrative Science Quarterly* 56, no. 2 (2011): 257–302, https://doi.org/10.1177/0001839211429102.

9 Adam D. Galinsky et al., "Power and Perspectives Not Taken," *Psychological Science* 17, no. 12 (2006): 1068–74, https://doi.org/10.1111/j.1467-9280.2006.01824.x.

10 John R. P. French Jr. and Bertram Raven, "The Bases of Social Power,"

in *Studies in Social Power*, ed. Dorwin Cartwright (Ann Arbor, MI: Institute for Social Research, 1959).

11 Elaine Hatfield, John T. Cacioppo, and Richard L. Rapson, "Emotional Contagion," *Current Directions in Psychological Science* 2, no. 3 (1993): 96–100, https://doi.org/10.1111/1467-8721.ep10770953.

12 Elliot Aronson, Ben Willerman, and Joanne Floyd, "The Effect of a Pratfall on Increasing Personal Attractiveness," *Psychonomic Science* 4 (2014): 227–28, https://doi.org/10.3758/BF03342263.

13 Susan Fiske et al., "A Model of (Often Mixed) Stereotype Content: Competence and Warmth Respectively Follow from Perceived Status and Competition," *Journal of Personality and Social Psychology* 82, no. 6 (2002): 878–902, https://doi.org/10.1037/0022-3514.82.6.878.

14 Aronson, Willerman, and Floyd, "The Effect of a Pratfall."

15 Enns and McFarlin, "When Executives Successfully Influence Peers."

16 Hyunsun Park, Subra Tangirala, and Insiya Hussain, "The Unintended Consequences of Asking for Employee Input," *Harvard Business Review*, February 18, 2022, https://hbr.org/2022/02/the-unintended-consequences-of-asking-for-employee-input.

17 Ella Miron-Spektor, Julia B. Bear, and Emuna Eliav, "Think Funny, Think Female: The Benefits of Humor for Women's Influence in the Digital Age," *Academy of Management Discoveries* 9, no. 3 (2023), https://doi.org/10.5465/amd.2021.0112.

18 A. Konovalov and I. Krajbich, "Neurocomputational Dynamics of Sequence Learning," *Neuron* 98, no. 6 (2018): 1282–93, https://doi.org/10.1016/j.neuron.2018.05.013.

19 John F. Dovidio and Steve L. Ellyson, "Decoding Visual Dominance: Attributions of Power Based on Relative Percentages of Looking While Speaking and Looking While Listening," *Social Psychology Quarterly* 45, no. 2 (1982): 106–13, https://doi.org/10.2307/3033933.

20 Michael Fleming, "Becoming a Trusted Advisor: The Ten Behaviours," KWC Global, April 19, 2013, https://www.kwcglobal.com/blog/becoming-a-trusted-advisor-the-ten-behaviours/.

PROBLEM 4: INDIVIDUAL PERFORMANCE

1 Alan Benson, Danielle Li, and Kelly Shue, "Promotions and the Peter Principle," *Quarterly Journal of Economics* 134, no. 4 (2019): 2085–134, https://doi.org/10.1093/qje/qjz022.

2 Michael Bazigos and Jim Harter, "Revisiting the Matrix Organisation," *McKinsey Quarterly*, 2016, https://www.mckinsey.com/capabilities/people-and-organizational-performance/our-insights/revisiting-the-matrix-organization.

3 J. Lepine, N. Podskoff, and M. Lepine, "A Meta-Analytic Test of the Challenge Stressor-Hindrance Stressor Framework: An Explanation for Inconsistent Relationships Among Stressors and Performance," *Academy of Management Journal* 48, no. 5 (2005): 764–75, https://doi.org/10.5465/AMJ.2005.18803921.

4 *Remote Workforce Report 2023: The Rise of Globally Distributed Teams* (San Francisco: Remote Technology, 2023).

5 D. Brown, "I Am Supposed to Believe This Man Is a Genius?," May 1, 2023, in *Flipping the Bird: Elon vs. Twitter*, podcast.

6 Brown, "I Am Supposed to Believe."

7 C. Treude, "Why Elon Musk's Focus on Code Misses the Mark," University of Melbourne Faculty of Engineering and Information Technology, December 15, 2022, https://eng.unimelb.edu.au/ingenium/why-elon-musks-focus-on-code-misses-the-mark.

8 *Performance Management: An Introduction* (London: Chartered Institute for Professional Development, 2024).

9 Adam Grant, *Think Again: The Power of Knowing What You Don't Know* (London: Ebury, 2021).

10 After negative feedback, employee engagement is 10.4 percent. After positive feedback, employee engagement is 50.5 percent. Cheyna Brower and Nate Dvorak, "Why Employees Are Fed Up with Feedback," Gallup, October 11, 2019, https://www.gallup.com/workplace/267251/why-employees-fed-feedback.aspx.

11 Marcus Buckingham and Ashley Goodall, "The Feedback Fallacy," *Harvard Business Review*, March–April 2019.

12 Pauline Rose Clance and Suzanne Ament Imes, "The Imposter

Phenomenon in High Achieving Women: Dynamics and Therapeutic Intervention," *Psychotherapy: Theory, Research & Practice* 15, no. 3 (1978): 241–47, https://doi.org/10.1037/h0086006.

13 In a recent study, 54 percent of women claimed to have experienced imposter syndrome, compared with 38 percent of men and 57 percent of nonbinary people. Research discussed in "Prescribing Success: How to Identify and Support People Suffering with Imposter Syndrome, to Create a More Confident and Productive Team," Executive Development Network, accessed April 30, 2024, https://edn.training/prescribing-success/.

14 Stephen Gadsby, "Imposter Syndrome and Self-Deception," *Australasian Journal of Philosophy* 100, no. 2 (2022): 247–61, https://doi.org/10.1080/00048402.2021.1874445.

15 Ruchika Tulshyan and Jodi-Ann Burey, "Stop Telling Women They Have Imposter Syndrome," *Harvard Business Review*, February 11, 2021, https://hbr.org/2021/02/stop-telling-women-they-have-imposter-syndrome.

16 While there has been some criticism of the research conducted on this topic, with changes in hormone levels being hard to replicate, the research backs up that people feel more confident and powerful when they adopt poses that are less contracted and more expansive. A summary of the research and controversy can be found here: Tom Loncar, "A Decade of Power Posing: Where Do We Stand?," *Psychologist*, June 8, 2021, https://www.bps.org.uk/psychologist/decade-power-posing-where-do-we-stand.

PROBLEM 5: ENGAGEMENT

1 "State of the Global Workplace: 2023 Report," Gallup, 2022, https://www.gallup.com/workplace/349484/state-of-the-global-workplace.aspx.

2 "World Economic Outlook Database," International Monetary Fund, April 2023, https://www.imf.org/en/Publications/WEO/weo-database/2023/April.

3 Stefan Stern, "If Staff Don't Want to Work Any More, Leaders Should Step Up," *Financial Times*, June 10, 2024, https://www.ft.com/content/eabd1aba-3ea9-4a11-af3d-e3e10c468b96.

4 Lian Parsons, "How to Engage a Disengaged Employee," Harvard Division of Continuing Education, November 8, 2022, https://professional.dce.harvard.edu/blog/how-to-engage-a-disengaged-employee/.

5 J. Stacy Adams, "Towards an Understanding of Inequity," *Journal of Abnormal and Social Psychology* 67, no. 5 (1963): 422–36, https://doi.org/10.1037/h0040968.

6 Armin Falk and Urs Fischbacher, "A Theory of Reciprocity," *Games and Economic Behavior* 54, no. 2 (2006): 293–315, https://doi.org/10.1016/j.geb.2005.03.001.

7 Ioana Lupu and Mayra Ruiz-Castro, "Work-Life Balance Is a Cycle, Not an Achievement," *Harvard Business Review*, January 9, 2021, https://hbr.org/2021/01/work-life-balance-is-a-cycle-not-an-achievement.

8 Jack Zenger and Joseph Folkman, "Do You Tell Your Employees You Appreciate Them?," *Harvard Business Review*, September 12, 2022, https://hbr.org/2022/09/do-you-tell-your-employees-you-appreciate-them.

9 Zenger and Folkman, "Do You Tell Your Employees."

10 Evangelia Demerouti, Arnold B. Bakker, and Jonathon R. B. Halbesleben, "Productive and Counterproductive Job Crafting: A Daily Diary Study," *Journal of Occupational Health Psychology* 20, no. 4 (2015): 457–69, https://doi.org/10.1037/a0039002.

11 Maria Tims and Daantje Derks, "Proactive Personality and Job Performance: The Role of Job Crafting and Work Engagement," *Human Relations* 65 (2012), 1359–78, https://doi.org/10.1177/0018726712453471.

12 Albert Bourla, "The CEO of Pfizer on Developing a Vaccine in Record Time," *Harvard Business Review*, May–June 2021.

13 Joey Coleman, *Never Lose an Employee Again: The Simple Path to Remarkable Retention* (London: Portfolio, 2023).

14 Anthony Klotz, Shawn McClean, and Pok Man Tang, "Research: A Little Nature in the Office Boosts Morale and Productivity," *Harvard Business Review*, July 21, 2023, https://hbr.org/2023/07/research-a-little-nature-in-the-office-boosts-morale-and-productivity.

15 Simone Stolzoff, *The Good Enough Job: Reclaiming Life from Work* (London: Portfolio, 2023).

16 "What Is an Employee Value Proposition (EVP)?," Hays Employer Insights, https://www.hays.com.au/employer-insights/recruitment-information/define-your-evp.

PROBLEM 6: TEAMWORK

1 David A. Garvin, "How Google Sold Its Engineers On Management," *Harvard Business Review*, December 2013.

2 Andreas Holmer, "Project Aristotle: Conversational Turn-Taking, Social Sensitivity, and Psychological Safety," LinkedIn Pulse, December 23, 2022, https://www.linkedin.com/pulse/project-aristotle-conversational-turn-taking-social-safety-holmer/.

3 David Rock and Heidi Grant, "Why Diverse Teams Are Smarter," *Harvard Business Review*, November 4, 2016, https://hbr.org/2016/11/why-diverse-teams-are-smarter.

4 Daan van Knippenberg et al., "Diversity Faultlines, Shared Objectives, and Top Management Team Performance," *Human Relations* 64, no. 3 (2011): 307–36, https://doi.org/10.1177/0018726710378384.

5 Stephen B. Goldberg, Jeanne M. Brett, and Beatrice Blohorn-Brenneur, *How Mediation Works: Theory, Research and Practice* (London: Emerald Publishing, 2020).

6 Lianne Davey, *You First: Inspire Your Team to Grow Up, Get Along, and Get Stuff Done* (London: Wiley, 2013).

7 Ed Smith, *Making Decisions: Thinking Bigger, Seeing Further* (London: HarperCollins, 2022).

8 Arthur C. Brooks, *From Strength to Strength: Finding Success, Happiness and Deep Purpose in the Second Half of Life* (London: Green Tree, 2023).

PROBLEM 7: HYBRID AND REMOTE WORKING

1 Ghassan Karian, *Making the Case for the Office* (Lendal, England: Ipsos, Karian and Box, 2023).

2 "State of Remote Work Report 2023," Buffer, https://buffer.com/state-of-remote-work/2023.

3 Karian, *Making the Case*.

4 Chinchih Chen, Carl Benedikt Frey, and Giorgio Presidente, "Disrupting Science," April 2022, working paper 2022-4, Oxford University, Oxford, England.

5 "Work Trend Index Annual Report: Making Hybrid Work Work," Microsoft, March 26, 2022, https://www.microsoft.com/en-us/worklab/work-trend-index/great-expectations-making-hybrid-work-work/.

6 "State of Remote Work Report 2023."

7 Alexandra Lechner and Jutta Tobias Mortlock, "How to Create Psychological Safety in Virtual Teams," *Organizational Dynamics* 51, no. 2 (2022): 100849, https://doi.org/10.1016/j.orgdyn.2021.100849.

8 Lechner and Tobias Mortlock, "How to Create Psychological Safety."

9 Joan C. Williams and Marina Multhaup, "For Women and Minorities to Get Ahead, Managers Must Assign Work Fairly," *Harvard Business Review*, March 26, 2018, https://hbr.org/2018/03/for-women-and-minorities-to-get-ahead-managers-must-assign-work-fairly.

10 Karian, *Making the Case.*

11 Cal Newport, *Slow Productivity: The Lost Art of Accomplishment Without Burnout* (London: Portfolio, 2024).

12 Williams and Multhaup, "For Women and Minorities."

13 J. Harper, "Splitters and Blenders: Two Different Relationships with Work," *Harvard Business Review*, December 8, 2022, https://www.gallup.com/workplace/405392/splitters-blenders-two-different-relationships-work.aspx.

14 Sean Graber, "Why Remote Work Thrives in Some Companies and Fails in Others," *Harvard Business Review*, March 20, 2015, https://hbr.org/2015/03/why-remote-work-thrives-in-some-companies-and-fails-in-others.

15 Sid Sijbradij, "GitLab's CEO on Building One of the World's Largest All-Remote Companies," *Harvard Business Review*, March–April 2023.

16 Gleb Tsipursky, "What Is Proximity Bias and How Can Managers Prevent It?," *Harvard Business Review*, October 4, 2022, https://hbr.org/2022/10/what-is-proximity-bias-and-how-can-managers-prevent-it.

17 Lisa Britz and Robert Norwood, "How LinkedIn Redesigned Its HQ

for Hybrid Work," *Harvard Business Review*, October 21, 2022, https://hbr.org/2022/10/how-linkedin-redesigned-its-hq-for-hybrid-work.

18 Britz and Norwood, "How LinkedIn Redesigned."

19 Karen Cygal et al., *Remote Work: The Road to the Future* (New York: Deloitte, 2022), https://www2.deloitte.com/content/dam/Deloitte/us/Documents/Tax/us-tax-remote-work-the-road-to-the-future.pdf.

PROBLEM 8: DELIVERING ON THE STRATEGY

1 Francis J. Flynn and Chelsea R. Lide, "Communication Miscalibration: The Price Leaders Pay for Not Sharing Enough," *Academy of Management Journal* 66, no. 4 (2023), https://doi.org/https://doi.org/10.5465/amj.2021.0245.

2 "In Defense of Middle Management," July 18, 2023, in *HBR IdeaCast*, podcast, https://hbr.org/podcast/2023/07/in-defense-of-middle-management.

3 Arlie Russell Hochschild, *The Managed Heart: Commercialization of Human Feeling* (Berkeley: University of California Press, 1983).

4 "Study: The Risks of Ignoring Employee Feedback," Leadership IQ, 2017, https://www.leadershipiq.com/blogs/leadershipiq/study-the-risks-of-ignoring-employee-feedback.

5 Elad N. Sherf, Subra Tangirala, and Vijaya Venkataramani, "Research: Why Managers Ignore Employees' Ideas," *Harvard Business Review*, April 8, 2019, https://hbr.org/2019/04/research-why-managers-ignore-employees-ideas.

6 Al Comeaux, *Change (the) Management: Why We as Leaders Must Change for the Change to Last* (Austin, TX: Lioncrest, 2020).

7 David J. Collis and Michael G. Rukstad, "Can You Say What Your Strategy Is?," *Harvard Business Review*, April 2008.

8 "Agree and Commit, Disagree and Commit," Stanford Technology Ventures Program, video, 2:38, posted November 15, 2006, https://ecorner.stanford.edu/videos/agree-and-commit-disagree-and-commit/.

9 Frances Frei and Anne Morriss, *Uncommon Service: How to Win by Putting Your Customers at the Core of Your Business* (Boston: Harvard Business School Publishing, 2012).

PROBLEM 9: CULTURE AND VALUES

1 Anthony Giddens, *The Constitution of Society: Outline of the Theory of Structuration* (Cambridge, UK: Polity Press, 1984).

2 This exercise is inspired by the Competing Values Framework, originally presented in Robert E. Quinn and John Rohrbaugh, "A Competing Values Approach to Organizational Effectiveness," *Public Productivity Review* 5, no. 2 (1981): 122–40, https://doi.org/10.2307/3380029.

3 William H. Whyte, *The Organization Man* (New York: Simon & Schuster, 1956).

4 Donald Sull et al., "Why Every Leader Needs to Worry About Toxic Culture," *MIT Sloan Review*, March 16, 2022, https://sloanreview.mit.edu/article/why-every-leader-needs-to-worry-about-toxic-culture/.

5 Edgar H. Schein, *Organizational Culture and Leadership* (San Francisco: Jossey-Bass, 1985).

6 Sull et al., "Why Every Leader Needs."

7 Sivapragasam Panneerselvam and Kavitha Balaraman, "Drivers of Toxic Cultures and What We Can Do About It!," *South Asian Journal of Human Resources Management*, 2024, https://doi.org/10.1177/23220937241245288.

8 Elizabeth Stokoe, *Talk: The Science of Conversation* (London: Robinson, 2018).

9 Anne-Laure Fayard and John Weeks, "Who Moved My Cube?," *Harvard Business Review*, July–August 2011.

10 "Inside Fruit Towers: Innocent's London HQ," Mix Interiors, May 30, 2020, https://www.mixinteriors.com/project/inside-fruit-towers-innocents-london-hq/.

11 Martha Kearns, "Fury over Air Chief's 'Steal Don't Buy' Advice to Staff," *Irish Independent*, December 20, 2003, https://www.independent.ie/irish-news/fury-over-air-chiefs-steal-dont-buy-advice-to-staff/25919488.html.

12 Joey Coleman, *Never Lose an Employee Again: The Simple Path to Remarkable Retention* (London: Portfolio, 2023).

13 Jon R. Katzenbach, Ilona Steffen, and Caroline Kronley, "Cultural Change That Sticks," *Harvard Business Review*, July–August, 2012.

14 Adam Bryant, *The Leap to Leader: How Ambitious Managers Make the Jump to Leadership* (Harvard, MA: Harvard Business Press, 2023).

15 David A. Buchanan and Andrzej A. Huczynski, *Organizational Behaviour*, 11th ed. (London: Pearson, 2023).

PROBLEM 10: LEADING CHANGE

1 "Five Skills Leaders Need for the Future—Global Leadership Forecast 2023," DDI, https://www.ddiworld.com/global-leadership-forecast-2023/leadership-skills.

2 "Losing from Day One: Why Even Successful Transformations Fall Short," McKinsey, https://www.mckinsey.com/capabilities/people-and-organizational-performance/our-insights/successful-transformations.

3 Daniel Kahneman, *Thinking, Fast and Slow* (London: Penguin, 2011).

4 "Work-Related Stress and How to Manage It," Health and Safety Executive, https://www.hse.gov.uk/stress/overview.htm.

5 Derek Pugh, "Understanding and Managing Organisational Change," in *Managing Change*, ed. Christopher Mabey and Bill Mayon-White (London: Paul Chapman / Open University, 1993).

6 Bent Flyvbjerg and Dan Gardner, *How Big Things Get Done: The Surprising Factors Behind Every Successful Project, from Home Renovations to Space Exploration* (London: Macmillan, 2023).

7 Bernard M. Bass and Ronald E. Riggio, *Transformational Leadership*, 2nd ed. (Mahwah, NJ: Lawrence Erlbaum Associates, 2005).

8 Louise A. Nemanich and Robert T. Keller, "Transformational Leadership in an Acquisition: A Field Study of Employees," *Leadership Quarterly* 18, no. 1 (2007): 49–68, https://doi.org/10.1016/J.LEAQUA.2006.11.003.

9 David A. Garvin and Michael Roberto, "Change Through Persuasion," *Harvard Business Review*, February 2005.

10 Darius Adamczyk, "The Chair of Honeywell on Bringing an Industrial Business into the Digital Age," *Harvard Business Review*, March 2024, https://hbr.org/2024/03/the-chair-of-honeywell-on-bringing-an-industrial-business-into-the-digital-age.

11 Laura London, Stephanie Madner, and Dominic Skerritt, "Seven

Percent Solution? How Many Employees Should Be Involved in Your Transformation?," McKinsey, September 23, 2021, https://www.mckinsey.com/capabilities/transformation/our-insights/how-many-people-are-really-needed-in-a-transformation.

12 Peter G. Northouse, *Leadership: Theory and Practice* (London: Sage, 2021).

CONCLUSION

1 Robert I. Sutton and Huggy Rao, *The Friction Project: How Smart Leaders Make the Right Things Easier and the Wrong Things Harder* (London: Penguin, 2024).

Index

Credit: Jannine Newman

Dr. Katie Best is the founder and director of KatieBest Associates, a leadership development consultancy that works with leaders at companies including EY, Goldman Sachs, and Verizon. She leads the MBA Essentials executive education program at the London School of Economics and is a visiting senior research fellow at King's College London, where she earned her PhD in management. She lives in London.